Reconstructing Times Square

STUDIES IN GOVERNMENT
AND PUBLIC POLICY

Reconstructing Times Square

Politics and Culture
in Urban Development

Alexander J. Reichl

University Press of Kansas

Portions of the text previously appeared in "Historic Preservation and Progrowth Politics in U.S. Cities" by Alexander J. Reichl, in *Urban Affairs Review* 32(4): 513–35. Copyright © 1997 by Sage Publications, Inc. Reprinted by permission of Sage Publications.

Published by the University Press of Kansas (Lawrence, Kansas 66049), which was organized by the Kansas Board of Regents and is operated and funded by Emporia State University, Fort Hays State University, Kansas State University, Pittsburg State University, the University of Kansas, and Wichita State University.

Library of Congress Cataloging-in-Publication Data

Reichl, Alexander J., 1960–
    Reconstructing Times Square : politics and culture in urban
development / Alexander J. Reichl.
        p.   cm. — (Studies in government and public policy)
    Includes bibliographical references.
    ISBN 0-7006-0949-0 (cloth : alk. paper). — ISBN 0-7006-0950-4
(pbk. : alk. paper)
        1. City planning—New York (State)—Times Square (New York)
    2. Urban renewal—New York (State)—Times Square (New York)
    3. Special districts—New York (State)—Times Square (New York)
    4. City planning and redevelopment law—New York (State)—Times
Square (New York)   5. Tourist trade and city planning—New York
(State)—Times Square (New York)   6. New York (N.Y.)—Politics and
government.   7. New York (N.Y.)—Race relations.   I. Title.
    II. Series.
    HT168.N5R45   1999
    307.1'216'097471—dc21   98-55259

British Library Cataloguing in Publication Data is available.

Printed in Canada

10 9 8 7 6 5 4 3 2 1

The paper used in this publication meets the minimum requirements of the American National Standard for Permanence of Paper for Printed Library Materials Z39.48-1984.

For Mom and Dad,
and for Joan, my love

In the center of Fedora, that gray stone metropolis, stands a metal building with a crystal globe in every room. Looking into each globe, you see a blue city, the model of a different Fedora. These are the forms the city could have taken if, for one reason or another, it had not become what we see today. In every age someone, looking at Fedora as it was, imagined a way of making it the ideal city, but while he constructed his miniature model, Fedora was already no longer the same as before, and what had been until yesterday a possible future became only a toy in a glass globe. . . .

On the map of your empire, O Great Khan, there must be room both for the big, stone Fedora and the little Fedoras in glass globes. . . . Not because they are all equally real, but because all are only assumptions. The one contains what is accepted as necessary when it is not yet so; the others, what is imagined as possible and, a moment later, is possible no longer.

. . .

When you have forded the river, when you have crossed the mountain pass, you suddenly find before you the city of Moriana, its alabaster gates transparent in the sunlight, its coral columns supporting pediments encrusted with serpentine, its villas all of glass like aquariums where the shadows of dancing girls with silvery scales swim beneath the medusa-shaped chandeliers. If this is not your first journey, you already know that cities like this have an obverse: you have only to walk in a semicircle and you will come into view of Moriana's hidden face, an expanse of rusting sheet metal, sackcloth, planks bristling with spikes, pipes black with soot, piles of tins, blind walls with fading signs, frames of staved-in straw chairs, ropes good only for hanging oneself from a rotten beam.   —Italo Calvino, *Invisible Cities*

Contents

Photos are between pages 42–43 and 142–143.

Acknowledgments

This project grew out of my doctoral work at New York University, and I am indebted to the members of my dissertation committee—Tim Mitchell, Larry Mead, Paul Kantor, Christine Harrington, and Manny Tobier—for their valuable doses of support, encouragement, guidance, insight, and friendship. I am also grateful to Janet Abu-Lughod, Bill Kornblum, Bob Lake, Fred Papert, and Terry Williams for sharing their time, insights, and resources with me. The faculty and staff of the Department of Politics at NYU supported me in many direct and indirect ways. My fellow graduate students in the department were a remarkable group, and I depended heavily on their companionship throughout the process of completing my dissertation.

Three people in particular deserve credit for helping me transform my initial manuscript from a dissertation to a book. Richard DeLeon and Susan Fainstein provided extremely sharp reviews and identified the crucial issues and tasks that I had to address in order to develop my analysis fully. They showed me the path to the best possible book; that I have strayed should in no way detract from the value of their efforts. Eric Gorham, my friend and colleague at Loyola University New Orleans, is an invaluable resource in helping me sharpen my own ideas and arguments. This is a vastly better book because of the input of these scholars, and I am most grateful for their contributions.

I am proud to be associated with the University Press of Kansas. I owe a debt of gratitude to Director Fred Woodward for his support, encouragement, and professionalism in nurturing my rough manuscript into a publishable book. Susan Schott, Melinda Wirkus, and copy editor Irene Pavitt have also been a pleasure to work with. I am thankful to Rich DeLeon a second time for taking note of my work at an American Political Science Association conference and introducing me to the folks at UPK.

At Loyola University, I have found a comfortable and supportive environment for my work. Among the many people from the Loyola community who deserve thanks, I must single out three for their extra efforts in helping me complete this project: Phil Dynia, chair of the Department of Political Science; Gayle Mumfrey, departmental administrator; and librarian George Dansker.

The book is greatly enriched by the photographs of Forty-second Street and Times Square that help me tell my story. Their inclusion was made possible by the generous cooperation from staff at the Museum of the City of New York, the 42nd Street Development Project, the Times Square Business Improvement District (and its photographer, Philip Greenberg), Robert A. M. Stern Architects, Tishman Realty and Construction Co., and Photofest. I am especially grateful to Michael Ackerman for allowing me access to his photos, which capture the essence of another lost era in the history of Times Square. In addition, I must thank Zdeněk Pivečka for his technical assistance, and Loyola University for a Faculty Research Grant that helped defray the costs of acquiring and using the photos.

The contribution from my family cannot be put into words. Perhaps the most I can say is that they are the ones who make everything in life seem worthwhile. And Joan has made my life a pleasure.

Introduction

The ideas that underlie this study date from my experiences in New York City, which began when I migrated there for graduate school in the mid-1980s. Like most urbanists, I genuinely love cities, and the streets of New York served as a fascinating laboratory. My field of observation was greatly expanded when I began working for the New York City Department of Housing Preservation and Development (HPD) in 1987. My initial position involved combing the streets of the most physically blighted neighborhoods of the city—including the South Bronx, upper Manhattan, and central Brooklyn—in order to update maps of city-owned "in-rem" properties taken from tax-delinquent owners. Over the next five years, I made repeated visits to these communities as part of my work with several city programs to transform dilapidated buildings into affordable housing.

While I was collecting raw data from the streets of New York, I was also acquiring, as a graduate student, the intellectual tools necessary to make sense of the city. From my early mentor, Hank Savitch, I learned much about urban programs, urban theories, and urban development in New York City; but perhaps more important, I found that it was possible to read the physical form of the city as a guide to underlying patterns of political power. This essential idea—the political significance of the nature of the built environment—has continued to shape my understanding of the urban realm and is at the heart of this inquiry into the redevelopment of Times Square.

During my formative years as an urban scholar in New York, I had no trouble maintaining my optimism about the possibilities of city life, even though I was exposed to areas that many would consider to be the worst examples of urban failure. In fact, my experiences in the "bad neighborhoods" of New York were overwhelmingly positive. While Tom Wolfe, in *The Bonfire of the Vanities,* depicted the Bronx County Courthouse as a besieged fortress in a war zone and those who worked there as afraid to set foot on the surrounding streets, I was lunching peacefully in a nearby neighborhood park. Increasingly, I became aware of the vast discrepancy between what I felt to be the potential for cities as places that could thrive on their social diversity and the popular acceptance of cities as places of social conflict where diversity meant little more than the threat of the "other."

As I conducted research on the redevelopment of Times Square, I was struck by the sense that the politics surrounding the redevelopment effort revolved largely around this fear of diversity. Times Square in the 1980s was a troubled place, but it was also a rare area of diversity in the heart of Manhattan, primarily because

West Forty-second Street was home to an assortment of inexpensive entertainment (not including adult entertainment) that attracted lower-income African-American and Latino youth into the otherwise pricey Broadway theater district. It provided a relatively safe entertainment district for residents of the most troubled city neighborhoods. So although there was much to dislike about Times Square, there was something valuable about it, too. The unfamiliar mixing of classes, races, and cultures contributed to the unique energy and excitement of the area. Indeed, the essence of Times Square is found as much in its history as a contested social space as in its dramatic physical characteristics.

But the diversity of Times Square served as a powerful symbol that helped mobilize support for redevelopment of the area. Running through planning documents, media reports, and official statements was a dominant narrative—what I call public or political discourse—that defined Times Square as a symbol of urban decline in the United States. Public reports emphasized concerns about crime, drugs, violence, and pornography in the area; but the language of urban decline derives much of its potency from racial anxieties, and lurking beneath the surface of redevelopment proposals was the persistent theme that West Forty-second Street had become the domain of a menacing population of young African-Americans and Latinos. While urban development is a reasonable response to urban decline, the fact is that development is ultimately about making money, not solving social problems. Therefore, I became particularly attentive to the way in which the language of decline was being used to support a redevelopment agenda.

While racial anxieties formed a thinly veiled subtext to political debate about redevelopment, images of high culture figured prominently in the overt public discourse. Before Disney's arrival on Forty-second Street in the 1990s, the redevelopment effort was regularly portrayed in public reports as an attempt to restore a legendary "Great White Way." The project's proponents drew on the romantic imagery of the theater district that had stretched along Broadway and Forty-second Street in the early twentieth century to define their agenda. This characterization of the redevelopment effort had perhaps a slight basis in reality, in the sense that the project included the restoration of nine historic theaters on Forty-second Street (that showed mostly action movies, but also some pornography) for use as Broadway stages. But this nostalgic vision was hardly an accurate representation of the changes that would result from a redevelopment project involving more than 7 million square feet of conventional new construction.

And so, in public discourse, the redevelopment agenda was reduced to an appealing symbolic image of high culture, just as the existing conditions of the area were reduced to an appalling symbolic image of dangerous urban culture. While the public discourse played on fears of racial transition and lost historic culture, its real potency could be found in the interaction of these two discursive strands. In short, the redevelopment project promised to restore the magical Great White Way in an area that was identified with urban decline and racial takeover. Framed in this way, the proposed 42nd Street Development Project was an offer that New York could not refuse.

Once my early research on Times Square led me to the realization that political discourse and cultural politics were central to this case of redevelopment, I began to pursue questions that might verify this conclusion: to what extent did the actual history of Times Square correspond to the dominant discourse of the 1980s that depicted the area's decline from a glamorous theater district to a place of social breakdown? Did the elements of high culture that supported the vision of a new Great White Way—historic preservation and the arts—figure prominently in the formulation of redevelopment plan for Forty-second Street? Was the pattern of group alliances that supported the project shaped in an identifiable way by the focus in public discussion on the promised high culture of the Great White Way? And if political support for large-scale development was built around components of historic preservation and the arts in the Times Square district, was it possible to identify a political basis for the shift to preservation-centered development approaches more generally?

These questions establish the general framework of the book. The answers reveal how pro-growth forces drew on cultural images of Times Square past, present, and future to construct a political discourse that mobilized broad public support for the redevelopment plan that won final approval in the mid-1980s. But it was not until the 1990s that the redevelopment area of West Forty-second Street began to undergo the dramatic physical and social transformation that has made the street a tourist mecca. And more than anything else, it is the recent participation of the Walt Disney Company that has brought a new face and a new incarnation to Forty-second Street. In addressing the impact that Disney has had on the Forty-second Street project, I inevitably deal with fundamental questions about the influence of Disneyspace on cities.

Chapter 1 makes the case for investigating the political meaning that is inscribed in the built environments of postindustrial cities, with their glittering new office towers and trendy historic districts. An overview of the Times Square redevelopment story illustrates its value as a premiere example of the postindustrial transformation of U.S. cities.

The changes in urban politics and policies that underlie the distinctive features of contemporary cities are the subject of Chapter 2. The federal government and cities throughout the United States, including New York, promoted the shift to preservation-base redevelopment in response to the political opposition that increasingly confronted clean-sweep urban renewal in the 1960s. In this way, public policies led the transformation from the modern to the postmodern urban form.

Chapter 3 reveals how wholesale redevelopment was justified according to a constructed discourse that depicted the decline of Times Square from a glamorous theater district to a place of danger and depravity. In fact, the white-light theater district of Times Square had coexisted since the nineteenth century with a thriving red-light district, and Times Square served an important role as an entertainment area for low-income New Yorkers at the time of its redevelopment. Nonetheless, the dominant discourse enabled political and economic elites to mobilize support for their vision of a new Times Square.

The plan to redevelop Times Square was fueled by negative cultural images of the area—such as adult entertainment and young African-American and Latino males—and by positive images drawn from Times Square's legendary past. Chapter 4 documents the history of the 42nd Street Development Project and shows how pro-growth elites consciously adopted this cultural strategy by including the restoration of historic Broadway theaters alongside the construction of massive new commercial buildings.

Chapter 5 turns to the public hearings that were held on the Times Square project. The voices of supporters and opponents make explicit how cultural imagery fed into a dominant political discourse that unified a broad coalition of interests behind the agenda of pro-growth elites.

Chapter 6 shows how sponsors revised their plan to revive the flagging redevelopment effort. This involved a shift in the cultural strategy to emphasize Times Square's role as a place of popular entertainment. The arrival of the Disney Company then sealed the deal, and the future, for Times Square.

The ultimate normative question is addressed in Chapter 7: So what if Times Square has been transformed into Disneyspace? Both the question and the answer are relevant to the fate of premiere public spaces in cities around the globe.

Finally, I would like to make some remarks about the relevance of this book to understanding the changes taking place in cities more generally. This is a study of one case of urban development, and thus I make no claim that the conclusions I draw are universally applicable to redevelopment efforts elsewhere. Times Square is nothing if not a unique case. Nonetheless, many elements of the Forty-second Street redevelopment strategy are common to revitalization projects in cities throughout the United States, specifically the emphasis on historic preservation and the arts, and the attempt to replicate Disneyspace. I believe, therefore, that the Times Square case can shed light on the politics behind the new spectacular places of the postindustrial city.

For those who would model the study of politics on the "hard" sciences, this book will, by its nature, be lacking. But even such a scientific endeavor operates on a variety of levels, from the macro level of paradigm formation to the micro level of hypothesis testing. Both activities are useful and valid in their own ways, although scholars are not equally suited to both pursuits. In this book, I have followed what I believe to be my strength: drawing on an empirical case to theorize inductively about the operation of political power. I am explicit about the theoretical framework that guides my analysis, and I hope to demonstrate convincingly that it is firmly grounded in the case I am studying. If I am fortunate, someone will be intrigued enough by my analysis to test the usefulness of my framework against other cases. This, it seems to me, is an essential process in political inquiry. For those who remain unconvinced, I ask only that you enjoy a fascinating story of how Times Square has been reconstructed for the twenty-first century.

1
Times Square as Text

The Great White Way dazzles. . . . That's what Times Square could look like.
—"Five Reasons to Transform 42d Street," *New York Times* (1989)

The cheerful face of Mickey Mouse now greets visitors to Times Square from atop
a Disney superstore. Poised near the corner of Forty-second Street and Seventh
Avenue, Mickey looks out over an area that, until recently, was a national symbol
of urban decline. West Forty-second Street—the lower boundary of Times Square—
was synonymous with a frightening mélange of real and perceived urban problems,
including crime, drugs, pornography, prostitution, and menacing African-American
and Latino youths. Business, civic, and political leaders shared the conviction that
this part of Times Square—especially Forty-second Street between Seventh and
Eighth Avenues—threatened the economic and social health of the entire west side
of midtown Manhattan.

Today, however, the reassuring presence of Disney's harmless rodent heralds
the dramatic and ongoing transformation of West Forty-second Street into an
avenue of family fun and entertainment. In addition to the Disney superstore, Disney's corporate presence on Forty-second Street is evident in the historic New
Amsterdam Theater, restored as a showcase for Disney stage productions, and in
a planned hotel, vacation club, retail, and entertainment complex. Following Disney's lead, other corporate giants in the entertainment industry have left their mark
in a spectacular array of flashy new superstores, theme restaurants, theaters, high-
tech amusements, and other entertainment facilities.

If all continues according to plan, the area will soon be submerged, by day, in
the shadows of four huge new office towers on Forty-second Street at Times
Square. By night, the freshly sanitized Forty-second Street will be bathed in the
neon glow of a high-tech "billboard park" stretching along its rooftops and sheath-
ing its office towers. From the towers to the superstores to the orgy of lighted
advertisements, Forty-second Street and Times Square will epitomize the corporate dominance of public space. For the time being, Mickey Mouse smiles in antic-
ipation, waiting for the moment when the famous lighted ball will drop to usher
in a new millennium and signal a new era for Times Square.

On one level, this book is the story of the remarkable transformation of Times
Square from a symbol of urban decline to a symbol of urban renaissance. The story
goes back more than a century to explore the invention of Times Square with the

5

arrival of elegant Broadway theaters, a subway line, and the *New York Times*. It then traces the evolution of Times Square as an area of popular entertainment, commercial culture, public gatherings, countercultural activity, commercialized sex industries (legal and not), moral crusades, and real-estate speculation. The main focus of this book, however, is on the period since the mid-1970s, during which time economic and political elites successfully orchestrated a dramatic redevelopment effort for West Forty-second Street and Times Square.

On a second level, this book is about politics and power at the city level and their relationship to the development of urban space. In many respects, the transformation of West Forty-second Street reflects the processes and patterns of downtown redevelopment that are characteristic of those in other cities in the United States and beyond. Recycled historic structures, new arts facilities, and themed Disneyspaces are now common features of revitalized inner cities, often nestled alongside gleaming new office towers. The redevelopment of Times Square thus offers an empirical case for theorizing about the political and economic forces behind the production of the postindustrial urban form. The analysis of the Times Square case illustrates how several major theoretical approaches to the study of urban politics can be integrated into a coherent analytical framework for understanding contemporary urban development.

READING THE URBAN LANDSCAPE

The redevelopment of Forty-second Street and Times Square illustrates the fundamental shift in the nature of urban development that has taken place over the past several decades. The large-scale projects of clean-sweep destruction and modern rebuilding that characterized the urban renewal approach of the 1950s and 1960s have been discredited. Instead, development projects have come to center more and more around the preservation and restoration of architecturally significant historic buildings. Through the technique of adaptive reuse, old structures such as industrial buildings, railroad stations, warehouses, waterfront markets, and theaters (as in Times Square) have been recycled into thriving commercial districts. Prominent examples of such preservation-based redevelopment include Ghirardelli Square in San Francisco, Faneuil Hall and Quincy Market in Boston, Harbor Place in Baltimore, and the South Street Seaport and SoHo in New York City. But similar types of redevelopment projects can be found throughout the United States, in small and medium-size cities. Indeed, historic preservation is so prevalent that it has been identified as the only widely accepted strategy guiding urban development over the past three decades.[1]

As the Times Square case illustrates, historic preservation is related to broader cultural strategies that underlie contemporary urban development. The historic theaters on Forty-second Street served as a defining image in the redevelopment effort not just as physical landmarks, but as potential sites for the performing arts as well.

The redevelopment of Forty-second Street came to be framed as an expansion of the Broadway theater and entertainment district. Indeed, historic preservation and the arts—and other forms of cultural capital—are now common components of redevelopment projects that employ cultural strategies and images to create new urban spaces.[2]

This study of Times Square redevelopment is, therefore, also an analysis of the political significance of a widespread preservation-based cultural approach to urban development. As such, it fits into a line of urban study that has sought to discover the social and political messages encoded in the built environment. This type of inquiry views the urban landscape as a kind of three-dimensional, topographic map of power in society. The city is treated as a text, in the sense that its physical form tells a story. Lewis Mumford's *The Culture of Cities* remains a definitive example of such an analysis,[3] but other scholars have provided valuable insight into the social and political significance of urban forms. Indeed, urban forms tell many stories and are legible from a variety of perspectives.

For example, Carl Schorske's rich study of politics and culture in "fin-de-siècle Vienna" illustrates the way in which an ascendant liberal regime "inscribed its values in space and stone" through urban redevelopment.[4] It did so initially with monumental public buildings that drew on the symbols of classical Greek and Roman architectural styles; later, modernism provided the business and professional class with an architectural language of its own. Closer to home, Mike Davis recently surveyed the postmodern landscape of Los Angeles and revealed a militarized terrain where dominant urban institutions are protected—down to their trash receptacles—in fortresslike buildings that blend architecture and advanced security technology.[5]

Michel Foucault discovered entirely new and different levels on which to understand the operation of power in spatial arrangements.[6] Foucault revealed how knowledge and power converge in the modern disciplinary practices that order space, such as architecture, and shape patterns of behavior and social activity. Building on this analysis, Timothy Mitchell demonstrated how the modern urban-planning practices of structuring and enframing space—for example, laying out streets according to a grid pattern—were essential techniques by which Western powers established control in colonial societies.[7]

Social theorists have thus uncovered political significance in the construction of the built environment by careful examination of the particular urban forms of different times and places from a variety of perspectives.[8] The production of a new kind of built environment through preservation-based redevelopment requires similar analytic consideration. The social and political relevance of the historic-preservation approach is apparent in the distinctive nature of the places that are being constructed. In effect, historic structures are being infused with new life and new meaning, and the time is ripe to explore these new sites.

Current redevelopment projects make use of historic buildings in a variety of ways that may or may not have any direct connection to their historic function.

Indeed, the term "historic preservation" is a highly imprecise and misleading—perhaps even oxymoronic—designation for a process that creates new urban environments out of historic structures. Nevertheless, historic structures have become an invaluable resource in urban development. Developers manipulate the history of place, even in the most superficial ways, to construct a marketable image or a theme-park atmosphere for new urban places. Restored historic areas are manufactured as objects of consumption, forming the type of urban spectacle that attracts affluent residents and visitors and nurtures commercial activity.[9]

At the South Street Seaport in New York City, for example, a conventional museum of exhibits in glass cases is complemented by a "historic" waterfront area of restored nineteenth-century warehouses, piers, ships, cobbled streets, and low-rise brick buildings—as well as the pricey and antihistorical shops and restaurants they now contain. Similarly, Forty-second Street is being re-created as a fantasyland of Broadway theater, popular culture, and commercial glitz, based on historic images of Times Square. At the same time, enormous skyscrapers tower over both Times Square and the South Street Seaport; they, too, are an integral part of contemporary redevelopment projects.

Urban scholars have generally interpreted these new urban forms, combining office towers and spectacular historic theme parks, as a product of the shift from an industrial to a postindustrial economy. The decline of manufacturing and the rise of a service economy (based on finance, insurance, real estate, and advanced corporate activities) have produced a change in the defining image of the urban skyline from smokestacks to skyscrapers. The trend also has led to the transformation of the urban labor pool, with white-collar professionals replacing blue-collar laborers as the backbone of the urban economy. A parallel development involves the polarization of the workforce into highly educated, well-paid managers and professionals at the upper levels of the service economy, and low-skilled workers locked into dead-end jobs at the lower end.[10]

From this perspective, contemporary urban redevelopment is driven by the need to construct the places of work (office towers), entertainment (urban theme parks), and housing (luxury high-rises and gentrified neighborhoods) that will accommodate the advanced service economy and its workforce. There is a political dimension to this process as well: in the era of neoconservative politics, emphasizing private-sector initiative and government retrenchment and deregulation, cities have been forced into greater economic competition for survival. Thus city officials become eager and active participants in promoting downtown redevelopment to attract new forms of investment, thereby hastening the postindustrial transformation. The flip side of this process, of course, is a geographic polarization corresponding to the economic polarization in cities. Cities increasingly become divided into areas of consumption for the rich and areas of abandonment for the poor, with little ameliorative government intervention.

Various urban scholars have emphasized different aspects of this process while, for the most part, focusing on an underlying economic rationale. According to Christine Boyer, private capital has, in effect, appropriated the built form as an advertising tool aimed at enticing the consumption dollars of the affluent.[11] By placing commodities in the exotic settings of urban theme parks, it is possible to enhance their appeal and sustain an increasingly frenzied level of hyperconsumption. Private-sector domination of the urban environment has become possible because the state has essentially ceded its use of urban planning as a means of promoting social change. Instead, architecture and urban planning have succumbed to the superficiality of marketing strategies. The postindustrial city thus reflects the ultimate triumph of the market over a critical and reforming modernist aesthetic. At the same time, the landscape of themed urban spaces diverts attention from the areas of abandonment and the socioeconomic problems that they represent.[12]

Along complementary lines, David Harvey regards the changing urban form as an expression of a new "condition of postmodernity" rooted in the move from an urban economy based on production to one based on consumption.[13] For Harvey, changes in the urban environment reflect a re-rationalization of space in the service of capital accumulation.[14] With the shift from "Fordism" to more flexible modes of production, and the increasing importance of specialized business services in city economies, space no longer is a necessary factor of production; instead, space itself can become an object of consumption: "imaging the city through the organization of spectacular urban spaces became a means to attract capital and people (of the right sort) in a period (since 1973) of intensified inter-urban competition and urban entrepreneurialism."[15] At the same time, spectacular places and public festivals serve to obfuscate underlying class conflicts and inequalities. The postmodern city provides the "bread and circuses" necessary to uphold the late-capitalist socioeconomic order.

Pushing this line of analysis further, Sharon Zukin has proposed that we invert the Marxist tenet that holds the cultural realm to be a reflection of the material realm of production, and consider "the radical argument that the way consumption [is] organized . . . [has] become at least as important in people's lives as the organization of production."[16] She argues that a new "symbolic economy" in cities—centered on tourism, entertainment, and the media, and promoted through historic preservation and the arts—has become a driving force shaping fundamental economic activities such as business services and real-estate development. In the symbolic economy, Disney theme parks provide the model for urban development based on the principles of cleanliness, security, and visual coherence. The Disney-inspired urban strategy prescribes developing space according to a common visual and symbolic theme (historic districts are especially suitable), and then turning the area over to private management (for example, through business improvement districts). In this way, parts of the messy, "real" city can be made to replicate the reassuring security and social order of the Disney parks and walled communities that are so appealing to the suburban middle class.

Although Zukin, Harvey, and Boyer offer valuable insights into the social implications of contemporary urban development, they do not directly address its political underpinnings. Each focuses on the economic bases of this new pattern of market-driven urbanism, in which the city promotes capital accumulation through upscale consumption. Each recognizes that this process of urban economic restructuring has important political consequences: the urban poor (increasingly made up of immigrant populations and people of color) are displaced and marginalized; social problems are masked behind images of spectacular urban places; private-sector control and government retrenchment are justified by visible downtown redevelopment; and problems of unemployment, underemployment, and poverty are dismissed with statistics on increased investment and job creation.

Although there is a recognition of the political significance of urban restructuring, there has been less attention to the specific political arrangements that support contemporary redevelopment. Political factors have been treated more as consequences than as causes in a process of urban change driven by economic forces. These analyses therefore imply an economic determinism behind the creation of new urban forms, as cities are redeveloped to accommodate the service industries and professional workforce of the postindustrial economy.

The postindustrial transformation of American cities has been under way for at least half a century, though, and during this time the approach to urban development has changed dramatically. Both the clean-sweep urban renewal strategy of the 1950s and 1960s and the preservation-based approach of recent decades were aimed at furthering the process of postindustrial urban restructuring. Economic forces alone do not explain this change in urban development. It is necessary, therefore, to identify noneconomic forces that help account for contemporary redevelopment strategies. The argument presented here is that political factors play a central causal role in changing patterns of urban redevelopment. Without overlooking the importance of broad economic forces, this study of Times Square contributes to an understanding of the political dynamics that support the new cultural development strategies based on historic preservation and the arts.

THE CHANGING NATURE OF URBAN DEVELOPMENT

In order to understand the significance of the cultural strategies of urban development based on historic preservation and the arts, it is necessary to consider the changes in development politics during the twentieth century. Specifically, it is necessary to consider the legacy of the urban renewal approach to development, which was fully entrenched in the 1950s. Urban renewal reflected a cultural vision, based on urban modernism, for the redevelopment of American cities very different from that of historic preservation. It is in this historical context that the source of current development politics can be located.

Urban renewal at mid-century was symbolized by the image of a bulldozer plowing its way through the cityscape. Entire neighborhoods were razed, and new ones rebuilt, in a process justified as radical surgery on an ailing city corpus. Urban renewal thus epitomized the process that Harvey has called "creative destruction," whereby the built environment is continually torn down and rebuilt in the interest of economic necessity and greater profits.[17] Creative destruction was supported by the belief in social progress that was so integral to modern culture.[18] In this light, the shift to historic preservation, which is a fundamentally antimodern approach, marks an outright rejection of urban renewal.

The source of the move from renewal to preservation lies in a class-based political conflict over urban space. Urban renewal was a massive effort to restructure land-use patterns in American cities around an emerging postindustrial economy.[19] This strategy for revaluing downtown real estate ultimately depended on dislodging the poor, largely African-American populations that were clustered in dilapidated neighborhoods around inner-city business districts.[20] African-Americans were already perceived as having taken over the nation's inner cities, posing a fundamental threat to the social and economic health of cities.[21] The survival of cities seemingly required that they stem the exodus of the white middle class for the comfort and security of the suburbs. Urban renewal involved not only demolishing city slums, but also rebuilding the urban environment to accommodate a middle- and upper-income workforce.

Urban renewal also employed a particular cultural strategy, defined by modern architects and planners. The built landscape produced by urban renewal followed the principles of rationality and efficiency that characterized urban modernism. Modern architects and planners believed that the city should be constructed as a machine, with function alone dictating its form.[22] Newly constructed buildings invariably followed the stark International Style of modern architecture, which rejected the decorative features of classical architecture in the interest of pure geometric forms. Rich and poor alike were confined to faceless, boxy apartment buildings of pale brick or concrete, while glass and steel formed the pure "skin and bones" architecture of downtown office buildings. There was remarkably little in modern architecture to distinguish the apartment buildings of the rich and the poor, with the exception of telltale details like the chain-link fences caging in the balconies of the poor.

Urban renewal, guided by its cultural vision of urban modernism, failed to construct a new cityscape that appealed to middle- and upper-income people. On the contrary, these groups increasingly mobilized in opposition to renewal activities throughout the 1960s. Rallying behind Jane Jacobs's assault on the planning principles of modernism[23]—and the "marvels of dullness and regimentation" that they produced—higher-income city dwellers began asserting their commitment to the value of neighborhood preservation. Young professionals in particular began pioneering new housing opportunities in the wild frontier of marginal city neighborhoods.[24] In the process of restoring architecturally interesting historic homes, these urban pioneers were constructing new symbols of status and distinction.[25] Their residences offered a means of class differentiation, which was denied them by the Spartan aesthetic of modernist housing. After all, the International Style had its roots in European socialism and reflected its equalizing vision. Tom Wolfe's *From Bauhaus to Our House* stands out as a biting bourgeois attack on modern architecture for denying the decorative symbols of wealth and status to those with the money and good taste to desire them.[26]

Historic preservation remains a luxury for lower-income residents, since the costs of historically accurate restorations are generally prohibitive for those with limited means; indeed, this is the source of the appeal of preservation as a distinguishing status symbol. Because of the costs, preservation has often translated into gentrification, a process by which higher-income people reclaim and revalue older inner-city residential neighborhoods.[27] In this sense, gentrification represents another stage in an ongoing class struggle over the urban terrain.[28]

Residential gentrification clearly reveals the class-based appeal of historic preservation. But the same class orientation is apparent in commercial redevelopment strategies as well. The invention of the trendy SoHo neighborhood in New York City was aided by the designation of a special historic district that asserted—and thereby helped to create—the area's exclusive character.[29] Historic preservation melded nicely with a commercial theme based on the visual arts to produce a marketable atmosphere of high culture. The SoHo example illustrates how historic preservation has been integrated into the menu of cultural forms that serve to distinguish the taste of the upper class.[30] Indeed, historic preservation and the arts are often effectively linked as the focus of contemporary redevelopment projects.[31]

To the extent that preservation- and arts-based redevelopment is an effort to restructure and revalue downtown areas and accommodate higher-income populations, the process differs little in its economic functions from earlier urban renewal efforts. But the two approaches are fundamentally different because of the different patterns of political activity that undergird them. Whereas urban renewal increasingly became the focus of political conflict, preservation- and arts-based development has tended to enjoy broad public support. Understanding the evolution of development strategies points the way to a new theoretical approach to urban politics.

COMPETING PARADIGMS OF DEVELOPMENT POLITICS

The scholarly debate over the politics of urban development was defined during the 1980s by Paul Peterson's influential book, *City Limits*.[32] Skillfully applying the logic of economics to the urban realm, Peterson argued that cities in the American federal system are compelled to pursue economic development above all other goals. Economic development brings the jobs and tax revenues that ultimately benefit the city as a whole; therefore, city residents share a "unitary interest" in development. As a result, there is a broad political consensus in support of development projects. In the interest of efficiency, development policy is generally formulated behind the scenes by business elites and local officials and then endorsed by a supportive public. The same economic imperatives that compel cities to pursue pro-development policies also preclude them from pursuing costly redistributive programs.

Peterson's argument was compelling as a concise explanation of the pro-development orientation prevalent in municipalities during the late 1970s and the 1980s. But his policy-determines-politics approach provided a static picture that failed to account for the dynamic nature of development politics. Indeed, urban development politics had been increasingly conflictual, rather than consensual, during the 1960s and early 1970s. Because Peterson defined urban development policymaking as essentially nonpolitical, his analysis was unable to account for differences in patterns of political activity, including frequent conflict, surrounding development.[33]

Peterson's argument stimulated an effort by urbanists to rediscover the politics in urban development policymaking.[34] In a number of prominent studies, scholars formulated alternative analytical frameworks that identified, in slightly different ways, a combination of political and economic pressures at the heart of urban politics.[35] These works can be loosely joined under the label "regime studies" because they share an understanding that urban politics is about the decidedly political process of constructing and maintaining stable governing coalitions, or regimes.[36]

Foremost among the new approaches challenging Peterson's economic determinism was Clarence Stone's work developing and applying the regime concept.[37] Stone described development policy—indeed, all urban policy—as the product of a fundamentally political process of coalition building. He recognized that the business community occupies a central position in a local governing coalition because it possesses resources that are needed "to get things done." This productive capacity gives the business community "systemic power"—and thus a pervasive influence—in the local arena.

Nevertheless, Stone argued, the business community is not in a position to dictate unilaterally the terms of local policy because it lacks the numbers necessary for electoral power. As a result, business interests must form a coalition with other social groups in order to generate the electoral support necessary to accomplish their agenda. According to Stone, they do this by providing selective incentives, in the form of material benefits, to their allies in exchange for political support. A governing coalition based on stable patterns of cooperation among political leaders, the business community, and other social groups constitutes an established urban regime.

Stone's focus on politics and political strategy provides a useful point of departure for exploring the significance of historic preservation and the arts in contemporary urban development. Economic imperatives alone are insufficient as an explanation of the shift from urban renewal to a preservation- and arts-based development approach. Economic pressures may indeed require cities to pursue economic development and growth, even postindustrial restructuring, but they do not dictate how that development will proceed. Development processes must be constructed in a way that will generate the necessary political support and minimize opposition. This is precisely the key to understanding the emphasis on preservation- and arts-based cultural strategies in contemporary redevelopment projects. Historic preservation and the arts are a means by which widespread support for redevelopment efforts can be politically constructed. The interaction of political and economic pressures, not abstract economics alone, best explains the cultural strategies of contemporary urban development and their ability to generate consensus.

Although the regime approach provides the essential analytic basis for a theory of urban politics, its specific formulations reflect an overly narrow understanding of political processes. By focusing on tangible, material trade-offs between the business community and its coalition partners, the regime framework remains bound to traditional conceptions of politics and power that needlessly circumscribe the scope of political analysis. A fully developed regime approach must recognize the greater complexities of politics and account for multiple levels of political action. This requires greater attention to the way in which political issues and identities are constructed.

Scholars from various disciplines are coming to acknowledge "the malleability of social issues" and the attendant conclusion that a fundamental aspect of politics and policymaking involves the definition of issues themselves.[38] In a brilliant analysis of political conflict, E. E. Schattschneider argued that "the definition of the alternatives is the supreme instrument of power."[39] In a political universe where there are "billions of potential conflicts"[40] that divide the public in many different ways, success comes not from being on the popular side of the issues, but from bringing to the forefront those issues on which one is on the popular side. Schattschneider's genius was in recognizing the strategic importance of control over the political agenda; but he never adequately explained how such control is achieved, in part because he did not directly consider that even a given issue could be framed in a number of ways.

Political strategy is about not just determining which issues are most salient, but also shaping how issues are defined in public debate. As Murray Edelman has argued, political debate is not primarily concerned with objective facts; if it were, there would be little basis for ongoing conflicts.[41] Instead, political debate involves competing interpretations of reality. In this political contest, power is gained by constructing a potent representation of social reality, or "political spectacle," that will mobilize an apathetic public in support of a given agenda. Thus language itself—especially symbolic language—is an elemental tool of politics. Crime is a good example of a political issue whose salience is only loosely related to objective measures,[42] but whose substance provides a recurring political spectacle because of the many different agendas that it serves.

In his innovative and exciting work, Robert Beauregard demonstrated the relevance of political discourse to the analysis of urban politics and policy in the United States.[43] For Beauregard, it is crucial to recognize that "cities are narrative objects" that are defined by the meanings we ascribe to them.[44] Cities come to be represented, perceived, and understood in terms of interpretive frameworks that give meaning to a vast array of objective conditions. So, for example, Beauregard explored the concept of "urban decline" as a prevailing discursive theme in the public debate about American cities during the postwar era. Drawing on the "voices" of commentators in the media, academia, and government, he pieced together a relatively coherent narrative, or "discourse on urban decline," that has structured perceptions of cities in the United States. The discourse is "materially based but not materially determined"[45] because it draws selectively from a messy world of contradictory developments to convey a narrative tale of decline.

Those who study cities must be attentive to discourses on cities—the systems of meaning that are constructed and conveyed in public debate to represent cities— because they have important social, economic, and political ramifications. The particular ways in which cities are represented in public debate shape the choices made by individuals, investors, and public officials. For example, the discourse on urban decline contributed to the multitude of public and private decisions that furthered the postwar process of suburbanization.

A fundamental concern, then, is the relationship between public discourse and material interests. Beauregard rejects "a functionalist logic in which the discourse serves the needs of some larger entity,"[46] and he specifically denies the kind of economic determinism that might portray political discourse as an instrument in the service of capital accumulation. Nevertheless, he does acknowledge that the discourse on urban decline has contributed to "an ideology of development that legitimizes trends, fosters trust, and produces a modicum of acquiescence,"[47] thereby supporting patterns of capital investment. In this sense, political discourse is aligned, albeit imperfectly, with the interests of dominant economic and political elites.

In sum, Beauregard reveals a prevailing narrative that shapes (rather than determines) public and private choices about cities. The discourse is neither monolithic nor entirely coherent, but consists of certain dominant themes. It is not unrelated to objective conditions in cities, but the link between the two realms is tenuous. Nevertheless, as an interpretive framework that structures decision making, the discourse has important material effects and so can serve political and economic interests. Consequently, the discourse is relevant to the political economy of cities.

The work on political discourse points the way to a more sophisticated conceptualization of urban regimes that can provide a basis for urban political analysis. Specifically, the regime framework should be broadened to encompass the realm of political discourse in addition to the traditional focus on political exchanges involving tangible benefits. Urban regimes are constructed not only around direct material interests and trade-offs, but also around a shared discourse that defines and justifies to a particular urban agenda. A stable governing coalition requires a unifying vision, or representation, of urban policy that, in turn, structures the nature of material exchanges. From this perspective, the symbolic and material realms form two interacting sides of the political process: material interests shape the language of politics, and political discourse shapes the pursuit of material interests.

Thus the language of urban politics and urban development is a political force that affects how interests are subjectively perceived by both public and private actors. The narrative themes that are constructed in public debate shape how these participants think and act. In this way, a prevailing public discourse plays a fundamental role in structuring political behavior. The discourse can help mobilize political support for a given agenda and undermine others; it can help unify political allies and isolate enemies; and it can privilege certain political interests over others. Thus public discourse should be considered an essential instrument of politics, more so than Beauregard concedes.[48]

Attention to political discourse not only enriches an understanding of regime politics, but also explains the salience of cultural issues in contemporary urban politics and redevelopment. Conceptions of culture and cultures, in all their incarnations, have become central images in the urban political arena: consider, for example, the potent political symbolism of graffiti, historic districts, rap music and hip-hop styles, the ghetto "underclass," white Catholics, public-housing projects, art galleries and museums, the homeless, and yuppies. In part, the power of such images results from their role as codes in the language of urban politics. The way that cultural images are defined and deployed in political discourse is important to the construction and maintenance of political alliances.

THE TIMES SQUARE CASE

Just as cities are narrative objects, so are particular city spaces—none more so than Times Square. Times Square has been dubbed the "Crossroads of the World," and, indeed, it is very possibly the world's most famous and symbolic urban place. Both residents of and visitors to New York congregate there to welcome in the new year, celebrate the end of war, and experience the excitement of an exploding commercial culture. By the 1970s, however, the meaning of the area had changed, from a glamorous past to a horrific present.

It took two decades to transform Forty-second Street and Times Square from a symbol of urban decline into a thriving Disneyspace. The process began in the latter half of the 1970s with several initiatives from private-sector interests. New York City, having narrowly escaped bankruptcy, was ripe politically and economically for new investment; a pro-business political order was in place, and the city was embarking on an explosive real-estate boom that came to define the 1980s. Midtown Manhattan was ground zero for new skyscraper development and, therefore, Times Square was ripe for a blitz of new investment.

In the early 1980s, public officials at the city and state level, led by New York mayor Edward I. Koch, picked up on the private-sector plans for Times Square and initiated the publicly sponsored 42nd Street Development Project. The project called for the extensive redevelopment of about thirteen acres of prime real estate on Forty-second Street from Broadway to Eighth Avenue. The proposal included the construction of four office towers containing more than 4 million square feet of space, a 2.4-million-square-foot wholesale merchandise mart, and a 550-room hotel. It also provided for the renovation of the Times Square subway station and the preservation and restoration of nine historic theaters with entrances on Forty-second Street. In effect, the Forty-second Street Development Project was an essential component of the city's effort to complete the postindustrial transformation of midtown Manhattan.[49]

The price tag on this project—described as the largest public urban redevelopment effort in the history of New York State—began at more than $1 billion and ballooned to $2.5 billion by the late 1980s.[50] Most of the upfront costs (including land acquisition and construction) would be borne by private developers, but government officials sweetened the deal with substantial public subsidies. Estimates of the value of the complex incentive package for developers have varied; one early estimate placed the baseline value of the public subsidy at $650 million over fifteen years,[51] but other analyses found as much as "a hundred years of subsidy" potentially worth billions of dollars.[52]

This was, after all, the era of public–private partnerships in American cities, when public authority was harnessed to smooth the way for lucrative private development.[53] For the Forty-second Street project, New York State's economic development agency, the Urban Development Corporation (UDC), used its power of eminent domain and offered enticing financial incentives to attract substantial private investment. Equally valuable to developers was the UDC's ability to overrule local land-use laws and review procedures in New York City. In effect, UDC sponsorship of the project preempted direct public involvement and cleared the way for an insulated process of planning and implementation driven by political appointees, technocrats, and private developers.

Although the UDC enabled the project to circumvent the usual political roadblocks that confront development proposals in New York City, the plan did face one crucial political hurdle. The New York City Board of Estimate (BoE), composed of the city's major elected officials,[54] would have to approve the terms of the project as negotiated between the UDC and the designated developers. Thus much of the political wrangling over the project, which centered on the formulation and adoption of a specific plan, occurred in the period leading up to the BoE vote in late 1984. The redevelopment of Times Square was especially important to the political fortunes of Mayor Koch, and it was he who was most directly involved in shaping the proposed plan, forging a supportive pro-growth alliance, and securing BoE approval. Beyond that point, the process of implementation was largely left to project officials at the UDC. Indeed, Koch's successors, David N. Dinkins and Rudolph W. Giuliani, had very little direct involvement in the effort to redevelop this central place in their domain.[55]

Once the project received BoE approval, new obstacles emerged that threatened to derail the redevelopment effort. In New York City, as elsewhere, the courts serve as an important resource for antigrowth movements, and the Forty-second Street project was stymied by a barrage of lawsuits for the next half decade. The UDC finally won court approval to condemn properties and move forward with the project, but not until the close of the 1980s. By this time, the real-estate market emerged as the spoiler. The combined impact of a stock market crash that hobbled the postindustrial economy of New York City, and a decade of frenetic overbuilding spurred by city officials, left the city with a glut of office space. So precisely when the UDC was clearing West Forty-second Street for redevelopment, the prospects for a cluster of new skyscrapers were grim indeed.

Early in the 1990s, therefore, it appeared that the Forty-second Street Development Project was a colossal mistake. West Forty-second Street was being vacated and drained of all life, but the redevelopment plan could not proceed. Conceding defeat, UDC officials went back to the drawing board. They scrapped the office towers, for the time being, in favor of restoring existing buildings on Forty-second Street for a variety of entertainment uses. This plan, relying on the piecemeal addition of shops and attractions to pave the way for later office development, reflected a fundamental shift in strategy. Success seemed uncertain, and the project stumbled along at first because many investors were reluctant to commit to the uncharted territory of West Forty-second Street.

That all changed when project officials succeeded in luring Disney to Forty-second Street in the mid-1990s. As word spread that Disney might sign on, other prominent entertainment companies began flocking to Forty-second Street and Times Square. In a few years, Times Square emerged as the premiere tourism and entertainment district in the city. Furthermore, the real-estate market in the city was coming full circle, and developers were once again plotting monumental additions to the skyline. The time had finally arrived for new office towers on West Forty-second Street. The first of the towers envisioned nearly two decades earlier would join Disney on Forty-second Street in time for the new millennium.

The effort to redevelop West Forty-second Street and Times Square in New York City illustrates the significance of cultural politics and political discourse in contemporary urban development. Specifically, the case reveals how the historic-preservation and arts components of the redevelopment plan, centering on the restoration of Broadway theaters, provided the foundation for a pro-growth strategy that drew on cultural images of Times Square. These images formed the crux of a dominant political discourse that was important in solidifying a pro-growth alliance in support of the project—an alliance that could draw essential constituencies into Koch's broader pro-growth coalition, or regime.[56]

By all objective measures, the Times Square project approved by the BoE was for massive office construction and other conventional commercial development. In some respects—for example, the extent of property condemnations and the scale of new construction—the plan was reminiscent of the urban renewal projects of an earlier era. What makes this case so interesting, however, is the extent to which the focus of the public debate over the original project was on the elements of historic preservation and the arts related to the theater restorations. Although these restorations promised to expand the city's stock of Broadway theaters by as much as 20 percent, they accounted for only a tiny fraction of the total project cost.

Yet in the statements of politicians and planners, and in media coverage of the project, the office towers and other commercial sites were seemingly justified as simply a means of providing the cross-subsidy necessary for the restoration of the historic theaters.[57] This was particularly apparent in the coverage by the *New York Times,* the newspaper after which Times Square was named, whose headquarters borders the project area.[58] This characterization of the project as a mission of historic preservation and re-creation was reflected in the phrase "the return of the Great White Way," which frequently was used to evoke starry-eyed visions of the Times Square theater district during its romanticized heyday in the early twentieth century. The image of the Great White Way was the defining discursive theme for the project until it was revised in the 1990s and redefined by Disney.

This vision is a key to understanding the cultural and racial politics that supported the redevelopment effort. Given the widely held perception in the 1980s of West Forty-second Street as a "ghetto street"—a key element of the discourse on Times Square—there was an obvious political appeal to a project that professed to restore a sparkling Great White Way. In effect, the Great White Way was marketed as a Great White Hope for the future of Times Square and New York—and perhaps even for urban America.

At the same time, the symbolic language of the Times Square discourse tapped into the realm of cultural politics to generate support for redevelopment through more subtle mechanisms. As Beauregard has pointed out, the issue of urban decline has a potent symbolic impact because it overlaps with more general social anxieties and fears that have prevailed in the United States during the postwar era.[59] Concern about urban decline is deeply entangled with anxieties regarding racial transition, the erosion of elite culture and civilization, even the loss of national superiority. The discourse on Times Square was also a discourse on urban decline that drew on deeper anxieties in mobilizing support for redevelopment among middle- and upper-income whites, groups that were crucial to the endurance of Koch's regime. Thus the Times Square discourse drew on symbolic imagery from the realm of cultural politics in ways that served dominant economic and political agendas.

2
From Urban Renewal to Historic Preservation

All this is another way of saying that the city itself, as a living environment, must not be condemned to serve the specialized purposes of the museum. . . . By confining the function of preservation to the museum, we thus release space in the rest of the city for the fresh uses of the living.
—Lewis Mumford, *The Culture of Cities* (1938)

The Congress finds that . . . the historical and cultural foundations of the Nation should be preserved as a living part of our community life and development in order to give a sense of orientation to the American people.
—National Historic Preservation Act (1966)

In October 1963, demolition began on Pennsylvania Station, located at Thirty-third Street and Seventh Avenue in New York City. The station, completed in 1910, was a monumental granite structure occupying two entire city blocks. Its facade included a Doric colonnade along the Seventh Avenue entrance and carved eagles adorning the roof. Years later, Christopher Gray, in the *New York Times,* provided the following nostalgic description of the station's interior:

> Midway between Seventh and Eighth Avenues, the General Waiting Room ran north–south, a huge, high space with a vaulted, coffered ceiling, grand stairways and giant columns. At the Eighth Avenue end was the even bigger Concourse, a vast space open to the tracks below, lighted by an expansive curved steel and glass roof supported by riveted girders. The Waiting Room was modeled after ancient Roman baths, but the Concourse was pure Industrial Revolution. The entire complex was on an astounding scale—even the ancillary spaces were bigger than those in conventional public buildings.[1]

According to the Municipal Art Society, this building was "one of the great monuments of classical America."[2] By the 1960s, however, this architectural masterpiece was considered an impediment to a vastly more profitable use of its prime location. The financially strapped Pennsylvania Railroad Company was demolishing the structure in order to make way for the new $70 million Madison Square

Garden complex, consisting of a sports stadium and an office tower. As the president of the development concern observed, "In some areas the land is just too valuable to save anything that doesn't fully utilize it."[3] In order to accommodate the new development, the station itself was reduced to a series of claustrophobic subterranean tunnels.

Thirty years later, in the ultimate of ironies, Amtrak announced its plan to recreate the architectural grandeur of the demolished station by relocating it across Eighth Avenue to the site of the landmark General Post Office building.[4] Now called the James A. Farley Building, the post office is another classical Beaux-Arts granite structure. Completed in 1913, it was designed by the same architectural firm that created the original Penn Station—the prominent office of McKim, Mead, & White—as a companion to that building across the street.[5] It also occupies two city blocks and features a colonnade of twenty Corinthian columns more than fifty feet in height. Plans were already under way to relocate the main post office, and since the railroad's tracks and platforms extend under the post office building, its conversion to a train station would be feasible.

In 1993, Amtrak's development team released design sketches illustrating how the ceiling of the post office would be transformed into a soaring 120-foot-high arch of white steel girders covered by a sparkling glass skin. It was a design created with "deference to and reference to the old Penn Station."[6] The cost of reclaiming the past would be $315 million, with the federal, state, and city governments expected to pick up nearly two-thirds of the tab.[7] And yet, as Herbert Muschamp, architecture critic for the *Times,* put it, this offered the city a rare second chance to remedy "one of the greatest traumas New York City ever suffered" with the loss of Penn Station.[8]

The case of New York's Penn Station stands as a particularly illuminating example of the transformation that has taken place in urban redevelopment over the past three decades. The urban renewal approach to development, which involved tearing down the old and building anew, has been widely discredited. Architecturally significant older structures, once considered obstacles to profits, have become the marketing vehicle for successful redevelopment efforts. Historic preservation (and adaptive reuse) is arguably the one identifiable and coherent principle guiding urban development in the postmodern era.[9]

THE POLITICS OF URBAN RENEWAL

The federal urban renewal program, established by the Housing Act of 1949, represented an unprecedented commitment of public funds to facilitate the physical and economic restructuring of the nation's cities.[10] During the twenty-five-year life span of the program, more than $10 billion in federal grants were approved for over 2,100 urban renewal projects.[11] The program left its mark on hundreds of cities of all sizes that took advantage of the federal subsidies to promote downtown revitalization projects.

The urban renewal program relied on local renewal agencies to initiate and sponsor projects. These agencies exercised their power of eminent domain to condemn large assemblages of "blighted" inner-city land targeted for redevelopment. The federal government then provided the localities with a subsidy to write-down the cost of land acquisition and clearance.[12] The condemned land, cleared of its dilapidated structures, could then be transferred to private developers at a fraction of its value for purposes of redevelopment. The federal program thus embodied the principle of demolition and new construction as the basis of urban redevelopment.

Dennis Gale has identified two essential principles that supported the urban renewal program.[13] The first, which he calls the "Tabula Rasa Imperative," was the assumption that urban revitalization could succeed only by tearing down deteriorated slum areas and building anew from the ground up. This was the essence of the urban renewal approach.[14] Renewal efforts were often likened to a process of radical surgery that involved cutting out the blighted areas that acted as a cancer on the body of the city.[15] Implicit in this approach was the conviction that revitalization would require removing the poor, largely minority populations surrounding central business districts.

The second principle identified by Gale is what he calls the "Publicism Imperative," which held that only massive efforts combining federal and local government action could reverse the decline of city neighborhoods. Private-sector initiatives alone could not stem or reverse the spread of inner-city slums. The two imperatives went hand in hand: urban revitalization required clean-sweep redevelopment of entire areas, and such massive intervention required government power and money. Urban renewal fit the bill, combining local condemnation power with federal subsidies.

The concept of a Publicism Imperative is somewhat misleading, since it implies the possibility of development processes operating in the absence of government intervention. Gale himself acknowledges the omnipresence of government involvement, but suggests that in the case of urban renewal the state's role ascended to a "level of overall control." It is equally true, however, that federal policy was central to the preservation-based development approach that replaced urban renewal.

The meaningful distinction between the era of urban renewal and that of historic preservation is not so much in the degree of government involvement as in the nature of the strategy embodied in development policies. In the 1950s, there was widespread support for the urban renewal approach among dominant local interests; indeed, many mayors built powerful pro-growth coalitions around renewal agendas. Federal policy therefore facilitated this strategy of clean-sweep redevelopment. When support for the urban renewal approach began to erode during the 1960s, federal policies became an important force in the construction of a preservation-based development approach that would supplant the discredited slash-and-burn tactics of renewal.

POLITICAL CHALLENGES TO THE URBAN RENEWAL APPROACH

In the 1960s, two political challenges emerged to confront the urban renewal process. On the one hand, various groups of city residents began to resist the violent destruction that renewal activity entailed. On the other hand, scholars, professionals, and other opinion leaders began to formulate intellectual critiques of the urban renewal approach. Together, these movements raised the political cost of urban renewal efforts to an increasingly high level. Ultimately, these challenges led to the demise of urban renewal and, consequently, the need for a new political strategy to guide urban redevelopment.

Urban renewal projects exacted a high price from the residents of the lower-income communities that were forced to relocate. Entire neighborhoods were razed, but construction of public housing lagged far behind. The price was particularly heavy for minority communities. Racial discrimination had confined African-Americans to the oldest, most dilapidated housing stock, which generally surrounded the central business district. This was precisely the geographic target that local elites aimed at in their pursuit of economic development.

With the ongoing threat of white flight to the suburbs, urban revitalization meant not only rebuilding downtowns, but also relocating their minority populations away from the city center.[16] In effect, revaluing downtown areas required wresting control from the impoverished minority populations that had seemingly come to dominate them and, thereby, to pose a fundamental threat to the social order.[17] African-Americans and other minority groups thus bore a disproportionate burden in terms of displacement.[18]

By the 1960s, civil-rights activists had given urban renewal the unflattering label of "Negro removal," and they began to target development efforts with demonstrations and sit-ins. The rioting that erupted in the nation's cities during the 1960s reflected in part the increasing frustration with and resistance to a renewal process that involved the destruction of African-American communities. As John Mollenkopf points out, "Many of these riots occurred in or near urban renewal areas, and they constituted a kind of revolt against the heritage of New Deal urban programs."[19] Susan Fainstein argues that these urban rebellions were the primary force compelling a change in development strategies.[20]

But it was not just the opposition of low-income minority communities that stood in the path of the renewal bulldozer. In an important sense, the function of urban renewal—to rebuild the nation's cities around a postindustrial economy—contained the seeds of a more salient opposition movement. As urban renewal proceeded to build a new service-based economy, it drew a population of young, educated, middle-class professionals into the cities.[21] These residents, later dubbed yuppies, often acted as "pioneers" forging new housing opportunities in the rugged, untamed wilderness of marginal urban neighborhoods.[22] In the process, they became an additional force for community preservation. The middle-class professionals were powerful allies for the low-income communities fighting renewal because of their greater political influence and resources.[23]

But the community movement among higher-income residents went beyond simply protecting social communities to elevating historic preservation as a value in itself. Gentrification normally took place in older city neighborhoods with a declining stock of architecturally rich buildings. Restoration of the historic housing offered status and distinction to upwardly mobile young investors willing to take a chance.[24] Such housing was a welcome alternative to the uniformity and anonymity of the modernist boxes being constructed by the renewal process.[25] Where successful, historicity would serve as the marketing device for a revalued residential neighborhood. Middle-class taste thus transformed the preservation movement from a defense of use values to a source of exchange values.

In this respect, the middle- and upper-class preservation movement represented a new phase in an ongoing class struggle over urban space.[26] Gentrification became a process of class definition and differentiation. Historic preservation remained something of a luxury for the lower-income residents of gentrifying neighborhoods, since it imposed costs that were usually prohibitive.[27] As a result, preservation often triggered a reverse invasion–succession pattern, with upper-income pioneers driving out lower-income residents.

Thus, there was a fundamental division between the two sides of the neighborhood movement. Increasingly, historic preservation became a tool by which to revalue residential inner-city neighborhoods by promoting their transition to an upscale character.[28] In this sense, historic preservation offered to pick up where the urban renewal process was failing. It provided a redevelopment strategy that enjoyed the support of the higher-income populations that increasingly opposed the renewal approach.

Regardless of these class divisions, urban renewal had triggered an overwhelming movement of community opposition in the 1960s. The growth of neighborhood resistance to renewal was cumulative, becoming more organized and active over time. By 1963, the Housing and Home Finance Administrator acknowledged that "in nearly every major city in the country and many small cities there are heated debates over urban renewal projects that are underway or under consideration."[29]

This community movement posed a fundamental challenge to the method of urban renewal, demanding that wholesale clearance be abandoned in favor of neighborhood preservation and restoration. Even though amendments to the urban renewal program attempted to accommodate rehabilitation in place of clearance, the destructiveness of the process remained its outstanding feature. By 1963, nearly 130,000 structures had been demolished (for an average of about 10,000 a year), and program activity was still accelerating.[30]

Neighborhood opposition to urban renewal was supported and reinforced by intellectual critiques that emerged in the early 1960s. They reflected a fundamental rethinking of the renewal approach within a range of academic disciplines, including urban planning, architecture, and sociology. Perhaps the most devastating and enduring of all the challenges to urban renewal was Jane Jacobs's assault on the modern planning philosophy that supported it.[31] Jacobs argued that the lifeblood of city neighborhoods was found in "a diversity of uses that give each other constant and mutual support, both economically and socially."[32] This diversity of uses depended in large part on a diversity of building types that, in turn, depended on the preservation of some older structures in the process of community redevelopment.

For Jacobs, urban renewal not only destroyed buildings but also undermined the complex social dynamics that supported a community. The uniform, large-scale modernist developments that were constructed as a result of urban renewal segregated uses and removed pedestrians from the street, thereby precluding the diversity of people and activities that contributed to a vibrant city neighborhood. The big money of urban renewal projects acted as "cataclysmic money," destroying rather than rebuilding city neighborhoods.

Sociologists like Herbert Gans also helped construct a social, rather than geographic, understanding of what constituted a neighborhood. Gans's study of Boston's West End neighborhood, an area slated for urban renewal, depicted a lively "urban village" built around a network of supportive social relations.[33] What appeared to the outsider, or city planner, to be an area of dilapidated physical structures was in fact a living and viable community that sustained its inhabitants. City neighborhoods were recognized as having a social value independent of their physical appearance. Other scholars had even begun to explore "some sources of residential satisfaction in an urban slum."[34]

Urban renewal even came under sharp attack on economic grounds. Martin Anderson's influential critique of "the federal bulldozer" portrayed urban renewal as a costly and inefficient program for redistributing urban land from low-income to higher-income populations.[35] Anderson presented data on more than a decade of renewal activity that challenged virtually all the major arguments used to justify the program. His conclusions indicated that the program was harming the poor, especially minorities; was contributing to the spread, rather than the elimination, of slums; was wasting public funds on projects that would have been built anyway; was possibly undermining rather than enhancing local tax revenues; and was adding little or nothing to the national economy.

Architects, too, were challenging the premises of urban renewal. Historic preservation became an established part of the field of architecture in the mid-1960s when it was introduced into the curriculum of the architecture program at Columbia University by James Marston Fitch. Fitch and other social theorists argued that retaining physical manifestations of the past was essential to the emotional well-being of individuals and the stability of society.[36] Around the same time, architects began resurrecting historical styles in an emerging postmodern movement that represented "a wider social protest against modernisation."[37]

The combined challenges of neighborhood activists and academic critics created a political climate in which renewal practices were no longer tenable. It then became necessary to devise development approaches that would circumvent these sources of political opposition.

The new urban programs of the Great Society, including Model Cities and the Community Action Program, were an attempt by Democratic politicians to harness and channel potentially disruptive community activism.[38] By mandating "maximum feasible participation," the federal programs sought to empower local communities in the processes of government planning and service delivery and thereby establish a direct link between organizations in poor neighborhoods and the national government.

Certainly, the programs of the Great Society represented an effort to reintegrate restive inner-city minority communities into the political system. At a more subtle level, though, federal policy was also beginning to formulate a new approach to urban development based on the value of historic preservation to higher-income groups. The intellectual critiques of the destructiveness of renewal activity offered a means by which middle-class city residents could articulate the value of preservation. Before the 1960s, as Marshall Berman has noted, the language simply did not exist through which to defend neighborhood preservation.[39]

It is widely believed that the decline of urban renewal marked the beginning of the end of government intervention in urban development and a return to private-sector control,[40] but that assumption is deceptive. Urban development was undergoing an important transformation in the 1960s, and government policy at the federal, state, and local levels served as a part of the new development practices that were replacing the renewal approach.

HISTORIC PRESERVATION AND FEDERAL POLICY

On October 15, 1966, President Lyndon Johnson signed into law the National Historic Preservation Act, marking the first official statement of a national policy on historic preservation. Before that time, federal involvement in preservation had been limited: Congress had provided some protection for a handful of historic sites and monuments of national significance, and in 1949 had chartered the nonprofit National Trust for Historic Preservation to promote preservation and maintain a national listing of historic places. But in 1966, historic preservation was a modest movement largely confined to the efforts of private groups. After passage of the act, historic preservation emerged as a focus of federal government activity.

The National Historic Preservation Act was widely portrayed as a response to the destructiveness of urban renewal.[41] The stated purpose of the act, set forth in the preamble, was "to give a sense of orientation to the American people" in the face of "ever-increasing extensions of urban centers, highways, and residential, commercial, and industrial developments."[42] Thus it was presented as a government initiative motivated by concern for the public interest, and it reflected the influence of the intellectual critiques of urban renewal.

The law declared an intention to encourage coordinated preservation efforts through a partnership among all levels of government. To support this approach, the act created a program to provide 50 percent matching grants-in-aid to both the states and the nongovernmental National Trust for Historic Preservation to assist in the acquisition and restoration of historic properties. In order to receive the grants, states were required to submit preservation plans for approval. (The preservation grants were administered by the new Office of Archeology and Historic Preservation in the Department of the Interior.) In this way, the program spurred preservation activity by the states themselves; by 1969, all fifty states were participating in the program.

The authorization for the grant program was initially set at $2 million, but grew to $100 million in little more than a decade and was then set at $150 million annually from 1981 through 1997.[43] Actual grant allocations peaked at slightly more than $50 million in 1980 and then leveled off at about $25 million a year through the mid-1980s. In 1976, Congress created the National Historic Preservation Fund in the Department of the Treasury, with revenues from the leasing of mineral rights on public lands and the continental shelf to serve as a permanent funding source for preservation.

The act also created the Advisory Council on Historic Preservation (ACHP) to guide federal preservation efforts. (The ACHP was initially established in the National Park Service of the Department of the Interior, but was made an independent agency in 1976.) Recognizing that federally funded development—particularly through urban renewal and interstate highway construction in cities—had been a primary force in the destruction of historic landmarks, the ACHP was empowered to review and comment on all federally supported projects that might have an impact on historic properties listed in the new National Register of Historic Places (so-called Section 106 reviews).

All federal agency heads were required to consult with the ACHP on any relevant projects under their direction. Urban renewal projects funded by the Department of Housing and Urban Development (HUD) were among those that would be subject to ACHP review. (Federal transportation and highway laws were also amended in 1966 to accommodate preservation as a priority.) An amendment to the National Historic Preservation Act passed in 1976 extended ACHP review to federal projects involving properties potentially eligible for the National Register as well as those already listed.

Initially, few properties were listed as national historic places, so the ACHP review process had limited application. But the creation of the National Register of Historic Places prompted an expansion of designated listings. At the end of the 1960s, only 1,212 sites were listed in the register, but the number of listings grew exponentially thereafter, reaching 11,233 in 1975, 26,360 in 1980, and 43,558 in 1985. Because many designated places are sites or districts with more than one building, the actual number of historic properties is even greater than the listings suggest.

As the number of listings expanded, so did the ACHP's role in reviewing and shaping federally supported development projects. In the late 1960s, it was reviewing only a handful of cases each year.[44] But by the early 1970s, the ACHP was receiving several hundred cases for review annually, and the numbers were increasing. The number of new cases tripled from about 250 in fiscal year 1973 to almost 750 in fiscal year 1975.[45]

The impact of this review power soon became apparent in the fate of major development projects. In 1967, an ACHP review resulted for the first time in the termination of a federally funded development project. In that case, preservationists successfully mobilized the federal law to block the construction of an elevated interstate highway in New Orleans that would have run between the city's historic French Quarter and the Mississippi River.[46] In 1972, an ACHP review of the urban renewal plan for Faneuil Hall and Quincy Market in Boston resulted in new design requirements to accommodate the historic properties.[47] Significantly, the redevelopment of Faneuil Hall and Quincy Market is now regarded as a model of successful commercial waterfront revitalization through preservation and adaptive reuse, reportedly attracting more annual visitors than Disneyland. And in New Orleans, the riverfront has become the site of extensive tourist-oriented development that successfully capitalizes on the resource of the historic French Quarter.

In 1971, President Richard Nixon further expanded the responsibilities of federal agencies in preservation efforts through Executive Order No. 11593, requiring agency officials to work with the ACHP to identify and nominate historic properties under their jurisdiction for inclusion in the National Register. This mandate, incorporated into the preservation act itself in 1980, contributed further to the expansion of the National Register.

A variety of other changes in federal law also promoted preservation in federal land-use activities. In 1972, the General Services Administration (GSA) was allowed to transfer historic properties to state and local governments at no cost for appropriate uses. In 1974, the GSA was encouraged to acquire and use historic properties for the location of federal offices. The Amtrak Improvement Act of 1974 attempted to integrate historic railroad stations into the Amtrak system, and a law passed in 1976 directed the ACHP to work with the Department of Transportation for the adaptive reuse of historic stations. The National Environmental Policy Act of 1969, requiring environmental impact statements for all federally sponsored projects, included historic preservation as a focus of concern to be addressed in measuring environmental costs.

Federal urban development programs both reflected and encouraged the shift to a preservation-based development approach as well. Even during the urban renewal era, HUD (and its predecessor, the Housing and Home Finance Agency [HHFA]) began an attempt to reorient the program toward preservation, having been "stung by the preservationists' criticisms of the 'slash and burn' modus operandi of earlier versions of urban renewal."[48] The shift was promoted in agency documents like *Historic Preservation Through Urban Renewal* and *Preserving Historic America.*[49]

The Demonstration Cities and Metropolitan Development Act of 1966 reduced previous restrictions on the use of urban renewal funds for historic preservation and authorized new programs for preservation.[50] Almost $3 million in matching grants for preservation projects was approved by HUD from 1968 to 1970 through a program specifically aimed at historic preservation.[51] In 1970, this Historic Preservation program was consolidated with the Open Space and Urban Beautification programs in a new plan intended to "encourage more aesthetic urban development [and] to preserve sites of historic or architectural value."[52] The combined program provided almost $600 million in grants for more than 4,500 development projects before the overall restructuring of development programs in 1974.

The most significant change in the structure of federal urban development programs came in 1974 under the rubric of Nixon's New Federalism. The urban renewal program was officially terminated as such and was consolidated with ten other development programs into the Community Development Block Grant (CDBG) program. The CDBG program allowed localities the discretion to use federal funds as they saw fit. It was motivated by a political attempt to return control over development activity to local elites, whose authority had been undermined by the community participation requirements of the categorical grant programs of the 1960s.[53]

Historic preservation was among the specified purposes for which CDBG funds could be used, and the program became an important tool for preservation-based redevelopment. Between 1975 and 1977, cities used $71.5 million from the CDBG program for historic restorations, reflecting a new awareness of the economic benefits of such projects.[54] According to a HUD survey, for every $1 that had been spent on rehabilitation loans and grants under the urban renewal program, $13 were spent to acquire property for demolition; in contrast, spending for demolition and rehabilitation was nearly even under the CDBG program.[55] Because the use of CDBG funds was largely left to local discretion, the program's positive or negative impact on historic properties ultimately depended on the terms of individual projects.[56] The same was true of the Urban Development Action Grant (UDAG) program, created in 1977, and the Rental Rehabilitation program, created in 1983, both of which authorized preservation as an acceptable use of funds.

While the focus of federal development programs shifted away from traditional urban renewal to preservation, federal tax policy also underwent a fundamental change to create an economic context favorable to historic preservation. By the early 1970s, preservationists recognized the detrimental impact that the tax code was having on the preservation cause.[57] The tax code allowed a business deduction for the cost of demolition and provided accelerated depreciation for a new building, while the straight depreciation of a rehabilitated property reduced tax liabilities at a slower rate. As a result, restoration was simply not an economically competitive alternative to demolition and new construction.[58]

Efforts to reverse this incentive structure succeeded with the Tax Reform Act (TRA) of 1976, which eliminated the deduction for the demolition cost of a historic landmark and allowed no accelerated depreciation for a new structure built on the site of a destroyed landmark; instead, accelerated depreciation was granted for rehabilitated historic structures. The new tax provisions applied to all revenue-producing, or commercial, structures listed in the National Register as well as those with an approved state or local historic landmark designation. A study conducted by the Commerce Department later found that the tax reforms had indeed reversed the "distinct bias in favor of demolition and redevelopment" and now "tipped the tax scale in favor of historic preservation."[59] Before the reforms, rehabilitation was found to be between 4 and 9 percent more costly than demolition and new construction; after the reforms, rehabilitation was between 13 and 28 percent less costly.

The attempt to restructure the economic context of development through the tax code did not stop there. Two years later, President Jimmy Carter approved a 10 percent investment tax credit for rehabilitation projects, greatly enhancing the value of preservation. In the four years following the passage of the Tax Reform Act, the National Park Service certified almost 2,300 private rehabilitation projects as qualifying for the tax incentives.[60] President Ronald Reagan's Economic Recovery Tax Act (ERTA) of 1981 provided an additional boost to preservation activity by substantially expanding the tax credits for rehabilitation. It created a three-tier system of tax credits for the restoration of older buildings, providing credits of 15 percent for thirty-year-old buildings, 20 percent for forty-year-old buildings, and 25 percent for historic landmarks.

These little noticed provisions of ERTA were probably the single greatest stimulus to the adaptive reuse of historic structures as a development strategy. In the four years following the passage of ERTA, the National Park Service received about four times the number of applications for project certification than it had during the previous five years, when the more limited preservation tax incentives were in effect.[61] The number of proposed rehabilitations more than tripled, and estimated expenditures on approved projects was more than five times the value of projects during the earlier period. The qualifying rehabilitation expenditures for 1982 and 1983 alone exceeded $6 billion, with more than $2 billion attributed to the restoration of historic landmarks. Through 1985, ERTA stimulated investment worth $8.8 billion in more than 11,700 historic properties.[62]

The significance of these changes in tax policy should not be underestimated. The value of the tax credits earned through restorations during 1982 and 1983 alone was estimated at $1.3 billion.[63] Tax expenditures of this magnitude compare with the value of approved urban renewal grants for any two-year period during the heyday of that program. This impact clearly established the tax code as an enormous subsidy program for preservation-based commercial development.

The Tax Reform Act of 1986 curtailed the use of rehabilitation tax credits by reducing their value—to 20 percent of the rehabilitation cost for a historic landmark, and 10 percent for nonlandmark buildings built before 1936—and placing additional restrictions on their use. The changes led to a sharp decline the following year in the number of proposed projects and the value of new investment. But the drop in activity leveled off, and in 1989 the tax program was regarded as "still an effective catalyst in the restoration and rehabilitation of urban historic properties."[64] In fact, preservation was one of the few investment credits retained in the simplified tax code, reflecting its importance as a tool in the preservation-based development approach.

The 1980s marked a steady movement away from federal grant programs for urban development.[65] Even the National Historic Preservation Fund became less a source of direct grants for preservation projects than a source of support for the administration of state and local preservation offices. This overall retrenchment is often misunderstood as a retreat of the federal government from the development arena that has allowed the free market to determine investment activity; indeed, politicians have marketed the change in just these terms.

This survey of policy change reveals the disingenuous nature of such an interpretation. Federal policy was actively creating a new economic context for profitable urban development centered around historic preservation, with generous tax credits replacing grants as the primary source of federal influence over investment patterns. Of course, state and local tax incentives often provided even greater benefits for developers in the 1980s and 1990s.

The new arrangements to facilitate preservation-based urban development were a response to changing political realities. By the 1970s, the potential of historic preservation as an economic strategy for commercial development was apparent. Early examples like Ghirardelli Square in San Francisco and Faneuil Hall and Quincy Market in Boston were attractive models of successful preservation-based revitalization efforts. Government studies such as *The Contribution of Historic Preservation to Urban Revitalization* provided evidence of increased property values and tax revenues from revitalized historic districts, where historic preservation promoted the tourism industry and contributed to social improvements.[66] Federally sponsored documents advocated preservation as an economic approach for local officials, in some cases even emphasizing its potential for reducing local political conflict.[67]

LOCAL ZONING AND LANDMARKS PRESERVATION LAWS

Sharon Zukin's insightful study of New York's SoHo district illustrates the crucial role that local governmental policies have played in restructuring development practices around historic preservation.[68] SoHo was created out of an area of underutilized nineteenth-century industrial lofts that were preserved and adapted to serve as an arts district. The buildings are distinctive for the use of cast iron to imitate more expensive classical stone facades. SoHo demonstrates the flexibility of historic preservation as a basis for redevelopment, since often little more than building facades are preserved. Indeed, SoHo has become a vibrant urban theme park drawing tourists and affluent residents to its trendy galleries, shops, restaurants, cafés, bars, and boutiques; and it also offers coveted loft living for the very rich. Starving artists should look elsewhere.

The "revalorization" of SoHo is particularly informative because it reflects the transition from urban renewal to preservation-based development in the 1960s and 1970s.[69] During the 1950s, large areas of lower Manhattan, including what is now SoHo, became the target of grandiose urban renewal schemes that aimed to demolish the "commercial slums" of downtown and replace them with office buildings and luxury housing.[70] By the 1960s, however, renewal proponents faced organized opposition from preservationists, artists, old-guard social elites, and educated middle-class residents—especially those from nearby Greenwich Village who were "mobilized behind the Jane Jacobs credo of neighborhood and building preservation."[71] In the face of this politically potent backlash, few of the renewal proposals for downtown Manhattan were completed.[72]

Instead, recognizing the appeal of historic preservation and the arts to the upper-middle class, city policy began to accommodate the conversion of industrial lofts to arts-related purposes—even though this reuse would undermine the very manufacturing base of the city whose demise officials were publicly lamenting. The range of local actions promoting the transformation of SoHo included the addition of a series of amendments to the building code that legalized residential use of lofts by artists and eased restrictions on loft conversions, the creation of a special artists' zoning district, and, perhaps most important, the designation of the SoHo Cast Iron Historic District. The city's landmarks law allowed the designation of historic districts having a "special character or special historical or aesthetic interest or value." This, in turn, had the effect of a self-fulfilling prophecy because the designation not only recognized the neighborhood's unusual architecture, but also established its social distinction and status.

The preservation- and arts-based strategy for revalorizing SoHo was ultimately so successful that the artists who pioneered the transformation were priced out of the area. The extent of its commercial success has even prompted the derogatory description of SoHo as the "Disneyland of the aesthete."[73] Still, the SoHo case is important because it illustrates the evolution of development practices. The lesson of arts- and preservation-based development was not lost. SoHo represents a stage in a process of social learning that has shaped subsequent development strategies, including the efforts to reconstruct Times Square.

Local zoning and landmarks preservation laws were important tools in the construction of SoHo; indeed, they have become essential components of contemporary development processes. By examining the case of local historic-preservation laws, as an aspect of zoning practices,[74] it is possible to gain better insight into the policy structure shaping contemporary urban development and the political motivations behind it.

Municipalities began enacting preservation laws more than three decades before the passage of the National Historic Preservation Act of 1966. The earliest ordinances were passed in Charleston, South Carolina, and in New Orleans in the 1930s.[75] Other cities, especially in the South, followed in the 1940s and 1950s.[76] The early municipal ordinances provided for the designation of historic properties and districts, and created local preservation commissions to oversee and regulate development activities involving historic properties. This established the standard local approach that was adopted later in other municipalities nationwide.

Faced with the social conflict triggered by the destructiveness of the urban renewal policies in the 1960s, local officials became a leading force advocating historic preservation as a national priority. The U.S. Conference of Mayors was a major participant in a study, sponsored by the Ford Foundation, that produced a report on preservation entitled *With Heritage So Rich*.[77] The recommendations in this report formed the basis of the National Historic Preservation Act, which, in turn, prompted further state and local preservation activity by providing federal grants to approved preservation offices. (Localities were fully integrated into the system by amendments to the National Historic Preservation Act passed in 1980.) By 1986, almost 300 local governments were certified for participation in the federal preservation grant program, and some 1,250 local preservation offices were members of the National Alliance of Preservation Commissions.[78]

Cities were the terrain on which conflict produced by the destruction of the built environment was played out during the 1960s. As inner-city minority populations became increasingly rebellious, middle-class whites continued to flee the city for refuge in the suburbs. The middle- and upper-income residents remaining in the city were increasingly resistant to renewal tactics, instead asserting the competing values of community and historic preservation. This was the context in which many more municipalities throughout the country were enacting laws to preserve their historic landmarks.

The New York City case is illustrative. The passage of a landmarks law in New York is widely understood as a reaction to one particularly egregious incident of creative destruction, the demolition of the original Penn Station.[79] Initially, opposition to the razing of Penn Station was confined to a small, rather elite assemblage of architects who showed up to picket as the demolition began.[80] But once the wrecking process was under way, influential opinion leaders like the *New York Times* expressed belated outrage at the tragedy. A *Times* editorial on the day after demolition began described it as "a monumental act of vandalism" that was driven simply by a "profit motivation great enough" to justify it.[81]

Soon the sense of irreparable loss became widespread, and public sentiment was mobilized in support of a historic preservation law that would prevent similar atrocities. Reporting on the Landmarks Preservation Act, passed in April 1965, Thomas Ennis declared that "New York at last has joined a preservation movement that has spread throughout the country under the impetus of public opinion aroused by landmarks vanishing in the explosive growth of cities."[82]

As did those in other cities, the Landmarks Preservation Act in New York created the Landmarks Preservation Commission (LPC), which had the power to designate historic landmarks and districts, subject to legislative approval, and closely regulate development involving them. The commission was empowered to prevent the owners of landmark buildings from carrying out unauthorized demolition or facade alterations, although the law did provide a limited "escape clause." Specifically, if an owner could demonstrate that the landmark restrictions would interfere with a reasonable rate of return on the property—defined as a net annual return of 6 percent profit on the assessed value—the LPC would work with the owner to develop an acceptable preservation plan. If a preservation agreement could not be reached, the city would still have the right to purchase the property or take it through condemnation; otherwise, it could not restrict redevelopment. Still, the LPC was ultimately not bound to consider the economic hardship that designations might impose.

This landmarks preservation law (which was amended in 1973 to eliminate certain loopholes) has had an enormous impact on the city's built form and the way it can be used for economic gain. By the end of 1991, some 19,000 buildings— about 2 percent of all properties in the city—were protected by a landmark designation,[83] and the preservation net continues to expand. But how do we interpret such an extensive regulatory system? The New York case seems to exemplify an autonomous liberal state acting to restrict the destruction and rebuilding of the built environment—and the powerful economic interests behind it—in the interest of the quality of life for city residents. Landmarks preservation suggests a defense of use values against the frenzied search for ever-increasing exchange values. This is precisely the logic expressed by the preservation movement itself.

Mayor David Dinkins, in his Foreword to the *Guide to New York City Landmarks,* declared that, in spite of the appeal of the city's landmarks to tourists, "the chief importance of New York's landmarks is for ourselves, for New Yorkers. Within our communities, landmarks . . . become sources of neighborhood stability, self-worth, and pride. They are monuments, great and small, which serve as the touchstones of our civic identity—the irreparable places without which New York becomes a different, and a poorer, city."[84] In the same document, preservationist Brendan Gill suggested that the Landmarks Preservation Commission is protecting not simply historic buildings, but ultimately "the psychological good health of millions of anonymous New Yorkers."[85] Landmarks are, according to Gill, a source of "emotional nourishment" for the city's inhabitants and thus are "indispensable to our well-being."

Real-estate developers, less concerned with emotional nourishment, still subscribed to the interpretation of landmarks laws that was implicit in the preservationists' argument. For both sides, these laws represented the interference of an independent state into market practices in the pursuit of some social objective.

Their disagreement stemmed from conflicting evaluations of that objective and the costs to be borne in achieving it. For those with large investments in real estate, the quality-of-life concerns were simply unable to justify the assault on the sacred institution of private property that the law represented. Consequently, developers sued the city, charging that the preservation law amounted to an unconstitutional taking of property by denying owners of designated landmarks the ability to develop their properties to their full economic potential.

From a broader perspective, though, historic preservation laws represent a far more complex role for the state in the economy. As the SoHo example indicates, preservation can also be an important tool for revaluing urban areas and thereby facilitating capital accumulation. Preservation laws, therefore, have contradictory goals, both imposing restrictions on capital and creating opportunities for profitable investment. In this respect, preservation laws are much like other zoning laws, which seek to reconcile the competing pressures of private and social goals.[86] A closer look at the impact of historic preservation in New York City reveals a process of policy evolution by which the landmarks law that was triggered by quality-of-life concerns became integrated into lucrative redevelopment strategies.

TRANSFERABLE DEVELOPMENT RIGHTS:
CONJURING A COMMODITY OUT OF THIN AIR

The Landmarks Preservation Act was passed as a result of mounting public opposition to the widespread destruction of the landscape of New York City that was taking place in the 1950s and 1960s. This indicates that government was responding to public input, and even a vision of the public interest, by endorsing historic preservation. But an analysis of the landmarks law cannot end there. A thorough understanding of its significance requires a consideration of its actual impact on urban development. In this way, it is possible to recognize historic preservation as part of the evolving social arrangements by which economically and politically feasible development occurs.

Powerful real-estate interests launched a legal assault on New York's preservation law because it represented a fundamental change in the rules by which property rights were defined. In the most important test of local preservation powers, the Penn Central Transportation Company challenged the ruling of the New York City Landmarks Preservation Commission that forbade Penn to build a $100 million, fifty-five-story office tower above Grand Central Terminal, following its designation as a historic landmark. Penn argued that the refusal of the LPC to approve this construction represented an unconstitutional "taking" of its property without "just compensation."[87] Penn was not suffering the loss of property in any physical sense; rather, the loss, it asserted, was in the form of potential profits that would be realized from redeveloping the prime parcel of midtown land on which the station was located. In fact, Penn had already entered into a lease that would generate at least $3 million a year for the company once the tower was built.

Penn's legal claim was based on the zoning laws that regulate land-use patterns in New York City. The laws restrict the development of each parcel of land, or lot, such that every building must conform to an allowable density (measured in terms of a floor-area ratio, or FAR) within an "envelope" of legally defined parameters. While zoning thereby imposes limits on development potential, it also defines a positive property right to construct up to the allowable limits specified in the zoning code. In this way, zoning establishes and defines the "development rights" of a property owner. Arguably, this can be regarded as creating the kind of expectation of a property right that establishes a legal entitlement.[88]

The concept of development rights formed the basis of Penn Central's legal claim. Grand Central Terminal contained floor space equal to 1.5 times its lot size (FAR 1.5), although it was located in an area of the city zoned for FAR 18 (floor area up to 18 times the lot size). The landmark designation therefore prevented Penn from developing additional floor space equal to 16.5 times the lot size, an area that constituted the unused portion of the development rights zoned for the site. Landmarking the station thereby altered the established basis of Penn's property rights.[89]

Penn Central lost its legal battle when the United States Supreme Court upheld New York's preservation law against this challenge in 1978. Nevertheless, the Penn Central case represents much more than the subordination of private property rights to broader social goals. It contributed to the creation of development practices that centered on historic preservation by prompting new conceptions of property and property rights. Penn's case must, therefore, be recognized as part of the process by which space is socially constructed as a commodity. The same preservation law that restricted the development potential of Grand Central Terminal also gave rise to an entirely new property and commodity form that provided the basis for preservation-based development opportunities.

In 1968, the New York City Planning Commission (CPC) approved a zoning amendment intended to facilitate historic preservation by permitting the owner of a landmark structure to transfer unused development rights (the difference between the maximum allowable floor area and the actual floor area of the existing structure) to adjacent lots for purposes of development. The transfer of development rights, sometimes called air rights,[90] would enable the owner of the lot who received the development rights to build a structure up to 20 percent larger than the zoning code would otherwise allow. Such transfers were limited to lots that were adjacent to or across the street from the landmark site.

This zoning amendment represented a remarkable innovation in the conceptualization of space: a new form of property—and a new commodity—was created literally out of thin air. The new property form, transferable development rights (TDRs), consists of an invisible and imaginary block of air space, wholly lacking in substance but defined precisely in law, that can be transferred from one owner and one physical location to another—for the right price. Its existence stems from the practice of enframing space through zoning codes and demonstrates quite vividly how enframing underlies the invention of space in its modern forms. Without a spatial framework of zoning envelopes, it would be meaningless to speak of a block of air space, separable from the land over which it hovers, as a commodity that can be bought and sold. While this commodity may seem unique, having been conjured out of the blue, it exemplifies the nature of all capital as being socially constructed.

Since this new commodity was created, it has undergone a process of expansion and revision that demonstrates the malleability of property and commodity forms. Under pressure from the lawsuit filed by Penn Central against New York, the City Planning Commission adopted a further zoning change "aimed at restoring some measure of profit to the business of owning a landmark."[91] The zoning amendment, which was announced on the same day in 1969 that Penn Central filed its suit against the city, allowed owners of landmarks to transfer unused development rights not only to adjacent lots, but also to any lot connected to the landmark site by a chain of lots under the same ownership.

The amendment also eliminated the 20 percent limit on the amount of additional floor space that a receiving lot could obtain through the transfer of development rights in certain high-density districts (the only areas where it imposed a significant constraint). Furthermore, it allowed the owners of landmark properties to divide their unused development rights into portions that could be sold to different owners of eligible lots, thus opening up new methods of packaging and marketing the transferable development rights commodity. These zoning changes were specifically tailored for Penn Central, which had extensive holdings of land around Grand Central Terminal.[92] Penn's properties formed a chain of commonly owned lots that connected the station with at least eight surrounding sites, several of which would have the potential for office development. The Supreme Court noted these economic advantages made possible by TDRs in upholding the landmarks law;[93] thus the Court recognized the opportunities as well as the restrictions created by historic preservation.

A zoning amendment approved in 1970 authorized the transfer of development rights from publicly owned landmarks on the condition that the owner of the receiving lot provide an improvement to pedestrian circulation or a transportation system, in addition to paying the city the purchase price of the development rights. The Planning Commission's general counsel explained that "developments incorporating formerly publicly owned air rights are therefore held to a higher amenity standard."[94] Although the CPC was thereby asserting a public interest, this zoning change was made to accommodate a particular developer who wanted to obtain almost 800,000 square feet of unused development rights— roughly the size of the entire Woolworth Building—from the landmark United States Custom House at the southern tip of Manhattan in order to build a massive structure on an adjacent site.[95]

The City Planning Commission also proposed a change in 1970 to promote the construction of luxury high-rise apartments on Manhattan's Upper East Side by allowing developers to purchase and use development rights from the smaller townhouses that occupied mid-blocks in the area.[96] The plan was again couched in terms of the public interest, with the CPC arguing that it would preserve the smaller scale of mid-block buildings in exchange for larger structures along the avenues. But the public did not buy the argument offered on its behalf, and the idea was shelved in face of strong opposition from the affluent neighborhood. Still, the proposal was significant in challenging the concept of transferable development rights as being limited to landmark sites. And, in fact, developers began using transferable development rights as planners had proposed through the unregulated process of zoning-lot mergers. This made possible the dramatic overbuilding of the East Side before planners moved to restrict the practice in the early 1980s.[97]

Since the transferable development rights commodity was devised in the late 1960s, the proposals for defining the conceptual contours of this property form have become increasingly peculiar. Much of the innovation has revolved around the development rights belonging to Grand Central Terminal, most of which have yet to be utilized. With between 1.6 and 1.9 million square feet of unused development rights tethered above the station, enormous interests are at stake. The development rights add perhaps tens of millions of dollars to the value of the terminal,[98] but it has proved difficult to find projects that meet the restrictions on the transfer of eligible development rights. Transfers can be made only to sites connected to Grand Central through a chain of lots under common ownership. By the early 1990s, only one sale had occurred from the vast pool of Grand Central's development rights; in 1979, Penn Central sold about 75,000 square feet, which were used in the construction of the Philip Morris headquarters at Forty-second Street and Park Avenue.[99]

In 1986, a development team of G. Ware Travelstead and the First Boston Corporation unveiled a proposal to use 800,000 square feet of the development rights in building a seventy-two-story office tower on Madison Avenue between Forty-sixth and Forty-seventh Streets. The skyscraper would contain over 1.4 million square feet of space and soar higher than 1,000 feet, making it the fourth tallest building in New York City.[100] Its floor-area ratio would make it even denser than the old Equitable Building, whose enormous bulk undermined the property values of neighboring buildings and contributed to the adoption of the city's first zoning resolution in 1916.[101] Thus the proposed tower posed a threat to the integrity of the city's zoning code.

The major obstacle that the developers faced was that the building site was located some four blocks from Grand Central Terminal and lacked an apparent link through a chain of commonly owned lots. They claimed, therefore, that the development rights could be transferred along a subsurface chain of lots owned by Penn Central; in effect, the air rights would be wheeled along Penn's underground railroad tracks to their new location four blocks to the north. Penn's lawyers denied that this was a suspect case of "development rights sneaking through the passageways and erupting like dragon's teeth at 383 Madison Avenue."[102]

The City Planning Commission rejected this novel approach to the transfer of rights, noting that it would theoretically enable development rights to be transported from midtown Manhattan all the way to Yonkers, just across the city's northern border.[103] In what has become the typical method of negotiation, the developers then filed suit, charging that the city had unconstitutionally taken their development rights and seeking $480 million in damages. Four days after the suit was filed, the Department of City Planning (DCP) recommended to the CPC the creation of a special district around Grand Central within which development rights could be transferred regardless of ownership patterns. A similar strategy had been enormously successful in transforming the historic South Street Seaport into a popular waterfront tourist attraction of low-rise nineteenth-century buildings surrounded by massive office towers.[104]

The Grand Central district would connect twenty-one buildings to the station, extending the eligibility for development rights transfers to part or all of fifteen additional blocks. The change would add eight eligible sites in particular with the potential to use development rights from Grand Central, including the Travelstead/First Boston site at 383 Madison Avenue.[105] But the new rules would limit a building there to about 1 million square feet, far short of what the developers had proposed, and so the conflict between the developers and the city-planning officials continued.

In 1989, developer Donald Trump suggested a method of creating and transferring development rights that was even more curious than rail transport. In the *New York Times,* David Dunlap reported that Trump was "plumbing the depths of the Hudson River" in order to dredge up development rights from parts of his waterfront property submerged offshore.[106] Trump would then "haul those rights ashore for use in the proposed Trump City project on the Upper West Side of Manhattan." The transfer would contribute as much as 4.5 million square feet to Trump City, a proposed development of fourteen residential and office buildings that was to include a 150-story tower. (The proposal has since been approved in a scaled-down form with the less self-aggrandizing name Riverside South.) Discussing the peculiarity of the proposed "underwater zoning," a Trump executive demurred, "I'm sure we didn't invent something." In fact, the Trump Organization was actively participating in the process of inventing and defining a new form of property.

The transfer of development rights has been both praised and criticized with regard to the public interest. The legal scholar John Costonis has articulated the most coherent intellectual case for transferable development rights as a means of furthering the public's interest in historic preservation.[107] Prompted by the destruction of the architecturally important Chicago Stock Exchange Building in the early 1970s, Costonis—with support from the National Trust for Historic Preservation and the Chicago chapter of the American Institute of Architects—produced the comprehensive "Chicago Plan" for unrestricted transfers of development rights.[108] Preservationists hailed this plan as the silver lining to the loss of the Exchange Building, since it would establish a mechanism for protecting the public from similar tragedies in the future.[109] City-planning officials in New York have likewise emphasized the public purpose of development rights transfers.[110]

While Costonis justified his plan by the public's interest in protecting its cultural heritage, he firmly embraced the realities of real-estate economics as the means to achieve this goal. Historic landmarks would survive only if they were made profitable, and the transfer of development rights was the technique by which this could be accomplished. Yet by interjecting profitability concerns into landmarks preservation, this approach was also exposed to criticism. The New York system has been portrayed as little more than a means of compensating property owners who faced any imposition from the landmarks law.[111] In the process of providing these owners with excessively profitable alternatives, the public's interest was arguably sacrificed with new buildings vastly larger than reasonable zoning regulations would allow.[112]

Ultimately, the case of transferable development rights illustrates how conflicting political and economic pressures shape and reshape development policy through continual interaction and negotiation. The process by which this commodity form was created in New York City began when, in the face of mounting political pressure, the city enacted a landmarks preservation law that restricted destructive urban renewal development. Shortly thereafter, in response to pressure from property owners and development interests, city officials created transferable development rights to restore the development value of landmarked properties. The ability to transfer development rights provided an important financial resource not only for developers, but also for preservationists and the cultural institutions that often owned and operated in landmark buildings.

Nevertheless, the process of defining the exact nature of transferable development rights has been marked above all by ongoing conflict between the city-planning officials and major real-estate interests. This illustrates the "dynamic of support and opposition between planners and businessmen" that Richard Foglesong describes as an inevitable feature of contemporary urban planning. According to Foglesong, "It is a dynamic that is inherent in capitalism, given the contradiction between the private ownership and control of property and the social needs, including the social needs of capital itself, that private property must serve."[113]

The contradictory nature of capitalist planning, as a source of both restrictions and opportunities for capital, is evident in the specific case of transferable development rights. On the one hand, this commodity continues to exist in a very limited form in New York despite the attempts of powerful developers to invent forms of development rights that will enhance the profitability of their projects. As early as 1972, Costonis had presented his comprehensive plan for historic preservation, which envisioned an extensive market, virtually unrestricted, in transferable development rights. But New York City has resisted such a major expansion of this commodity form, thereby obstructing the interests of some property owners and developers. Indeed, the enormous development potential of Grand Central Terminal has gone unrealized for more than a quarter century because city planners have repeatedly rejected the proposals offered by developers.

In New York City and elsewhere, on the other hand, the transfer of development rights has become an important means to construct the new places of the postindustrial, postmodern urban landscape. It provides valuable benefits to developers, preservationists, and the cultural institutions often housed in historic landmarks. By linking historic preservation and the arts with the development of high-rise office buildings and luxury residences, transferable development rights provide a mechanism for drawing higher-income city residents back into the progrowth coalition. In this way, public policy generates political support for contemporary urban development. Nowhere is the link between public policy and private interests more evident than in the revitalization of Times Square.

or most of the twentieth century, Times Square has been defined by the dramatic lights and signs
hat surround the intersection of Broadway and Seventh Avenue: The Crossroads of the World.
Photograph by Philip Greenberg)

At the turn of the century, New York City's entertainment district had spread into Longacre (or Long Acre) Square, at the intersection of Broadway and Seventh Avenue. The area would not become known as Times Square until the arrival of the *New York Times* in 1904. (Photograph by Byron, *Long Acre Square, 1900;* Museum of the City of New York, The Byron Collection)

In the first decades of the twentieth century, Forty-second Street between Seventh and Eighth Avenues was among the most prominent areas for legitimate theater, with thirteen theaters having entrances on the block in the 1920s.

By the 1920s, Times Square had emerged as ground zero in the explosion of commercial culture in the United States. (Photofest/Icon Archives)

In the 1930s, many of the elegant stages on Forty-second Street were converted for use as movie theaters.

The demolition in 1963 of the original Pennsylvania Station in New York City, whose main waiting room is shown in this photograph, contributed to the passage of the city's landmarks preservation law. (Photograph by Geo. P. Hall & Son, *Pennsylvania Station—Interior main waiting room;* Museum of the City of New York)

efore its redevelopment, Times Square and Forty-second Street allegedly had been taken over by a
ıenacing population of African-Americans and Latinos engaged in drugs, crime, and loitering.
Photograph by Michael Ackerman)

Sex-related businesses were not a subtle presence on Forty-second Street before its redevelopment. (42nd Street Development Project)

3

Times Square Discourse:
From the Great White Way to
the Dangerous Deuce

A belt of white electric bulbs girds the Times Building at Forty-second Street and Broadway, spelling out spot news in moving letters that can be read several blocks away. And to the north a wall of light and color, urging the onlooker to chew gum, drink beer, see the world's most beautiful girls, or attend the premiere of a Hollywood film, lights the clouds above Manhattan with a glow like that of a dry timber fire.

This is the Great White Way, theatrical center of America and wonder of the out-of-towner.

—Federal Writers' Project, *The WPA Guide to New York City* (1939)

People are still hung up on the goddamn corny image of what's there in Times Square, and yet Times Square is horrible. There's not one great thing about it.
—John Portman, developer (1973)

The name Times Square literally refers to the lower portion of the bowtie-shaped traffic islands formed by the diagonal intersection of Broadway and Seventh Avenue, between Forty-second and Forty-seventh Streets. (The upper portion is officially named Duffy Square after Father Francis P. Duffy, the heroic World War I army chaplain who was a pastor in the Times Square area.) In a truer sense, however, Times Square refers to a larger, more diffuse area that radiates from this spot and to its diverse images. The literal Times Square is a high-energy public arena defined by the huge, dramatic, lighted signs that surround it; this electrified focal point has provided the "central experience" of Times Square.[1] But Times Square, in the broader sense, also includes the Broadway theater district, which extends as far north as Fifty-third Street; Restaurant Row, a tourist creation on Forty-sixth Street between Eighth and Ninth Avenues; and, of course, it includes Forty-second Street between Seventh and Eighth Avenues, until recently known for its sleaze, but now the site of redevelopment and renaissance.

Times Square was officially created in 1904 with the opening of the New York Times Tower and the Times Square station of the city's first subway line. Shortly thereafter, the area emerged as the fulcrum of New York's most fashionable theater and entertainment district. Broadway from Times Square north to the Fifties was dubbed the Great White Way because of its continuous spectacle of brightly lighted marquees. West Forty-second Street, too, fit this dazzling image. Through the mid-1920s, the block of Forty-second Street between Seventh and Eighth Avenues was so prominent for theater that even theaters constructed on Forty-first and Forty-third Streets had their entranceways built through the block in order to locate their marquees at a Forty-second Street address. At its peak in the 1920s, no fewer than thirteen theaters had entrances and marquees on this one-block stretch of Forty-second Street.

By 1960, the *New York Times* declared that the same block was "the worst block in town," that it "[had] been so for many years," and that "if it is not getting worse it is certainly not getting better."[2] Images of the area during the 1960s were crystallized in John Schlesinger's award-winning film *Midnight Cowboy* (1969), which depicted the Times Square and Forty-second Street area as a distinctly rotten core of the Big Apple. Here was a grim underworld of violence, crime, con games, and male prostitution, where hopeful innocents from small towns were propelled into a tragic fall from grace.

Subsequent decades yielded few positive developments; on the contrary, the increase in homelessness and the invention of crack as a means of marketing cocaine to low-income users added to the area's troubled populations. From the 1960s through the 1980s, Times Square—particularly West Forty-second Street—had come to serve as a metaphor for urban decline in the United States, symbolizing for many the plagues of crime and drugs and the takeover of central cities by a menacing population of racial and ethnic minorities.[3]

The story of the rise and fall of Times Square and Forty-second Street was a familiar and widely accepted historical narrative that combined elements of myth and reality to form a dominant discourse on Times Square by the 1980s. In symbolic terms, the discourse portrayed the area's devolution from the Great White Way to the Dangerous Deuce.[4] (The Deuce, shortened from the Forty-deuce of police jargon, was a slick moniker of recent decades that effectively captured the images of hustlers, con artists, and small-time crooks associated with the area.) Examined with any care, the history of the area is much more complex, but it was the discourse on Times Square that served as a constructed political spectacle to generate support for the redevelopment agenda.

At the planning level, the Times Square discourse supported a project of massive economic redevelopment, including major new office construction, as the only viable solution to the social and economic problems of Forty-second Street and Times Square. It served this policy agenda in two ways: by constructing an idealized past around the symbolism of the Great White Way that would both highlight the exceptional severity of the contemporary problems and provide a grand vision to guide redevelopment, and by defining the area in the 1970s and 1980s as without any redeeming social function and home to only a depraved subculture so deeply entrenched that it would repel all but the most determined assault.

THE PHYSICAL AND SOCIAL CONSTRUCTION OF TIMES SQUARE

Times Square has always been a highly contested urban space.[5] The construction and reconstruction of Times Square over time, as both a physical and a social space, reflects a complex interplay of political, economic, and social forces. Public policy decisions made in the nineteenth century established the infrastructure that motivated the particular patterns of economic development that occurred during the early decades of the twentieth century. The built environment was largely set by the late 1920s, and virtually no new construction took place in the immediate area of West Forty-second Street over the following half century. But during that time, the area underwent significant changes in its social and economic characteristics. Socioeconomic conditions were shaped and reshaped through the competition and cooperation among urban subcultures, public officials, and economic interests.

A number of important public policy decisions dating back to the early nineteenth century established that midtown Manhattan, and specifically Forty-second Street, would be a central focus of the economic and social life of the New York City region far into the future. In New York, as elsewhere, urban political regimes in the nineteenth century were heavily dominated by economic elites, and decisions about infrastructure in particular were closely tied to economic interests and personal fortune-building.[6] These early policy decisions reflect an often indistinguishable mix of political and economic objectives.

In 1811, city officials adopted the Commissioner's Plan, which outlined the organization of Manhattan from 14th Street to 155th Street according to a grid pattern of streets. This framework facilitated the transformation of Manhattan land into property—that is marketable lots—an essential requisite for capitalist urban development. The plan designated Forty-second Street as one of fifteen major crosstown transportation axes. At the time, the region around the proposed West Forty-second Street was an "uptown" area of farmland divided into several large suburban estates. When Forty-second Street officially opened in 1837, all the estates had been subdivided into ordered lots.[7]

Before 1850, Broadway from Twenty-third to Forty-second Street was "but a winding road through pleasant countryside."[8] Railroad construction soon changed that, clearing the way for industrial and commercial development of the Middle West Side. In 1851, the Hudson River Railroad opened with a station at Thirtieth Street and Eleventh Avenue. A year later, the Eighth Avenue Railroad introduced a line between Fifty-first Street and downtown Chambers Street. When warned by friends against building his Hudson line through such sparsely populated country, rail baron Commodore Cornelius Vanderbilt firmly informed them: "Put the road there and people'll go there to live."[9]

Vanderbilt was, of course, correct. In the 1850s, lumberyards, brickyards, lime kilns, stables, warehouses, distilleries, and other industrial plants crowded together with "malodorous slaughterhouses" in the upper Thirties on the West Side. Workers followed the plants, packing themselves into "wooden shacks and shanties" and "jerry-built tenements" constructed in the area during the 1860s. The first rapid transit system in the city, the Ninth Avenue elevated train, began operating below Thirtieth Street in 1871 and expanded northward five years later. Although it destroyed "the charm and property values of Chelsea's most sedate avenue," it earned huge profits for speculators who were building tenement housing.[10] Public outrage at the squalid living conditions emerged in the early 1860s and even constituted "a vigorous but ineffectual reform movement." The industrialization of the West Side continued throughout the 1860s and 1870s.

In 1857, the City Council banned steam locomotives and the movement of cattle south of Forty-second Street in response to growing concerns about fire and pollution expressed by owners and insurers of large downtown commercial properties. This was a primary determinant behind the decision to locate the first Grand Central Terminal at Forty-second Street and Fourth Avenue (present-day Park Avenue) in the late 1860s.[11] From the beginning, the terminal served as a magnet for commercial development in midtown, drawing hotels and restaurants and other commercial activities that formed the basis of an uptown business district. Grand Central Terminal went through several stages of redevelopment before construction was completed on the current landmark building in 1913.

By the 1870s, elevated trains ran up a number of avenues in Manhattan (including Second, Third, Sixth, and Ninth Avenues), and all these lines had stops at Forty-second Street. Perhaps the most significant decision, however, establishing the centrality of Forty-second Street in the evolving transportation system came in 1901 with the announcement that construction would begin on the city's first subway line.[12] The project was indicative of the close cooperation, even unity, between public and private actors in the way that it accommodated a wide variety of economic interests. It was planned by a public commission, every member of which was also a leader in the New York State Chamber of Commerce. It was built by the Independent Rapid Transit (IRT) Company, a private corporation established by leading bankers and railroad men of the time. A municipal-bond guarantee subsidized the bonds that financed the project.

The subway route that was finally agreed on—from Wall Street and City Hall, up the East Side to Grand Central Terminal, crosstown along 42nd Street to Broadway (at what is now Times Square), and then up Broadway to 155th Street on the Upper West Side—was carefully designed to serve various real-estate and other economic interests. It respected the franchises of elevated lines already serving the Upper East Side; it accommodated downtown property owners along Broadway and Fifth Avenue who had had their opposition to rail lines enacted into law; and it served Upper West Side property owners who felt that their land values suffered unfairly from the absence of adequate transportation development. Ironically, the locational advantages that the subway line gave to the Times Square area were largely an unintended by-product of the series of political accommodations that had been reached.

Land values around present-day Times Square, which was then called Longacre Square, jumped overnight following the announcement of the subway route.[13] Adolph Ochs, owner of the *New York Times,* sensed an opportunity to link the prestige of his newspaper to that of an emerging commercial center and so bought the triangle of land at the square as a new location for his newspaper's headquarters. On New Year's Eve 1904, several hundred thousand New Yorkers gathered for the formal opening of the twenty-three-story, Italianate Times Tower, the second tallest building in the city at the time. Thus began the tradition of ushering in the New Year at Times Square.

The new IRT subway was completed in 1904 as well. Ochs convinced the City Council to change the name of the square from Longacre to Times Square and to name the subway stop Times Square station, in honor of his newspaper's new presence. A decade earlier, the owners of the *Herald Tribune* had adopted a similar geographic strategy by locating its headquarters a few blocks south, around the intersection of Broadway and Sixth Avenue, an area that then became known as Herald Square. As these cases illustrate, newspaper businesses have been important players in the urban growth machines of nineteenth- and twentieth-century America.[14]

The mass transit systems that were built during the following decades continued to reinforce the centrality of Forty-second Street and Times Square.[15] By 1928, five subway lines, four elevated train lines, eleven surface lines, five bus routes, and a ferry all had terminals or stops on Forty-second Street. The annexation in 1898 of the four boroughs surrounding Manhattan, which created the modern five-borough, five-county city of New York, had already furthered the importance of Manhattan and its midtown transportation systems because Manhattan's advanced economy and central location made it the focus of the entire metropolitan area.

These early public policy decisions and infrastructure developments both contributed to and responded to a particular pattern of economic development in Manhattan. The development of Manhattan began at the southern tip of the island and proceeded northward throughout the nineteenth century. Real-estate speculators consistently turned to uptown farmland on which to build exclusive suburban residential neighborhoods.[16] With the growth of the city's industry and commerce, however, less profitable commercial enterprises also migrated uptown in pursuit of larger spaces, lower land costs, and cheaper rents. As these businesses encroached on fashionable residential areas, affluent New Yorkers again moved farther uptown to newly constructed respectable neighborhoods. The areas they abandoned either were rebuilt to serve manufacturing and other commercial needs or were adapted to house working-class tenants through the subdivision of town houses into rooming houses.

This process demonstrates that suburbanization, or the migration of wealthier residents to less developed areas outside the central city, has long been an integral part of New York City's historical development. Only when the annexation of new suburban development was precluded by the incorporation of independent localities did the negative consequences for New York City—in lost population, jobs, and tax revenues—become apparent.

This pattern of development served to delineate cultural boundaries and insulate the city's elite from contact with lower economic classes.[17] Spatial segregation was regarded as a necessary solution to problems of potential conflict by imposing order and predictability on the urban terrain. Real estate derived its value from the "moral character" of its population, which was reflected, in turn, in its economic status. This pattern did not hold, however, in Times Square, where a new commercial culture was emerging and where economic value supplanted moral value as the basis of the real-estate market.

The development of the Longacre/Times Square area followed the same general pattern of real-estate investment that shaped other parts of Manhattan, beginning with exclusive residential construction and then shifting to a commercial character. In the mid-nineteenth century, large tracts of land in the area were bought by real-estate speculators and developed into exclusive suburban neighborhoods. William Astor alone built some 200 elegant brownstones on Forty-fourth through Forty-seventh Streets northwest of Longacre Square. By 1860, the area consisted of many magnificent row houses occupied by "a superior class of residents."[18]

By the 1870s, however, commerce had already reached West Forty-second Street and was expanding with the construction of small hotels and other lodging houses, commercial buildings with storefronts at street level and offices above, stables, carriage houses, and spaces for light industry.[19] By 1890, Forty-second Street was a major commercial thoroughfare, and the area was no longer "uptown." Because of the large number of carriage manufacturers, harness shops, and livery stables, the area known as Times Square today was then called Longacre Square after the similar district in London.

CRIME AND PROSTITUTION GREET THE BIRTH OF TIMES SQUARE

The industrialization of the Middle West Side that began in the mid-nineteenth century was accompanied by a concentration of working-class Irish and Italians in squalid and overcrowded tenements—"the lowest and filthiest in the City"[20]—in the area west of Longacre Square. This neighborhood, which became known as Hell's Kitchen (present-day Clinton), was considered "one of the most dangerous areas on the American continent" in the latter half of the nineteenth and early twentieth centuries.[21] As the *New York Times* reported in 1881, this was "a locality where law and order is openly defied, where might makes right and depravity revels riotously in squalor and reeking filth. The whole neighborhood is an eyesore to the respectable people who live or are compelled to do business in the vicinity, a source of terror to the honest poor, and an unmitigated nuisance to the police of the 20th Precinct."[22] It was a description that might be equally likely to appear in a *New York Times* report on Times Square a century later.

A commentator in the 1930s, writing in the spirit of the times, noted that residents of the area were "shackled by low-wage industry to desperate poverty and barbarous living conditions" and often resorted to crime and violence.[23] Draft riots had erupted in Hell's Kitchen in 1863, and later in the decade disaffected residents began forming organized gangs. The Hell's Kitchen Gang was one of the more infamous, with a "repertoire [that] included extortion, breaking-and-entering, professional mayhem, and highway robbery."[24] It merged with the Tenth Avenue Gang and "for decades terrorized the neighborhood," until the rival Gophers "achieved hegemony" in the area with some 500 men. "Gangster rule" prevailed in Hell's Kitchen until about 1910, when the New York Central Railroad—whose West Side yards were a repeated target of looting and vandalism—retaliated by organizing its own special police force: "Clubbing, shooting, and arresting indiscriminately, they soon had most of the Gopher leadership in hospitals or behind the bars."[25] While some gang activity continued in the area through the Prohibition era, its scale was greatly diminished.

Still, in its early years the Great White Way bordered on one of the most dangerous areas in the United States. The West Side gangsters made the local police station, then on West Forty-seventh Street between Eighth and Ninth Avenues, one of the busiest in New York City.[26] Ironically, this is the same distinction that was bestowed on the precinct house for the Times Square area almost a century later, when the cries for redevelopment—and a return to the glory years of Times Square—reached their crescendo around 1980. By the turn of the century, Longacre Square at the intersection of Broadway and Seventh Avenue was known less affectionately as "Thieves' Lair," as the once-respectable brownstone neighborhood had become a nightlife and entertainment district with alarming levels of crime and prostitution.[27]

Historically, there has been a close geographic connection between prostitution and commercial theater in the United States.[28] In New York City, prostitution was a central part of the entertainment economy throughout the nineteenth century, as theaters and brothels operated side by side.[29] Industrial and commercial development downtown forced the interrelated entertainment and prostitution industries to migrate together up the island and into Longacre Square by the 1880s and 1890s. Thus at the time of its invention, Times Square was already known for a thriving sex industry; commercialized sex has proved to be a lasting and stubborn feature of the area ever since.

The theater and entertainment district settled in the area south of Houston Street (present-day SoHo) in the early nineteenth century, but then migrated uptown along Broadway in pursuit of larger and cheaper spaces. Along the way, it located, in turn, around Fourteenth Street/Union Square in the mid-1850s, Twenty-third Street in 1870, and Thirty-fourth Street/Herald Square in 1885 before moving into the "Roaring Forties" around Longacre Square.[30] The move from Thirty-fourth Street to Forty-second Street began in 1883 with the construction of a new Metropolitan Opera House on Thirty-ninth and Fortieth Streets between Broadway and Seventh Avenue. In 1893, the Empire Theater was built at Forty-first Street and Broadway, and in 1894 Oscar Hammerstein crossed the Forty-second Street line, constructing his Olympia Theater on Broadway between Forty-fourth and Forty-fifth Streets. By 1900, Hammerstein's Victoria (1895) and Republic (1900) Theaters stood side by side on Forty-second Street at the corner of Seventh Avenue, joined by rooftop gardens featuring an enclosed glass bar, a live menagerie, and a dance hall with ponds, fountains, and waterfalls.[31] The image of Forty-second Street as the fashionable theater block had been set.

From 1903 to 1907, nine more theaters were built in the immediate vicinity of Forty-second Street and Times Square, and soon seventeen theaters were located on the two square blocks between Forty-first and Forty-third Streets, and Seventh and Eighth Avenues, alone. Between 1893 and 1927, some eighty-five theaters operated in the greater theater district, of which Times Square had become the focal point. This is more than double the number of legitimate Broadway theaters, around thirty-five, that have been active in the area during the 1980s and 1990s. During the peak theater season, which occurred in 1927 and 1928, 264 shows opened in 76 area theaters.[32]

Prostitution, too, had been centered in a multitude of brothels in the area south of Houston Street in the mid-nineteenth century and was driven out, along with theater, by the construction of manufacturing lofts in the 1860s. By the 1880s, prostitution had followed the theaters to the area around Thirty-fourth Street and Broadway, forming the notorious "Tenderloin" district. As many as nineteen brothels might be found on a single block,[33] and "one-half of all the buildings were reputed to cater to vice."[34] As theaters and other leisure institutions began moving north to a new geographic center at Forty-second Street, so did the Tenderloin: "By 1885, prostitutes were a prominent and visible part of the 42nd Street community."[35]

At the turn of the century, moral crusaders identified more than 130 addresses out of which prostitutes were working in the thirty-three blocks surrounding Longacre Square, and the majority were located on the eight blocks from Thirty-ninth to Forty-seventh Streets between Seventh and Eighth Avenues.[36] More than sixty of these addresses were row houses, including many of the elegant brownstones built by Astor a generation earlier as luxury residences (owners who moved to more respectable areas found that renting them as brothels was their most lucrative option), while the other seventy were tenements and apartments. Hoards of prostitutes also solicited along Broadway, Forty-second Street, and Sixth to Eighth Avenues. Commentators reported that on Broadway there were ten to twenty prostitutes on every block, forming a "two-mile parade of prurient commerce" from Twenty-seventh to

Sixty-eighth Street.[37] This prostitution existed side by side, in a symbiotic relationship, with the exclusive theaters and restaurants that catered to the city's elite crowd.

A crusading minister of the era, outraged at the abject wickedness of the Tenderloin, denounced the city that tolerated it as "a modern Gomorrah."[38] A century later, another religious leader leveled the same condemnation of the city during public hearings on the 42nd Street Development Project. Apparently, conditions had not changed much over the years, a point conveniently overlooked in the discourse of Times Square decline.

By the turn of the century, the Longacre/Times Square area had emerged as the center of both a dazzling white-light district of theater and entertainment and a thriving red-light district of brothels and streetwalkers. The area had also become a central contested space, with investors, public officials, business organizations, moral crusaders, prostitutes, and "sporting men" all acting to define the area in different ways. According to Timothy Gilfoyle, "By 1910, Times Square was a cultural battleground for competing forms of leisure, entertainment, and sexuality."[39]

Within the following decade, prostitution was largely reduced to a clandestine activity operating discreetly through area hotels and nightclubs. Progressive reform politicians, property owners' associations, and various citizens' leagues had joined forces in a sustained attack that had begun before the turn of the century. Especially important in this effort were the voluntary citizens' organizations, such as the Committee of Fourteen, which gradually moved away from moral suasion as a tactic and began to exert pressure on owners of businesses and properties who benefited from the illegal sex market. These groups have been described as, in effect, "private state" agencies that usurped regulatory and enforcement powers from the corrupt public authorities who shared in the illegal profits of the underground economy.[40] (Previous crackdowns by the authorities had simply raised the cost of doing business as usual.)

The successes of the crusaders were short-lived, though, and it was not long before the sex market that had been forced off the streets was appearing in a new guise on the stages of area theaters. Indeed, commercial sex, in its variety of forms, has proved to be a remarkably resilient component of the Times Square economy throughout the twentieth century.

TIMES SQUARE AS SHOWPLACE OF COMMERCIAL CULTURE

There was perhaps a brief period in the late 1910s and early 1920s when the Forty-second Street and Times Square area closely resembled the romantic imagery that now defines its early days.[41] It was a thriving entertainment district with little of the overt sexual commerce that has characterized much of its past. The importance of Times Square even extended beyond its role as an entertainment district, with the area becoming by the 1920s a kind of national—even international—stage for the display and promotion of a new commercial culture.

The Times Square area contained the largest concentration of advertising space in the world, with marketing displays of unprecedented proportions.[42] Signs were distinguished by their enormous sizes, spectacular designs, and remarkable use of new illumination technologies. A single sign might be 80 feet high and 200 feet long, containing in excess of 17,000 bulbs.[43] The entire ambience was created by innovative uses of light, glass, colors, and images in signs, billboards, and shop windows. In effect, Times Square embodied what William Leach calls a new "commercial aesthetic." As he describes it, "By 1920 this aesthetic was remaking or deeply affecting the way Americans experienced everyday reality. Its purpose was to move and market goods, to produce a pecuniary climate, and to excite the spirit of acquisition and appropriation. At the same time, it was intended or had the possible effect of 'thrilling' onlookers and conveying a sense of wonder and awe."[44]

By 1920, the American psyche needed to be rebuilt. A revolution in production had begun in the second half of the nineteenth century with the Industrial Revolution. New techniques of standardization and mass production facilitated ever-expanding capacities for output. For this process to be profitable, it required a corresponding acceleration of consumption, so that the economy would combine "running full" and "selling fast."[45] This system of hyperconsumption, in turn, depended on rapid "social and moral engineering" to encourage adaptation to the industrialized society. Times Square thus served an important function in promoting the new consumer culture to support the mass-production techniques. Its magnificence and scale also reflected its central position in a new industry of domestic urban tourism that was taking shape early in the century and aiding in the dissemination of this commercial culture.[46]

The zoning resolution enacted in New York City in 1916 to regulate land use, which was the first comprehensive zoning regulation in the nation, set the stage for the role of Times Square as the center of the emerging commercial culture. The ordinance did not specifically create a theater and entertainment district in Times Square; rather, it established a mixed-use commercial district that allowed for the construction of giant billboards.[47] There was immediate opposition from Fifth Avenue property owners and merchants who were opposed to the signs in their area, and in 1922 the city's Board of Alderman banned giant billboards from the more exclusive Fifth Avenue (and parts of Madison Avenue and Thirty-fourth Street), while permitting them on Broadway.

Of course, members of the Fifth Avenue Association were often advertisers in Times Square (for example, Gimbel's and Macy's department stores), and they certainly wanted the business of Times Square tourists. But, they also wanted to protect their own turf from becoming a "carnival spectacle" that would attract the "wrong kind of people" and cause property values to drop.[48] In the end, the ordinance rewarded both the Fifth Avenue Association and the Broadway Association, which wanted no controls on signs in its area, and in so doing promoted the concentration of signs in Times Square.

In Times Square, commercial entrepreneurs had the opportunity to create a mecca of mass consumption, and commercial values alone drove patterns of real-estate investment. In this respect, the development of Times Square differed from that of other parts of the city where the value of an area or a neighborhood was determined by the "moral character" of its users. Real-estate developers often relied on this equation in creating and separating exclusive residential neighborhoods and working-class tenement districts.[49]

Since at least the beginning of the twentieth century, entrepreneurs were constructing entertainment facilities around Times Square aimed specifically at mass audiences. One such attraction was the huge, spectacular, carnivalesque Hippodrome, built in 1906 at Fortieth Street and Sixth Avenue and dubbed a "plaything for the masses."[50] The Hippodrome occupied an entire city block and provided a wide variety of entertainment for a range of prices, thus offering something for everyone.

Commercial success clearly superseded notions of moral character as the measure of real-estate values in Times Square. In this sense, the commercial culture in Times Square represented a breakdown of traditional class-based cultural boundaries. The early coexistence of elite and popular entertainment attractions contributed to the creation of Times Square as a contested space where different social classes vied for their own entertainment forms. Thus early forms of commercial development established the basis for the patterns of social and cultural conflict that have continued in the area. Indeed, it is likely that this contested nature of Times Square has been the source of its vitality and excitement—and thus of its appeal.

THE DECLINE OF THE GREAT WHITE WAY

While Times Square enjoyed a brief heyday around 1920 as a thriving entertainment district and the center of a flashy commercial culture, other forces were already at work to reshape the contest over this place. Some of the most fundamental changes in Times Square were triggered by Prohibition, which altered the social and economic dynamics of the area during the 1920s and early 1930s in ways that had lasting consequences. Prohibition represented a moral attack on urban culture and an effort to impose traditional values on urban immigrant populations.[51] In New York, however, Prohibition simply pushed the nightlife culture underground, where it continued to flourish, albeit with close ties to organized crime. On Forty-second Street, the primary effect of Prohibition was to precipitate the decline of legitimate theater and contribute to the emergence of other forms of entertainment, including movies and burlesque.

In order for the Times Square theaters to survive in the face of increasing land values stimulated by the emergence of a midtown business district and the twenty-four-hour crowds brought into the area by the extensive transit system, most of them had relied on additional income generated by rooftop gardens, cabarets, and restaurants that could operate on the premises for long hours. The profitability of the theaters themselves was limited by the short season and the inability to put on more than one or, at most, two performances a day. Prohibition killed many of these secondary entertainment activities, and the demise of the theaters inevitably followed.[52]

Motion pictures were becoming a popular form of entertainment in the 1920s, and many of the Forty-second Street theaters were converted for use as movie houses where shows could be run repeatedly each day. The major film companies, however, were constructing their own elaborate first-run movie houses elsewhere in the greater Times Square area. The Forty-second Street theaters consequently were converted into "grinders," the movie houses that were continually grinding out B-quality action and adventure movies oriented primarily to a male audience. Beginning in the 1930s, other failing theaters on Forty-second Street came to accommodate the expansion of burlesque entertainment to its new uptown location in the Times Square area.

By the mid-1930s, of the thirteen elegant theaters that had operated on Forty-second Street between Seventh and Eighth Avenues a decade earlier, three continued as legitimate theaters, five were grinder movie houses, two featured burlesque shows, and three were dark. Although the decline of legitimate theater is often blamed on the advent of the movie industry, in the Times Square area it is more likely that theater was already doomed by its relative lack of profitability in the late 1920s.[53] In fact, the elaborate theater houses themselves probably have survived through the twentieth century only because movies provided a profitable alternative use to which they could be easily converted. In the 1930s, the theater district could no longer continue its migration to cheaper areas uptown, as it had in the past; because of the rapid development of uptown areas, there was nowhere left to go.

The Great Depression of the 1930s exacerbated the downscaling of uses on Forty-second Street.[54] Along with the grinders and burlesque theaters came other businesses catering to a high-volume, quick-turnover crowd. These included "dime museums" that featured "freaks" with physical oddities and "sex education" exhibits of dubious informational value, bookstores that sold "sun-bathing" magazines and "marriage manuals," and arcades that offered a variety of amusement-park–style games. Street crime began to be considered a real threat, in contrast to the more romanticized Hollywood image of gangsters in Times Square that had prevailed during the 1920s.

The WPA Guide to New York City still bestowed the title of Great White Way on the Times Square of the late 1930s, describing the area as "the theatrical center of America and wonder of the out-of-towner."[55] The description proceeded, however, in a different tone, exposing an aging face behind the gaudy makeup of Times Square:

By day, Times Square is a jumble of skyscrapers, antiquated and remodeled commercial structures, and shabby taxpayers [small, cheaply built commercial structures] topped by the huge skeletons of electric signs. Without the beneficent flood of light descending from above, the area exhibits . . . a certain drabness. Adjoining elaborate hotel and theater entrances and wide-windowed clothing shops are scores of typical midway enterprises: fruit juice stands garlanded with artificial palm leaves, theater ticket offices, cheap lunch counters, cut-rate haberdasheries, burlesque houses, and novelty concessions.[56]

During the 1920s, property values along Forty-second Street had been rising, prompting major redevelopment plans, but the Depression brought these efforts to a halt. A real-estate study conducted in 1927 had found that three of the ten most valuable properties in the city were located on Forty-second Street, including one at the intersection of Broadway at the base of Times Square. Shortly thereafter, newspapers were reporting private efforts to assemble land along West Forty-second Street in order to build skyscrapers with theaters at street level and office space above.[57] These plans were abandoned, however, after the stock market crash of 1929.

During the 1930s, then, Times Square took on the "honky-tonk" character that has continued to shape images of the area in the public mind, albeit in an ambivalent way.[58] Commentators at the time decried the transition of Times Square to a new "Coney Island,"[59] with a "carnivalesque" and "cut-rate, amusement park ambiance."[60] As this imagery indicates, there had been a perceived decline to more "popular" forms of entertainment, in the most negative sense of the term, that catered to "low-class" crowds.

As the center of commercial culture since the early years of the twentieth century, Times Square had attracted a crowd that reflected a mix of socioeconomic classes, since it contained theaters and entertainment forms that appealed explicitly to "mass" audiences. Nevertheless, the legitimate theaters that dominated Forty-second Street through the 1920s were almost exclusively the domain of the "leisured class" and the "clerical/business class"; these two groups, in roughly equal numbers, constituted virtually the entire theater audience, with only the barest minimum of "working-class" people.[61] So even though the development of entertainment in Times Square had always reflected a variety of competing cultural values, the Broadway theaters formed the basis for a prominent "genteel" culture in the area.

Thus the shift to new entertainment forms—such as grinders, burlesque, dime museums, arcades, and bars and nightclubs (especially after the repeal of Prohibition in 1933)—certainly reflected a greater "democratization" of the area. *The WPA Guide to New York City* noted that Times Square had become "a district of glorified dancing girls and millionaire playboys and, on a different plane, of dime-a-dance hostesses and pleasure-seeking clerks."[62] In the 1930s musical *Forty-second Street,* the change was captured in more memorable verse:

> Where the underworld can meet the elite
> naughty, bawdy, gaudy, sporty, 42nd Street.

Opinions on whether the changes in Times Square were for better or worse have varied with observers. Contemporary historians such as Brooks McNamara and Lawrence Senelick have argued that the transformation did not indicate a decline, but a redefinition of the area aimed at accommodating a broader, more popular audience.[63] At the time, however, many observers were not so sanguine, firmly believing that democratization translated into decline. For the most part, the resistance to the new cultural definition of the area came from the Forty-second Street property owners and merchants. Their primary target was the highly successful burlesque industry, whose presence threatened to dominate Forty-second Street by the late 1930s.[64] Many of the more respectable businesses that had coexisted easily with the legitimate theaters were unwilling to operate side by side with the new sex entertainment establishments.

While the cleanup campaign launched by the 42nd Street Property Owners' Association was sometimes couched in terms of religious outrage, the essential motivation was decidedly economic. The burlesque theaters seemed capable of defining the nature of the entire street. As long as burlesque had remained downtown around Fourteenth Street and Union Square, it was largely left alone. But its presence on Forty-second Street was perceived as creating a "slum-like" atmosphere. As Peter Buckley succinctly puts it, "Land value came before moral value."[65] Concerned property owners reacted accordingly.

Reform politicians had been closely associated with efforts by moral crusaders and clergy to regulate entertainment and sexuality.[66] In the late 1930s, reform mayor Fiorello LaGuardia picked up this moral cause and, together with his license commissioner, acted to ban burlesque.[67] By 1942, burlesque had been officially eliminated from the city, although some shows went underground and the dime museums continued to present acts such as belly dancing for live erotic entertainment.

The eradication of burlesque marked the disappearance of the last successful form of live theater along Forty-second Street. The theater industry overall was suffering greatly by the late 1930s. In the 1927/1928 theater season, seventy-six theaters were operating in the greater Times Square theater district, but within a decade the number had dropped to thirty-three.[68] None of the Forty-second Street theaters were among those remaining in operation as legitimate theater at the end of the 1930s. Still, the greater Times Square area continued to house many businesses and institutions that supported and supplied the entertainment industry.

Although property owners and merchants had succeeded in their attack on burlesque, it is doubtful whether their cleanup campaign was able to improve the moral climate of the area significantly.[69] Forty-second Street had been taken over as a male domain during the 1930s, if not earlier, and the grinders, arcades, bookstores, and novelty shops continued to cater to a predominantly male clientele. World War II brought new crowds of soldiers and sailors into Times Square, reinforcing the tendency toward a male-dominated cultural space and bringing back a market in commercial sex.

Prostitution, particularly among gay men, flourished. By the 1930s, Times Square already had become one of the most important centers of gay life in New York.[70] Gays had succeeded in constructing their own "sphere of relative cultural autonomy" in the area. Male prostitution was visible as early as the 1920s, with flamboyant "fairies" operating along Forty-second Street. The Depression added a new, tough crowd of men ("rough trade") who were willing to sell themselves for cash. The influx of soldiers and sailors only expanded this market in the 1940s. Although there were frequent efforts to clean up the area by rounding up "undesirables" and using the State Liquor Authority to close gay bars, a homosexual culture had been firmly established and continued to adapt and survive.[71]

By the 1940s, property and business owners in the Times Square area again turned to the city to help redeem the value of their investments.[72] This time, their concerns focused on the arcades, galleries, and souvenir shops that opened onto the sidewalks and thrived with the arrival of soldiers and sailors in the area. The Department of City Planning and the Board of Estimate responded with various zoning amendments that were enacted in 1947 and 1954 to prohibit such "outdoor public nuisances." Only later did it become apparent that these zoning ordinances had backfired, since they encouraged the spread of enclosed pornographic bookstores by driving out the primary competitive uses on the street.

The trends that developed in the Times Square area during the 1930s and 1940s continued into the 1950s. The construction of the Port Authority Bus Terminal in 1950, just south of Forty-second Street on Eighth Avenue, further reinforced the area's position at the center of the city's transportation infrastructure; but it also drew more "vagrants" into the area, thereby sharing the fate of many inner-city bus stations.[73]

In the 1960s, Times Square provided fertile ground for an emerging counterculture based on libertarian values and lifestyles that involved experimentation with drugs and sex. A number of Supreme Court decisions that expanded First Amendment protections for sexually explicit materials facilitated the growth of the commercial sex industry in Times Square.[74] Adult entertainment in Times Square took on increasingly brazen and bizarre forms.[75] By the 1970s, consumers could choose from a smorgasbord of books, magazines, films, peep shows, private one-on-one peep booths (usually, but not always, divided by a glass partition), stripteases, and even live sex performances in the Times Square establishments. Prostitution was thinly veiled behind the facades of these and other enterprises, such as hotels, topless shoe-shine stands, and, especially, the many massage parlors of Times Square. Other Supreme Court decisions that expanded the rights of the accused and provided protection against unlawful search and seizure also may have contributed to the growing drug culture in Times Square, although the area had been a center for "cheap reefers" as early as the 1930s.[76]

At the same time, Times Square was affected by national trends involving the migration of population, jobs, and investment dollars. The riots that spread through the nation's major cities in the 1960s accelerated the pace at which private capital and middle- and upper-income populations were abandoning urban centers for the safety and comfort of suburban lawns, thereby reinforcing the trends that had been under way by the 1950s. This out-migration meant a loss of crucial tax revenues for cities, which, when federal aid began to decline in the late 1970s, were increasingly incapable of addressing the problems of poverty, housing abandonment, crime, and drugs that were seen as driving the middle-class exodus. In the public mind, Times Square symbolized this seemingly irreversible process of urban failure and decline that justified flight from the nation's decaying cities.

MOBILIZATION FOR CLEANUP AND REDEVELOPMENT

As noted earlier, New York City's elites already considered Forty-second Street between Seventh and Eighth Avenues as "the worst block in town" as early as 1960, and this decade also marked the beginning of a spate of new redevelopment proposals aimed at returning the street to more profitable use. The sex industry was clearly profitable, but not on the scale of the office development that prevailed elsewhere in midtown Manhattan, especially on the East Side. Moreover, the sex-related establishments were regarded as depressing property uses and values in the larger West Side area of Midtown. Plans for the redevelopment of Forty-second Street and Times Square were therefore an attempt to integrate the West Side into the midtown business district and secure the postindustrial transformation of Manhattan.

In 1960, the Broadway Association offered a plan for the expansion of the Times Square pedestrian mall (the triangular traffic islands between Broadway and Seventh Avenue); in 1962, it added a proposal for the redevelopment of West Forty-second Street that called for the conversion of the historic theaters into supper clubs, cabarets, and gambling facilities. Other schemes that were floated in the 1960s included one from the Department of City Planning for the development of combined office and theater space, another from transportation officials for the creation of a pedestrian mall along Forty-second Street, and yet another from the West Side Association of Commerce for the construction of an office and retail complex.[77]

On a more modest scale, the administration of Mayor John Lindsay created the Special Theater District around Times Square in 1967 to promote development while protecting the theater industry.[78] Developers were given a 20 percent zoning bonus for constructing high-rise buildings in the district if they included new theater space. The provision was first used a year later when the historic Astor Hotel was demolished to make way for the construction of a fifty-story office tower at Broadway and Forty-fifth Street. But its overall impact as a stimulus to development was limited; it produced a total of five theaters in four new high-rises.

Lindsay also established the Times Square Development Council in 1971 to pursue redevelopment plans for the area, although it was later revealed that some members of the council owned blighted buildings in Times Square—as did other prominent people and organizations in the city, including bankers, reformers, and developers[79]—that were housing the undesirable uses regarded as obstacles to improvement. In 1972, the mayor created two "super-precincts" in the Police Department, Midtown North and Midtown South, to enhance the effectiveness of law enforcement in the greater Times Square area.

In spite of these policies adopted in the 1960s and early 1970s to promote development, the economic recession in 1974 brought a temporary halt to the various plans. For the second time in the century, an uncooperative business cycle left private capital unable to complete the process it had begun. New efforts to improve the Times Square area, through both cleanup campaigns and redevelopment, did not resume until the late 1970s, after New York City had weathered the worst of its fiscal crises.

In 1976, Mayor Abraham Beame established the Mayor's Office of Midtown Enforcement (OME), "a tactical, 20-member legal swat team" of police and inspectors from the Buildings, Fire, and Health Departments that was deployed to enforce safety codes extremely vigorously in commercial sex establishments.[80] Through the use of these focused, selective enforcement techniques, the OME successfully closed many sex-related businesses in Midtown, reducing their total number from 121 in 1978 to 65 just five years later.[81] The OME closed about forty massage parlors, and, in 1979, the city passed a zoning amendment controlling "physical culture establishments" that effectively banned new massage parlors from operating in the city.

In 1978, Operation Crossroads involved the creation of a new police substation at Times Square and an increase in the police presence in the core of the area, between Broadway and Ninth Avenue from Fortieth to Fiftieth Street. At any given time, there were up to eighty uniformed and twenty-five plainclothes officers on duty, in addition to officers from the Public Morals Squad and other special units that may be operating in the area. While these cleanup efforts had a definite impact on activities in the area, the various subcultures of the street proved quite resilient and capable of adapting to the new enforcement patterns; thus many illegal activities continued.[82]

On the redevelopment side, the 42nd Street Development Corporation was established in 1976 as a nonprofit local development corporation (LDC), initiating a public–private effort to spur economic development on far West Forty-second Street. The Forty-second Street LDC was successful with a number of projects on West Forty-second Street, including the conversion of the Crossroads Building at Broadway from porn to police use, the restoration of the McGraw-Hill Building between Eighth and Ninth Avenues, and the creation of Theater Row between Ninth and Tenth Avenues. The last project involved converting a number of dilapidated buildings that had housed adult entertainment into a complex of off-off-Broadway theaters, restaurants, rehearsal spaces, and offices.

The real gold mine for redevelopment, however, was the block of Forty-second Street between Seventh and Eighth Avenues, and in 1979 an offshoot of the 42nd Street Development Corporation presented a grandiose redevelopment plan called The City at 42nd Street.[83] It proposed three office towers at the intersection of Broadway, Seventh Avenue, and Forty-second Street, and an enormous fashion mart at the western end of the block. Its most spectacular feature was a 750,000-square-foot urban theme park that would include a museum, rides, theaters, movie houses, and other amusement and entertainment facilities. The City at 42nd Street formed the conceptual framework for the publicly sponsored development project that was ultimately approved by state and city officials, whose planning philosophy was grounded in the discourse on Times Square.

POLITICIZING THE PROBLEMS OF TIMES SQUARE

In June 1980, New York City signed a "memorandum of understanding" (MOU) with the New York State Urban Development Corporation (UDC), initiating the process that culminated in formal approval of the 42nd Street Development Project in November 1984. City and state officials promoted the redevelopment plan as the only solution to the problems of the Times Square area. Its large scale was defended as a necessity, given the magnitude of the problems that had to be addressed on Forty-second Street.

Officials argued that the redevelopment plan would eliminate blight and crime; restore the historic Forty-second Street theaters and reestablish the area as a center for theater, tourism, and entertainment; develop the commercial and retail potential of the district; upgrade public facilities; increase the area's economic contribution to the city; and be a positive influence on adjacent areas of the city.[84]

These goals were aimed at addressing a complicated mix of perceived ills, some of which were grounded in empirical analysis of the area and others of which were not. In the highly politicized contest over this space, it became almost impossible to disentangle perceptions of the area from the objective conditions that existed. Clearly, there were serious social problems on Forty-second Street; yet the particular way they were defined was essential to the determination of goals and the justification for proposed solutions. In this respect, the Times Square discourse played a fundamental political role in defining the redevelopment agenda.

The political discourse on Times Square had two primary components relevant to planning for redevelopment: the first depicted a romantic, idealized history of the Great White Way, and the second defined the hopeless severity of the area's current problems. As we have seen, the actual history of Times Square illustrates the inaccuracies of the sanitized story of the area's past. And the depiction of its current condition was also at odds with the complex social life of this dynamic and troubled public space.

THE TAKING AND RETAKING OF TIMES SQUARE TURF

A recurrent and fundamental theme in the political discourse supporting Times Square redevelopment was that this urban space—specifically, the heart of the Forty-second Street project area, from Seventh to Eighth Avenues—had been taken over by a menacing street culture engaged in a variety of illegal and dangerous activities. Aside from the illegal markets in sex and drugs, this street culture was said to support and be supported by an established economy of businesses that, although legal, were considered undesirable and offensive. Together, these social and economic forces allegedly created a dangerous and uncontrollable domain that was avoided by the majority of respectable New Yorkers and by investment dollars alike. Consequently, only intervention on a massive scale by the public and private sectors would succeed in redefining the nature of this area. The imagery frequently used likened Times Square to a "cancer" that must be surgically removed in order to save the economic health and social fabric of the city's West Side.

Perhaps the primary statement of the planning philosophy behind the 42nd Street Development Project is the draft environmental-impact statement (DEIS) prepared by the New York State UDC.[85] This document is likely the most extensive and thorough expression of the thinking among planners and promoters of the project.[86] The DEIS is, therefore, a key to understanding the Times Square discourse and its relationship to the redevelopment plan that was adopted.

The DEIS is permeated with the language of territorial takeover and control, in effect defining an enemy in a battle for Forty-second Street at Times Square. The document identified "hustlers and loiterers" as the most disruptive influence on West Forty-second Street: "In a real sense, 42nd Street is *their* territory, and others venturing through it perceive that they do so at their own risk."[87] It argued that economic and social forces in the area had combined to create a place that was "claimed by no legitimate social group."[88] Most people just passed through the area, and there was an "absence of office workers and other positive users having a territorial stake" to make "competing claims."[89] As a result, "sidewalks are left free and available to loiterers and over time 42nd Street has become their turf."[90]

The function of the redevelopment project, therefore, was to "effect a transfer of turf to new users," creating a climate where "new merchants and theater managers will have an incentive to defend this space."[91] An important question that arises, then, concerns the validity of this depiction of Forty-second Street as an area taken over by a menacing street culture. Was the image based on objective conditions, or was it primarily the product of a constructed political discourse?

An undisputed fact about Forty-second Street between Seventh and Eighth

Avenues is that it was one of the most heavily traveled spaces in all of New York City in the late 1970s and early 1980s.[92] Street studies estimated that between 3,700 and 7,000 pedestrians passed along this block each hour during midday and rush hours on weekdays.[93] On weekends, the number of pedestrians on the block might reach a remarkable 8,000 an hour. Yet contrary to widely held perceptions, especially among suburbanites, that Forty-second Street had become a "ghetto street," studies found that whites constituted a "numerically dominant group" of persons on the street at almost all times of day.[94] It was only after midnight that the number of African-Americans might exceed that of whites.

Indeed, a study of activity on West Forty-second Street conducted by sociologists at the City University of New York (CUNY)[95] in the late 1970s concluded that

42nd Street between 6th and 8th Avenues is probably one of the most racially integrated streets in the city. Particularly in the daytime, the racial and ethnic breakdown of pedestrians approximates the proportions of white, Black, and Hispanic persons in Manhattan's residential population. While Blacks and Hispanics may be somewhat over-represented compared to their numbers of the overall city population, neither are they the under-represented minority nor the ghetto majority which they are in most other areas of the city.[96]

The CUNY study went on to point out, however, that "the 'street people' along 42nd Street tend to be predominantly Black and Hispanic, a fact which does not go unnoticed by the general population."[97] There are certainly important misconceptions at work when racial integration is perceived as a minority takeover, but these anxieties are deeply rooted in a society that continues to be characterized by racial segregation and inequality.[98] In fact, the real pattern of dominance was based on gender with men greatly outnumbering women on the street[99]—a point largely ignored in the dominant discourse.

Some other characteristics of the Forty-second Street population that were discovered are worth noting for the light they shed on the nature of the area before its redevelopment.[100] On average, roughly half of the pedestrians on the street lived outside New York City. More people were in the area because they worked nearby than for any other reason, both on weekdays (41.0 percent) and on weekends (18.6 percent). On weekdays, the second largest group was made up of those who were in the area to shop (11.2 percent); on weekends, it was the patrons of action movies (15.7 percent). On weekends, almost 10 percent of the people on the street were there for sightseeing, while another 10 percent were there to patronize the mainstream movie theaters and restaurants and bars. The number of persons in the area simply because they were passing through never exceeded 14 percent of the total, and the fact that pedestrian counts reached their highest levels on weekend evenings, with as many as 8,000 people an hour, clearly supports the contention that the Forty-second Street area of Times Square was itself a destination, particularly for entertainment. Less than 2 percent of the pedestrians admitted to being there for the purpose of "hustling," while no more than 1 percent admitted to being there for sex-related entertainment. An additional 13 percent of the total reported that they were there simply to "hang out."

In and of themselves, these statistics hardly support the contention that this area had been taken over by a dangerous street population, even acknowledging an inevitable underreporting by hustlers and sexual voyeurs. But the DEIS went on to create a reality out of this perception. First, it combined those "hustling" with those "hanging out" into a single group, which then accounted for almost 15 percent of the pedestrian population on weekends. The group was relatively young (almost 33 percent were twenty-five or under), predominantly African-American (40 percent) and Latino (21 percent), and overwhelmingly male (90 percent). Next, the report argued that among those whose reason for being in the area fell in the category of "other" (6.5 to 7.5 percent of the total), "at least some of this 'other' group were, in fact, hanging out,"[101] indicating an even higher percentage in this new composite group.

The study then proceeded to suggest that because the audience for action movies had the same general demographic makeup as the hustlers, hangers-out, and others—young, minority, and male—all these persons should be combined into a single group for purposes of understanding the social characteristics of the block. The study concluded:

> Thus, a large (over 30% on the weekend) group of like people were on the street. Most of these came for legitimate purposes; however, the distinction between legitimate and illegitimate users of the street is not easily made and, in the ebb and flow of the 42nd Street crowds, those standing around or congregating in front of a movie often appear as ominous as the pushers, solicitors and others "doing business" on the street.[102]

Despite the need to acknowledge that most people were in the area for legitimate purposes, the statistics were manipulated to prove the assertion that Forty-second Street was a threatening place. The implicit conclusion was that African-Americans, Latinos, and whites cannot share the same entertainment district because non-Latino whites are unable to distinguish the criminal element from among a crowd of African-Americans and Latinos. Yet the authors of the DEIS had conducted no studies to determine precisely who was frightened, and how their fear affected behavior among the larger urban population.[103] In other areas of recreation in the city where there also was a significant population of young African-American and Latino males, such as Washington Square Park in Greenwich Village, no state of panic prevailed among whites. But with regard to Times Square, planners chose not to consider the presence of racial and ethnic minorities as a valued element of diversity to be worked with in a positive way; instead, the population was defined as a negative feature that provided a justification for remaking the area.

To add force to its claim about the menacing nature of Forty-second Street, the DEIS repeatedly employed the disconcerting concept of the "loiterer," which included such "representatives of the street culture" as drug sellers and buyers, alcoholics, prostitutes (mostly male), various con men, peddlers, and homeless people.[104] Because many of these groups constructed their own social structures in "undefended" spaces on the street—in the form of "strolls," "stations," and "hang-outs"—it was argued that they "lend the impression that 42nd Street is their territory."[105] The DEIS acknowledged that, in fact, the proportion of loiterers on the street was very small—less than 3 percent of the pedestrians at the very most— but it maintained that they had an impact far greater than their numbers would indicate. Again, this was due in large part to the "confusion in distinguishing the legitimate moviegoers from the loiterer population."[106] The DEIS recognized that loiterers even included people engaged in legal activities like standing around or pursuing an occupation such as shoe-shine men and "flyboys" distributing leaflets for sex establishments and other businesses. Indeed, as Herbert Gans noted, the concept of the loiterer was so broad and poorly defined that it would seem "New York is full of loiterers."[107] For purposes of the DEIS, however, it seemed to cover all those populations—nonwhite and lower-income—that the project developers wished to displace.

According to the DEIS, the inability to distinguish moviegoers or people just hanging out from "those engaged in (or about to engage in) illegal activities" had more than a psychological impact on a jittery public. It created an insurmountable problem for law enforcement as well, since the crowds provided "the market and the screen for the hustlers and pushers." That is, the crowd included the potential customers of the dealers and, at the same time, screened them because "those hanging around [were] often indistinguishable from the criminals."[108]

It is possible, of course, that crime rates alone could have supported the perception of Forty-second Street and Times Square as an exceptionally dangerous place. The DEIS indeed emphasized that the Midtown South Precinct, which included the 42nd Street project area, ranked first in the city in the number of felony complaints for the four years examined: 1978 to 1981.[109] It also stated that Forty-second Street, from Seventh to Eighth Avenue, received a greater level of "police attention" than any other block in the city. Certainly, these numbers are cause for concern. Nevertheless, while the DEIS presented numerous tables and figures indicating high levels of crime, it was notably silent on the relative danger of victimization in the area. The CUNY study did address this side of the issue:

> Given the vast numbers of tourists and commuters who pass through the Port Authority Bus Terminal and the 8th Avenue subway station, [the] numbers of felonies and felonious assaults, while disturbing in themselves, reflect extremely low rates of incidence. Considering the number of persons who would be "exposed" to the risk of such crimes each year, the actual probability that one is a victim is quite low.[110]

In his coverage of the CUNY report, Samuel Weiss of the *New York Times* noted that "one of the most interesting findings" was that despite widespread fears of violence in the area the actual incidence of such crime was relatively low.[111] This point might have made an informative headline, but, on the contrary, it was revealed only in the last sentence of the article whose ominous headline declared "Police Cannot Cure 42nd Street, Study Finds." Still, even the CUNY study itself expressed some ambivalence about the relationship of its own empirical data to ingrained perceptions of the area. For example, it declared that "New Yorkers and visitors to the city are realistically afraid when traversing the area," but then went on in the same paragraph to say that after hours "42nd Street remains the safest and most alive section of midtown Manhattan's West Side."[112]

In addition to the issues of menacing loiterers and high crime, there was also a perception that the types of businesses located on Forty-second Street deterred both new investment in the area and use of the area by mainstream New Yorkers and tourists. The economy of the street was defined in the public mind by its concentration of commercial sex establishments. On the single block between Seventh and Eighth Avenues, there were eighteen sex-related businesses as of November 1983, including movie theaters, bookstores, peep shows, live shows, and combination emporiums.[113] Several others were located nearby on Eighth Avenue and on Broadway, and on Forty-second Street between Sixth and Seventh Avenues. With sexually explicit promotional materials displayed openly on the street and aggressive "flyboys" hustling customers, these businesses did not constitute a subtle presence.

Although no more than 1 percent of the pedestrians admitted to being in the area for the sex-related entertainment, it is clear that this industry was supported by a very large clientele who had money. This conclusion was borne out in a mail-in survey on public attitudes toward the Times Square area conducted as part of the CUNY study.[114] About 20 percent of the respondents reported that they had patronized an adult bookstore in the Times Square area in the previous year. The sociologists logically "surmise[d] that, if anything, the data underrepresent the actual proportion of the metropolitan area population which patronizes commercial sex establishments."[115]

This finding was particularly interesting because, as the sociologists noted, theirs was not a random sample; indeed, it was "skewed in the direction of professional, middle-class, and upper-middle-class persons," who composed a "population with the most disposable income."[116] Moreover, based on the "relatively sophisticated" tastes of the respondents—with 66 percent identifying Theater Row on Forty-fifth Street as their primary place for entertainment—the sociologists concluded that it was a "sample of persons who include a disproportionate number of the region's 'cultural leaders.'"[117] Ironically, and tellingly, they were described as the people who "set trends and establish patterns of patronage for the arts and cultural institutions at every level of the city's popular and high culture."[118] Studies also showed that the patrons of the sex establishments were overwhelmingly male, and roughly half white (56 percent) and middle class (50 percent). The middle-income group constituted a clear majority of the patrons at the more costly adult-entertainment attractions, such as live sex shows and massage parlors.[119] Even the sponsors of the redevelopment effort described the "typical patron" for pornography as a "white collar, middle class male."[120]

Given the middle-class norms of the clientele, it was not likely that this would be an outwardly disruptive population. The CUNY study concluded that "the 42nd Street audience [for sex entertainment] is not visibly deviant; the deviants in the area are not likely to be paying customers of entertainment establishments."[121] In fact, it is arguable that the clients of sex entertainment are among the least likely to be lawbreakers.[122] The operation of sex businesses may actually depend on a kind of "hiding behavior" and anonymity among patrons that is produced by norms and rules of behavior that patrons internalize and observe. Simply put, patrons go out of their way not to draw attention to themselves. Since the late 1970s, moreover, the sex businesses in Times Square had had to distance themselves from prostitution and drugs in order to avoid being closed down for code violations. Consequently, the street studies were never able to identify the link between pornography and crime in the area that proponents of redevelopment had hoped to find.[123]

All commentators recognized that the commercial sex establishments were in Times Square because of their enormous profitability, which, in turn, depended on an affluent clientele. In fact, the sex businesses derived many of their patrons from the large crowds that were drawn to the area for other "legitimate" reasons, such as tourists, workers, and commuters.[124] According to the CUNY study, this phenomenon "supports [the] conclusion that economic development of the Bright Light District will not eliminate the commercial sex industry from the Times Square area, since that is where it finds its most concentrated market."[125] Even the DEIS itself acknowledged that these structural factors favored the relocation and continued operation of such businesses in the Times Square area, particularly around upper Times Square (on Broadway in the upper Forties).[126] In fact, the renaissance in Times Square has depended on not only evicting sex businesses from Forty-second Street, but also implementing tough new zoning restrictions in the mid-1990s that break up concentrations of adult establishments. The adult-use zoning was also needed to prevent the sex businesses that were displaced from Forty-second Street from reconcentrating in outlying city neighborhoods.

In the late 1970s, however, the greatest entertainment attraction to Forty-second Street in terms of the number of paying customers was not the sex industry, but the collection of movie houses showing first-run action and horror films at discount admission prices.[127] These theaters generally did not advertise or list show times in newspapers, but offered a "unique range of movie choices and time availabilities." The DEIS reported that there were eleven such theaters on Forty-second Street between Seventh and Eighth Avenues in the early 1980s. The CUNY street study estimated that from four to six times as many persons attended action movies as pornographic movies. Yet, as noted earlier, the action-film audiences were predominantly lower-income African-American (51 percent) and Latino (25 percent) males. Ironically, then, according to the logic of the DEIS, the commercial sex establishments attracted a less ominous and menacing population than did the mainstream movie theaters, even though the sex shops were perceived as the source of the street's negative image.

Given the potential of Times Square in the postindustrial economy as an extension of the midtown office district—long an expressed goal of city officials, planners, and developers—the space was vastly underdeveloped. The redevelopment project area, between Forty-first and Forty-third Streets and Broadway and Eighth Avenue, was zoned for the highest densities allowed in the city; but only one-third of the allowable as-of-right development rights were actually utilized. If zoning bonuses were included in the calculation, less than one-quarter of the maximum possible development had been achieved. Thus some 4.1 to 7.1 million square feet of development rights remained unutilized in a central area of heavily built Manhattan.[128] In part because of uncooperative business cycles, and in part due to increasingly negative perceptions, no new construction had occurred in the immediate environs of the Forty-second Street project area since the McGraw-Hill Building was built on Forty-second Street between Eighth and Ninth Avenues in 1931. Consequently, property taxes generated for the city from this area in the early 1980s, at slightly more than $5 million a year, were but a fraction of the potential;[129] in fact, the total tax revenue was less than that received from a single building a block east at Sixth Avenue.[130]

In terms of uses, more than half of the Forty-second Street project area was office and commercial space in June 1983 (although vacancy rates averaged 36 percent, compared with a midtown average of 5.4 percent), while hotels accounted for 16 percent of the built area; entertainment, 10 percent; parking, 9 percent; retail and food, 8 percent; and sex establishments, 3 percent.[131] High vacancy rates in upper floors were attributed to the nature of street-level uses on Forty-second Street, where, between Seventh and Eighth Avenues, there were eleven action-movie houses, three adult cinemas, and fifteen other sex-related businesses. The DEIS repeatedly emphasized the need for a publicly sponsored redevelopment plan on the grounds that the seventy-four properties in the project area were divided among more than fifty owners, making private site assemblage impossible. But the CUNY study reported that along Forty-second Street from Sixth to Eighth Avenue, where there were twenty-seven different owners, 80 percent of the property was controlled by three large organizations.[132] The fundamental problem was that the existing uses were actually quite profitable, even if they fell short of their full potential, and required no major capital investment for their upkeep. Therefore, owners could afford to wait for an offer they could not refuse before selling out to even more profitable office development.

The extent to which the area was underutilized depended, of course, on the development goals for it. That millions of square feet of development rights were available reflected the city's effort to promote office development in west Midtown by allowing the highest zoning densities in the city. Development pressures also reflected the desire among developers for an intensification of uses that would result from integrating the area into the midtown office district. Developers and planners shared a vision of west Midtown as the next stage in the city's postindustrial transformation.[133] The degree of underutilization thus measured the gap between reality and this particular vision for the area.

Yet it is the nature of this vision that is open to question. The sociological and economic data presented in the DEIS and the CUNY study provide only limited support for the way in which the area's problems were defined by planners. The Forty-second Street and Times Square district was a thriving entertainment center that catered to a lower-income clientele, primarily African-American and Latino. It was a popular tourist spot, with the largest crowds visiting on weekend evenings for sightseeing, attending legitimate theater, and patronizing restaurants and bars. The CUNY survey tapped into this paradox in public attitudes about Times Square. The public was truly ambivalent about the area: it "still regard[ed] West 42nd Street as a primary entertainment zone even if it increasingly ha[d] doubts about going there."[134] When half the patrons of sex businesses are middle-class white men, the image of a territorial takeover by a threatening minority population, which was carefully reinforced in the DEIS, betrays a political rather than an empirical basis. The political effort to portray the area in terms of a racial dichotomy between "us" and "them" rings false when the sex and drug markets were supported by "us" as well as "them." Yet, as Murray Edelman has pointed out, the construction of a symbolic enemy is often an indispensable tool in an effective political discourse.[135]

Thus there were alternative ways to define the problems of Times Square and, consequently, the nature of the solutions that should be attempted. But the class- and race-based agenda reflected in the effort to transform one particular kind of entertainment district into another prevailed. Arguably, there were valuable elements to this lower-income entertainment area that should have been retained. Moreover, by pursuing the approved redevelopment plan as a solution to politically defined problems there were two great risks: the project would not solve the complex problems that really existed in the area, since that was never its intention, and it would destroy the elements that made the area—despite its problems—one of the most integrated entertainment places in New York City.

It was not until later in the 1980s that a greater appreciation for the valuable social role of the area began to emerge from under the stifling discourse on Times Square. Members of the preservation movement had begun to look more closely at Times Square, in light of the impending redevelopment project, and they discovered a "far more complex and vital neighborhood" than the city had recognized.[136] In the area's bars and restaurants, they found "thriving places full of middle-class black patrons" that remained hidden to white New Yorkers—and to their media resources. Many of the businesses were family-owned and had been in existence almost as long as the theaters that defined the area's history in the public discourse.[137] And, contrary to the sacred dogma of the Times Square discourse, most catered to a middle-class, family crowd, albeit one composed of the "minority" populations that were becoming the majority of the city's residents. Even the Forty-second Street movie houses were a particularly valuable resource, since most theater chains had abandoned the city's poorer neighborhoods. Thus as preservationists began to see through the haze of the Times Square discourse, they were forced to consider whether the redevelopment plan was not "inadvertently racist."[138] Unfortunately, by this time the 42nd Street Development Project had been approved and the process of taking property and evicting tenants was under way.

AN ALTERNATIVE DEVELOPMENT STRATEGY FOR TIMES SQUARE

The most immediate result of the definition of problems on West Forty-second Street offered by planners was to preclude any attempt to stimulate incremental private efforts to upgrade and redevelop Forty-second Street through zoning, tax, or other incentives. For planners, the belief that such a strategy was doomed to failure and only major publicly sponsored construction would effect a turnaround was elevated to a guiding principle. In the DEIS, the possibility of piecemeal redevelopment was effectively dismissed on the grounds that a menacing population had established complete control over the area and that site assemblage for individual private development efforts would be too difficult and too costly.

By the close of the 1980s, however, things looked very different. Dramatic new construction had taken place in the Times Square area in the late 1980s; it was only the redevelopment project area on West Forty-second Street that showed no sign of change. Many knowledgeable observers concluded at the time that the zoning strategy that promoted development in the greater Times Square area had indeed succeeded, while the redevelopment plan for Forty-second Street had not.[139] It seemed that an important opportunity for Forty-second Street redevelopment had been lost.

When city and state officials signed the memorandum of understanding committing to the redevelopment of West Forty-second Street, in June 1980, city planners were already studying ways to encourage a shift of midtown office development from the congested East Side core to the west and south. The Department of City Planning (DCP) issued a draft report on midtown development in July 1980 and, after receiving extensive public comment from business, real-estate, and citizens' groups, issued its final report, *Midtown Development,* in June 1981.[140] The proposals in the report formed the basis for an amendment to the zoning resolution that created the Special Midtown Zoning District in May 1982.

It was clear from the start, however, that this comprehensive package of development and preservation incentives and design guidelines was never intended to stimulate development along West Forty-second Street itself. Rather, the DCP report declared the need for a large-scale, publicly sponsored redevelopment project on West Forty-second Street—one of several so-called turn-around projects for west Midtown—as an important element in attracting development "pioneers" to the West Side. By this point, then, the city planners had already taken the position that the problems of West Forty-second Street were so severe and intractable that the area could be revitalized only through massive publicly financed intervention. The new zoning incentives, therefore, did not apply to Forty-second Street between Seventh and Eighth Avenues. In pursuing an independent strategy for the redevelopment of this block of Forty-second Street, the city planners determined in advance that the area would be left unaffected by any improvement in greater Times Square.

Office development had begun a gradual migration westward during the construction boom of the 1960s, but came to a halt with the bust of the early 1970s. When development resumed in the late 1970s, it remained centered on the East Side, where rents had increased significantly relative to rents for West Side space (while development costs in the two areas remained essentially the same). Physical and social conditions on the West Side were considered to have deteriorated greatly in the interim, particularly around Times Square, where speculators had turned to sex-related establishments as a way to generate profits until the market recovered. In doing so, they had further reduced the desirability of west Midtown office space. The DCP report argued that the deterioration of Times Square symbolized the decline of the West Side overall, making uncoordinated development seem too risky for private investors.

In order to promote a shift in midtown office development from east to west, city planners proposed dividing Midtown into three zoning areas: a West Side growth area bounded roughly by Sixth and Eighth Avenues and Fortieth and Fifty-seventh Streets (but also including "growth corridors" along parts of Fifth, Sixth, and Seventh Avenues and Broadway in the Thirties); an East Side stabilization area generally extending from Fortieth to Sixtieth Street and Third to Sixth Avenue; and a small preservation area encompassing the mid-blocks around the Museum of Modern Art between Fifth and Sixth Avenues, from Fifty-third to Fifty-sixth Street.[141] The new zoning law would then provide incentives for westward development by allowing higher building densities (in the form of floor-area ratios, or FARs) in the West Side growth area than in the East Side stabilization area.

At the time, Midtown was, for the most part, zoned for a uniform FAR 15 to 18 (a base FAR 15 as-of-right, and FAR 18 with as-of-right bonuses), with no explicit density differences between avenues and mid-blocks. City planners proposed to increase the base as-of-right density by 20 percent, from FAR 15 to FAR 18, on avenues in the West Side growth area while retaining the allowable FAR 15 for mid-block sites. Avenues in the East Side stabilization area would remain at a base FAR 15, while mid-blocks would be down-zoned by 20 percent to FAR 12. The highest density of FAR 18 on the West Side was made subject to a sunset clause, ultimately set at six years, in order to accelerate the pace of West Side development and allow for a review of the zoning revisions; thereafter, it would revert to the same zoning regulations that applied to the East Side.

In effect, then, the new midtown zoning gave developers a brief window of opportunity during which new construction on the West Side could exceed previous limits, and East Side limits, by as much as 25 percent. With zoning bonuses of up to 20 percent, allowable densities could reach an astounding FAR 21.6 on avenues in the growth area, compared with FAR 18, including bonuses, in the stabilization area. In the world of Manhattan real estate, these incentives for development in west Midtown translated into very big buildings and very big money.

In addition to shifting development westward, a second major goal of city planners was the preservation of legitimate Broadway theaters, which the DCP described as a "key element" in the city's economy.[142] Thus theater preservation and high-rise development were linked in a way that would have applied easily to the redevelopment project area of Forty-second Street. In the late 1960s, the city had created the Special Theater District because the apparent spread of office construction to the west and the inevitable rise in land values there were regarded as potential threats to the health of Broadway theater. The city, therefore, offered a zoning bonus of up to 20 percent for all development in the special district that included the construction of a new theater.

By the early 1980s, however, the DCP had decided to shift its emphasis from construction to preservation: "We have learned that in many ways the old theaters work better than the new ones built under the Theater District provisions. Their preservation, not replacement, is key to maintaining a vital theater industry."[143] Consequently, the new zoning proposals focused on preservation incentives for developers. On the one hand, the forty-four theaters in the district could not be demolished without a special permit from the City Planning Commission or the Landmarks Preservation Commission; on the other hand, a zoning bonus of up to 20 percent could be provided for a development project that also promoted the preservation (in the form of renovation, reconversion, or perpetuation) of a listed theater. Planners proposed liberalized regulations to facilitate the transfer of development rights from designated theaters to avenue development sites (for example, allowing TDRs from theaters across zoning boundaries). The 20 percent bonus for new theater construction was retained, but under more limited conditions.

Through a variety of zoning mechanisms, therefore, the preservation and development of Broadway theaters were linked to new construction incentives in the Times Square area. These approaches would have been ideally suited to the 42nd Street Development Project area, where historic theaters awaited renovation and avenue sites that were suitable for high-rise construction existed in the surrounding area. But these strategies were never used in an effort to stimulate private development efforts on Forty-second Street.

With only slight modifications, the DCP proposals were incorporated into the zoning amendment that created the Special Midtown Zoning District and the Special Theater and Fifth Avenue Sub-Districts in 1982. Five years later, the DCP published its *Midtown Development Review,* which evaluated the effectiveness of the zoning regulations.[144] Its overall assessment was quite positive because many of the goals behind the zoning revisions were being achieved. In particular, new growth showed clear signs of shifting westward. Of the private development that had been approved in Midtown since the zoning amendment, 8.3 million square feet, or 58 percent, was located in the West Side growth area, compared with 5.9 million square feet, or 42 percent, in the East Side stablization area. (These numbers did not include the 42nd Street Development Project, which, with almost 7 million square feet of space, would raise the approved West Side development to 72 percent of the total.) These figures showed a marked change from the previous five-year period (1977–1982), when only 22 percent of the floor area approved for development was west of Sixth Avenue.

In terms of the absolute numbers of new buildings approved, more buildings were being developed on the East Side than on the West Side from 1982 to 1987; however, the difference in numbers was significantly smaller than it had been during the previous five years. From 1977 to 1982, twenty-eight buildings were authorized on the East Side and six on the West Side; from 1982 to 1987, twenty-one buildings were permitted on the East Side and fourteen on the West Side. Overall, buildings were smaller after the new zoning regulations took effect than they had been before, although the average size of new buildings in the growth area was almost double that of those in the stabilization area.

The new zoning regulations sparked a shift in land values as well. In 1984 alone, prices on the West Side more than doubled from their levels of the previous year. Whereas the average annual increase in land values for the previous five-year period was 57 percent on the East Side and 24 percent on the West Side, from 1982 to 1987 values on the West Side increased by an average 26 percent annually while those on the East Side increased only 17 percent.

Moreover, the indications at the time suggested that westward shift of new office development would continue. Of the nineteen projects (totaling 11 million square feet) proposed for development within the following three years, fifteen (accounting for a vast majority of the floor area) were located in the growth area. Nor was new construction on the West Side staying clear of the Times Square and Forty-second Street area. By 1988, thirteen buildings around Times Square were in the planning or construction phases in order to beat the sunset date for the higher zoning densities,[145] and only a few potential development sites remained in the area. A few years later, a number of imposing new skyscrapers lined Broadway and Seventh Avenue just north of the Forty-second Street project area. Some of them were located in the midst of a concentration of sex-related establishments, primarily along Broadway and Seventh Avenue around Forty-fifth Street, rivaling that of the worst stretch of West Forty-second Street.

In fact, Paul Goldberger, architecture critic of the *New York Times,* was prompted by the extensive new construction activity to announce "A Huge Architecture Show in Times Square" in September 1990.[146] Two skyscraper hotels had just opened, another was opening the following month, and a fourth was going into construction, while three major office towers were expected to be completed later in the year, following on the heels of two others finished the previous year. Goldberger noted further that "all this is without the biggest project of all, the subsidized, city–state venture called the Times Square Redevelopment Project." He continued:

> Back in 1981 one justification put forth for surrounding Times Square with huge office towers was that public investment on that scale was necessary to stimulate private investment in the troubled area. The buildings nearing completion prove that supposition wrong, of course, since what we are now seeing is the completion of a new, privately financed and privately built Times Square neighborhood, so filling the blocks of Broadway and Seventh Avenue just north of Times Square that only a handful of sites [are] undeveloped.

Still, Goldberger expressed some ambivalence about the nature of the changes in the area, suggesting that "Times Square is changing from a tawdry theater district to a tawdry hotel and office district," since the new skyline was seemingly having little impact on conditions on the street—perhaps a bad omen of things to come.

It is impossible to know what impact the new zoning regulations might have had on revitalizing the Forty-second Street project area, had it not been designated for publicly sponsored redevelopment, or to determine what effect the 42nd Street Redevelopment Project had, psychological or otherwise, on contributing to the new construction on the West Side after 1982. The DCP report *Midtown Development* considered Forty-second Street redevelopment and other public projects to be essential for attracting developers to the West Side. But because the sunset date for the most generous zoning incentives was 1988, much of the construction on the West Side was already under way in the mid-1980s, while the redevelopment of Forty-second Street was far from certain. Although there was a firm commitment by city and state officials to proceed with the project, it did not receive final approval from the Board of Estimate until late in 1984. There followed a barrage of legal challenges that might have prevented it from going forward. After the lesson of the multibillion-dollar Westway highway project, which was defeated in the courts because of its adverse impact on striped bass in the Hudson River,[147] even the most optimistic of the West Side pioneers must have harbored some reasonable doubts about the inevitability of the plan for Forty-second Street. Thus it seems that the 42nd Street Development Project was less crucial to the development of the surrounding area than planners had claimed.

It is clear that many important development objectives can be achieved through the creative use of zoning regulations and tax incentives. Even if the Special Midtown Zoning District had been insufficient to spur development on Forty-second Street between Seventh and Eighth Avenues, it is by no means certain that other zoning and tax incentives designed specifically for that block would have been unable to encourage private development. The 42nd Street Development Project allowed for office buildings at densities that far exceed those permitted anywhere else in the city. If planners were prepared to allow such high densities in Times Square, they could have been offered as a zoning bonus in exchange for renovating theaters on the target block of Forty-second Street.

Moreover, even without the 42nd Street Development Project, there were many signs of economic revitalization in west Midtown by the early 1980s that might have indicated the potential for incremental private development and upgrading of the Forty-second Street project area. Some $800 million in public funds was committed to projects either approved for or under construction on the West Side, the most prominent of which was the $375 million Jacob Javits Convention Center, located between Thirty-fourth and Thirty-ninth Streets at the Hudson River. The Midtown Planning Office listed thirty-eight actual or possible projects for the area, from street paving to new construction.[148] The Brandt Organization had even restored two of its theaters on Forty-second Street between Seventh and Eighth Avenues.

The Mayor's Office of Midtown Enforcement had been successful in reducing the number of sex-related establishments on the West Side through legal enforcement strategies and had initiated several demonstration block projects for focused cleanup efforts; coincidentally or not, the first of these attempts was on the block of Forty-third Street, from Seventh to Eighth Avenue, on which the headquarters of the New York Times Company is located. A six-month interim report on the "Times Square Action Plan," initiated in the fall of 1978, showed that sixteen of twenty-one proposed tasks had been implemented, resulting in less crime, improved cleanliness, fewer sex businesses, and a better economic climate in the area.[149]

In 1980, the nonprofit 42nd Street Development Corporation had completed Phase I of its Theater Row project, which involved rehabilitating six dilapidated buildings on Forty-second Street between Ninth and Tenth Avenues for use as a complex of off-off-Broadway theaters, rehearsal space, and offices. Phase II, a $6 million redevelopment project, was already creating television studios, theaters, and restaurants in the area. Mel Gussow, theater critic of the *New York Times,* acknowledged that a visitor to Theater Row "might find it difficult to believe that five years [earlier it] was a strip of massage parlors and cheap burlesque houses."[150] In addition to its own accomplishments on West Forty-second Street, the Forty-second Street LDC had helped organize a $700,000 commercial revitalization program for Eighth Avenue, combining the efforts of owners, merchants, and residents. The Manhattan Plaza apartment complex had opened in the late 1970s on Forty-second Street between Ninth and Tenth Avenues and, with 70 percent of its units set aside for people in the theater industry, was an important stimulus to revitalization on the rest of West Forty-second Street as well.

In early 1980, in the trend-setting "Weekend" section of the *New York Times,* Gussow heralded the arrival of "The New Hell's Kitchen." He announced that the "cultural revitalization" of far West Forty-second and Forty-third Streets, "once a dream on a drawing board," was now "approaching realization."[151] "On one square city block, between Ninth and 10th Avenues, there is more theatrical activity than on almost any other street in New York." With nine theaters, three cabarets, six restaurants, and a variety of shops, the area exhibited, according to the neighboring *Times*, "an atmosphere that may yet rival London's Covent Garden." These accomplishments farther west on Forty-second Street in the late 1970s certainly supported the possibility that a similar approach of piecemeal upgrading and redevelopment for entertainment uses might succeed on Forty-second Street between Seventh and Eighth Avenues.

And, indeed, as recently as January 1978, the DCP's *42nd Street Study* outlined a number of approaches to revitalizing West Forty-second Street without mentioning the need for a massive, publicly sponsored redevelopment project.[152] The report praised the efforts of the Forty-second Street LDC, which had acquired fourteen properties on West Forty-second Street and was negotiating the purchase of five more (despite the reputed difficulties of site assemblage emphasized in later years), and the Mayor's Office of Midtown Enforcement, which it credited with having closed eighty-three adult entertainment establishments in a two-year period.[153] The report maintained that the successes of the Forty-second Street LDC and the "positive psychological impact" of the Manhattan Plaza complex demonstrated the "feasibility" of redevelopment along West Forty-second Street. It saw many opportunities for the construction or reuse of buildings, with up to 5 million square feet of potential floor area available for development under the existing zoning densities in the theater district.

The report argued further that tourism was a leading growth industry in the city and that the Broadway theater district was its focal point. It declared that the theater industry was one of the most financially secure in the city; with roughly 8 million tickets sold in the 1977/1978 season, the industry had shown a growth rate of 100 percent over the previous four years, earning $250 million. Indeed, the following season, a record 11 million Broadway tickets were sold.[154]

The DCP offered a number of recommendations that could be used in formulating a more comprehensive plan for the revitalization of West Forty-second Street, including forming an umbrella organization of public and private interests to focus redevelopment efforts, pursuing proposals for adult-use zoning, converting single-room occupancy hotels to permanent upscale residences through J-51 tax incentives and then developing new hotels,[155] beautifying the streetscape through the use of attractive signs and the restoration and regulation of marquees, improving mass transit and vehicle and pedestrian circulation, promoting the expansion of the theater, restaurant, and culture industries, and preserving and restoring historic buildings. Thus the report actually suggested a multipronged revitalization strategy for West Forty-second Street that relied on zoning laws and modest public improvement projects.

The ultimate irony, of course, is that the renaissance of West Forty-second

Street at Times Square in the mid-1990s has come about precisely through the kind of gradual upgrading that planners had dismissed in the early 1980s. With the collapse of the market for office space in the early 1990s, and the severe overbuilding of the West Side stimulated by the special zoning incentives, developers and sponsors of the 42nd Street Development Project were forced to delay the construction of the office towers. Instead, they turned to an interim strategy of gradually renovating the existing buildings and restoring the theaters for a variety of entertainment and retail uses. The planned office towers now threaten to cast an oppressive pall over the lively entertainment district.

4
Planning the Revaluation of Times Square

The arts are critical to the economic development of the city. Without them New York City would be nowhere. It is the reason why all the major corporations are here.
—Frederic Papert, president of 42nd Street Development Corporation (1980)

In early 1980, Mayor Edward I. Koch was faced with a crucial decision about the future of West Forty-second Street and the Times Square area. He had to decide whether to grant city approval for a privately sponsored plan to redevelop completely the area bounded by Fortieth and Forty-third Streets from Broadway to Eighth Avenue. The plan, called The City at 42nd Street, was the product of the 42nd Street Development Corporation and was backed by some of the world's most powerful corporations. It called for large-scale demolition to make way for the construction of three forty-two-story office towers, a vast entertainment and exhibition complex, and an enormous merchandise mart. It would be funded almost entirely with private dollars; all that was needed from the city was an urban renewal designation for the area in order to facilitate the acquisition of land from recalcitrant property owners. It appeared that major developers had secured financing and were committed to the project; all seemed set to proceed, pending a green light from the mayor.

Koch brought this redevelopment effort to a screeching halt in June 1980 when, after some two years and $1.2 million had been invested in the plan, he refused to support it. One month later, however, he announced that the city and state would take over the task of redeveloping the same area of Forty-second Street and Times Square. The following year, city and state officials issued a set of design guidelines and a formal request for bids for the new, publicly sponsored 42nd Street Development Project. The plan closely resembled the one that Koch had rejected the previous summer, except that it was larger and was based on a different cultural theme. In short, the proposal firmly embraced the image of the Great White Way as its symbolic focus and principal justification. In so doing, the redevelopment plan came to serve important political interests of the mayor.

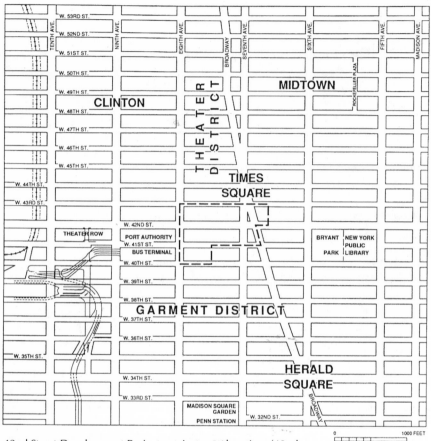

42nd Street Development Project, project area' location. (42nd
Street Development Project)

AN ARTS-BASED REDEVELOPMENT STRATEGY
FOR WEST FORTY-SECOND STREET

By the 1980s, Times Square was one of the last remaining pieces needed to complete the postindustrial transformation of Manhattan, which had been the focal point
of economic restructuring in New York City for half a century.[1] Because of its strategic location at the nexus of the city's transportation network and major industries,
Times Square had the capability to become the quintessential place of postindustrial work and play. It was ideally situated to draw on the synergy of the symbolic
economy—consisting of the theater district to the north and the garment and fashion district to the south—and the midtown office district to the east. Consequently,
the Times Square area represented enormous and untapped economic potential.

The 42nd Street Development Project had its roots in the plans to redevelop Forty-second Street that had emerged in the late 1970s. These efforts followed soon after the nadir of New York City's fiscal crisis in 1975, and so coincided with the arrival of a new pro-business era in which the business community enjoyed an enhanced bargaining position in relation to public officials.[2] With the election of pro-business Ed Koch as mayor in 1977, the city administration eagerly embraced the development goals of the private sector as its own.[3] Brendan Gill, an active preservationist in New York City, has characterized the late 1970s and 1980s as a period during which the city began handing out tax breaks as bribes to entice businesses.[4] Policy operated on the assumption that the construction of skyscrapers would restore confidence among those in the business community. Zoning laws were seemingly transformed into a mechanism for unbounded development.[5] In short, the political economy of New York City in the late 1970s and 1980s was extremely favorable to business and real-estate development.

The primary player in the revived efforts to redevelop Times Square was the 42nd Street Development Corporation, formed in 1976 to promote economic development on West Forty-second Street. (Two years later, the Forty-second Street local development corporation [LDC] expanded its target area to cover greater Times Square.) The Forty-second Street LDC was independent of any government agency and operated under its own initiative. It was established primarily with grants from the Ford Foundation, and the bulk of the funding during its early years came from private sector corporations and foundations. Over time, the LDC operated more on revenues and equity generated from the properties it acquired than on outside support.

Although it was a private, nonprofit corporation, the Forty-second Street LDC also enjoyed various forms of public support (in addition to its tax-exempt status) and so illustrates how blurred the line between public and private had become in urban development.[6] It received money from the city, the federal government, and the quasi-public Port Authority of New York and New Jersey.[7] As an LDC, it also enjoyed certain privileges, such as the right to lease or buy city properties without going through the normal process of competitive bidding, and status as recipient of some restricted federal grants. Given the ambiguous character of such an organization, Steven Weisman can be excused for describing the LDC erroneously as an "independent government entity."[8]

An essential characteristic of the Forty-second Street LDC was its close connection to the city's arts and preservation community. It had been established under the auspices of the Municipal Art Society (MAS), an elite civic organization that was active and influential on urban design and development issues in the city, especially those involving historic preservation. In fact, the MAS had been the primary organizational force behind the adoption of the city's landmarks law.[9] In large part, the Forty-second Street LDC came into being through the efforts of Frederic Papert, who planned and organized it as president of MAS. Papert was a former advertising man and "darling of Wall Street" who became active in preservation causes; he also had close ties to the Kennedy family, including Jacqueline Kennedy Onassis, a star of the preservation movement and MAS.[10] Upon the creation of the Forty-second Street LDC, Papert moved on to become its president, while retaining a position on the MAS board of directors. Accordingly, Papert has described the preservationist MAS as the "parent" of the Forty-second Street LDC.

The creation of the Forty-second Street LDC was, therefore, rooted in a particular vision of the city that valued its historic culture and resources. Papert explained that the idea of redeveloping West Forty-second Street emerged as "an extension of the effort to save Grand Central Station."[11] For Papert and others involved in that effort—including Jackie Onassis, who later contributed $25,000 to the Forty-second Street LDC and became one of its board members[12]—their fight to preserve Grand Central Terminal, on East Forty-second Street, gradually led them to shift their sights westward to the wealth of neglected historic resources around Times Square. A promotional brochure described the LDC's grand vision of preservation and redevelopment for Forty-second Street, which was

> to renew what have been the largely abandoned far westerly blocks and convert them into an incubator for the performing arts; to at least physically upgrade the blighted middle blocks; and then to link a strengthened west end with the booming east end of the street, creating in time a river-to-river Grand Boulevard that would become a magnet for private investment, visitors, jobs and tax revenues, and have a major impact on the economy of New York City and the Tri-State region.[13]

The origin of the Forty-second Street LDC in the arts and preservation movement is clearly evident in its early redevelopment efforts. It restored the landmark McGraw-Hill Building, an Art Deco tower on West Forty-second Street from the 1930s that stood vacant in the 1970s. The LDC also transformed the Crossroads Building, at Forty-second Street and Broadway, from an outlet for child pornography to a police substation. Papert then commissioned Richard Haas to paint a mural on the wall above the building (and another on the approach to Lincoln Tunnel, farther west), where he painted a ten-story trompe l'oeil re-creation of the original Italian Gothic New York Times Tower, which stood across the street at the birth of Times Square.[14] (The Times Tower had been reclad in the 1960s.) Although the changes were temporary, the LDC pointed to the presence of police and painting as symbolic of what was yet to come.[15]

In 1978, the Forty-second Street LDC registered a major victory on far West Forty-second Street with the completion of Phase I of its Theater Row project. This involved the conversion of six dilapidated tenement buildings between Ninth and Tenth Avenues—previously home to such disreputable establishments as the French Palace, the Body Rub Institute, and Studio $10 ("Complete satisfaction featuring the most beautiful conversationalists"[16])—into a complex of off-off-Broadway theaters with twelve floors of supporting rehearsal and office space and an upscale

French restaurant. In 1980, work began on Phase II of the creation of Theater Row, a $6 million project involving the construction of two 200-seat theaters and the renovation of an existing 99-seat theater, the rehabilitation of the former West Side Airlines Terminal for use as a television recording studio, the creation of additional rehearsal and restaurant space, and the improvement of a collection of outdoor public amenities, including new trees, sidewalks, signs, and gardens.[17]

A promotional publication of the Forty-second Street LDC touting the "artistry" employed in financing these and other projects hinted at the extent of Papert's connections and influence in business and government:

> Bridge loans, foundation grants, construction and long-term conventional debt, [federal] Community Development [block grant] funds, Federal and City mortgages, New York City's first major Urban Development Action Grant, sales and leasebacks to eliminate real estate taxes, private/public joint ventures, even the sale of investment tax credits and depreciation to private investors have been—or may soon be—used to pay for otherwise thinly financed undertakings.[18]

Even before work had begun on Phase II of the project, Mel Gussow began hailing the imminent "cultural revitalization" of far West Forty-second and Forty-third Streets that evoked comparisons with London's Covent Garden.[19] This exuberant reporting may have been at least mildly hyperbolic; it seemed so even to Papert, the man largely responsible for the changes. But it calls attention to the complex position of the *New York Times* with regard to the redevelopment of Times Square. The *Times* is itself part of Times Square; indeed, the neighborhood bears its name. Thus the newspaper is not only a source of reporting on Times Square and redevelopment efforts, but also a component of a major corporation whose headquarters is perched at the edge of the Forty-second Street area that was long targeted for redevelopment. Both its investments and its image have been at stake in the effort to revitalize and redefine Times Square. And the *Times* was a powerful voice in elucidating the cultural politics of the project. An important aspect of this effort involved producing a credible vision of a restored theater district, or Great White Way, to mobilize public enthusiasm.

In describing the changes in the area, the *Times* also noted, quite correctly, the crucial influence of the 1,698-unit Manhattan Plaza apartment complex, which opened on Forty-second Street across from Theater Row in 1978. What made this new housing resource so significant was the decision to set aside 70 percent of the units for people in the theater industry, with the remaining apartments split evenly between the elderly and neighborhood residents. In this way, the heavily subsidized housing project was made compatible with an arts-based revitalization strategy for West Forty-second Street.[20]

Not surprisingly, it was Fred Papert who first suggested designating Manhattan Plaza as a housing resource for the theater community. In doing so, he offered a clever solution to a dilemma faced by the private owners and developers who had invested in the area (including real-estate powerhouse Seymour Durst and Richard Ravitch, the future chairman of the New York State Urban Development Corporation) and the public officials who had approved the project. Manhattan Plaza was originally intended as moderate-income housing that would be created with a subsidy from federal housing funds. But rising interest rates and subsidized profits had priced it out of the market for the area before construction was even complete. Public subsidies would not make the project affordable to those with moderate incomes, and those with incomes high enough to pay the rent would be unlikely to live in the rugged location on far West Forty-second Street. Ironically, this pricey housing would have to be occupied by relatively low-income tenants who would qualify for federal Section 8 rent subsidies. Neither public officials nor private interests, however, wanted to see a low-income housing project go up in an area targeted for upscale redevelopment.

Papert's solution—designating most of the apartments for relatively low-income people in the theater industry who could receive Section 8 subsidies—thus offered an ingenious alternative whereby a low-income housing project, rather than posing a threat to neighborhood property values, would actually assist in revaluing the area. As a tenant of Manhattan Plaza remarked, the project then became a commercial success because it rewarded developers with "the next best thing" to market-rate housing: "People who looked like luxury tenants—but weren't. We're sort of like paper dolls on display to help sell the rest of the neighborhood."[21] The final outcome has been described by Robert Schur as no more than an "old style ripoff":

> Manhattan Plaza served a vital political and economic purpose for New York City's power brokers and master planners. In one fell swoop, the developers' hefty profits were guaranteed, and the "Wild West" of Times Square and Clinton was readied for a plush and gentrified future. Sacrificing almost all of the city's low-income subsidies to do so—on a less-than-needy population—was still, they figured, a bargain. After all, it wasn't they who had to pay.[22]

From the inception of the Forty-second Street LDC, Papert was explicit about the role of the arts in his agenda of economic redevelopment for the area. "When we began," he stated in 1980, "we didn't think we were doing artists a favor. We were doing renewal a favor. Performing arts are an anchor for renewal."[23] More than a decade later, Papert identified Lincoln Center for the Performing Arts as a conscious model for his early redevelopment strategy for West Forty-second Street. He was convinced that by creating facilities for the arts, together with supporting attractions such as restaurants and shops, and by bringing "a large arts-oriented population" into the community as residents, the foundation would be laid for further economic revitalization. This cultural strategy of the Forty-second Street LDC was summed up as follows: "It was the right time and the right place for art and economic development to converge: the artists needed the housing and the theaters; the renewal needed the artists; and the city needed the renewal."[24] In effect, Papert recognized early on the range of economic and political goals that could be achieved through the emerging cultural approach to urban development.

Logically, there was no reason why the strategy of incremental, preservation- and arts-based redevelopment could not be extended eastward to the block of Forty-second Street between Seventh and Eighth Avenues, which had long been condemned by influential opinion makers in the media and in city government as the worst block in town. Ironically, it was, at the same time, the site of a lively market in speculative real-estate investment. According to Papert, the properties west of Ninth Avenue that were acquired for the Theater Row project had been considered hopelessly undervalued, even "less than worthless." Thus the LDC "was able to acquire 16 properties for practically nothing, their true worth," from insurance companies and other owners.[25] But when the Forty-second Street LDC tried to acquire properties on "the worst block in town," it ran up against the alarming realities of a healthy real-estate market. Perceptions about the potential value of these sites for redevelopment drove up prices in a frenzy of speculation.

In the late 1970s, for example, the Ford Foundation, in its involvement with the Forty-second Street LDC, indicated an interest in leasing the New Amsterdam Theater, considered to be the most significant of the historic theaters on Forty-second Street. Ford was prepared to put up $500,000 to $1 million to restore the structure for use as a legitimate theater. The owner of the theater refused to lease the property, but offered to sell it. At the time, the owner was involved in ongoing litigation with the city in an effort to have the assessed value of the property reduced. The owner argued that the value should be set at $500,000, while the city had valued it at $1,175,000. When Papert made a compromise offer of $750,000 for the theater, the owner refused: the purchase price, he declared, was $8 million.[26] Clearly, the designation of this block as the worst in town reflected a political evaluation, not an economic one; real-estate investors saw dollar signs where politicians decried the decline of urban America.

SETTING THE DEVELOPMENT AGENDA

The block of Forty-second Street between Seventh and Eighth Avenues had long been eyed as a real-estate plum ripe for lucrative redevelopment by a variety of interested parties, and they were prepared to fund redevelopment efforts by the Forty-second Street LDC. In June 1978, a dozen private companies and organizations contributed a total of $110,000 for a preliminary study of renewal possibilities for the Times Square area.[27] The list of contributors included powerful financial institutions and entertainment corporations: American Broadcasting Corporation, American Express Foundation, Columbia Broadcasting System, Columbia Pictures, the Daily News, Hilton Hotels, League of New York Theaters and

Producers, Loews Corporation, Morgan Guaranty Trust, New York Times Company, Shubert Foundation, and Touche Ross & Co. The study was carried out by the Forty-second Street LDC together with the city's Office of Midtown Planning and Office of Midtown Enforcement. Its goal was to find ways to revive the "faded symbol [of Times Square] and again make it profitable."[28]

At the same time, the Ford Foundation, in conjunction with the Forty-second Street LDC, was preparing a proposal specifically for the renewal of Forty-second Street between Seventh and Eighth Avenues. During the summer of 1978, these groups began floating a general plan according to which the city would use its urban renewal powers to acquire the properties along Forty-second Street so that the structures could be demolished and the entire area redeveloped.[29] An urban amusement park would be constructed in their place.

According to several participants,[30] the active role of the Ford Foundation in early redevelopment efforts for West Forty-second Street was driven by its vice president, Roger Kennedy. Kennedy, a banker and historian, has been described as a "Renaissance man" with a strong interest in and commitment to the arts. Kennedy's interest in restoring a historic Forty-second Street theater for dance performances initiated Ford's involvement. This prompted the foundation to commission a study of the area by sociologists from the City University of New York and gradually evolved into much larger redevelopment efforts.[31]

Over the next several months, the Ford-sponsored plan began to take shape, and by early 1979 it envisioned the construction of an elaborate $175 million, 750,000-square-foot tourist and entertainment center filling the two square blocks bounded by Forty-first and Forty-third Streets, and Seventh and Eighth Avenues.[32] The project—tentatively called Cityscape—was described as a "mini world's fair," with exhibits, rides, and multimedia displays, underwritten by corporations, as well as restaurants, theaters, and shops.[33]

According to the proposal, the theme for the amusement park would be New York City and its cultural life. Corporate sponsors would create the actual exhibits and thereby provide a funding source for the project. Its centerpiece would be the retention of most of the historic theaters on the block, although they would be remodeled for a variety of entertainment-related uses. Some would be restored to use as legitimate theaters, while others would serve as exhibit areas, television production facilities, or rehearsal spaces. For the most part, the project would be privately funded through loans and contributions from corporations underwriting the exhibits. A key element of the plan, however, called on the city to designate the blocks as an urban renewal area, in order to force the sale of the properties through eminent domain, and to contribute $25 million toward acquisition costs.

For several weeks, Ford sponsors briefed city officials and potential investors at the "opulent headquarters" of the Ford Foundation on East Forty-second Street.[34] The Port Authority reportedly was "very excited" by the proposal and offered funding and staff support as the project proceeded. The New York Times Company, the largest corporation in the immediate area of the project, also offered financial support. Nevertheless, the Koch administration, while receptive to the concept, was reluctant to offer its full backing for the plan. In his report to the mayor, the chairman of the City Planning Commission, Robert Wagner, Jr., recommended that the city give only tentative approval to the "extraordinarily exciting" idea. The report cautioned that the concept of an urban theme park and entertainment center was untested and high-risk. The mayor, too, reportedly was "edgy" about the city's share of $25 million and declined to commit to such assistance. Still, Ford was moving forward aggressively with the project, providing a $500,000 grant to a group of planners, architects, mortgage bankers, lawyers, and theater specialists to develop the plan.[35]

As the planning team transformed the Cityscape concept into a detailed proposal, it began to reflect, more and more, the influence of powerful private real-estate interests. According to Papert, officials at the Equitable Life Assurance Society—a partner of the Forty-second Street LDC in its redevelopment efforts, and the most likely source of financing for the project—informed him that it would be impossible to secure private financing based on anticipated revenues from admissions prices alone, even though economic analyses showed that the project could support its debt service with these revenues.[36] Equitable insisted that the project would have to include the development of office space in order to meet conventional lending standards. So project planners began to negotiate with commercial developers, including some of the largest on the continent. The evolving nature of the project was symbolized by a change in its name from the amusement-park label "Cityscape" to the more sophisticated "The City at 42nd Street."

In May 1979, a new corporation, The City at 42nd Street, Inc., was formed as an offshoot of the Forty-second Street LDC to implement the redevelopment plan. The City at 42nd Street, Inc., shared directors, including Papert, with the LDC, and the two organizations were closely involved in all aspects of the project.[37] The individuals and organizations that composed the new corporation reflected the influence of powerful private interests and arts-based civic groups. For example, John Gutfreund, the managing partner of Salomon Brothers, was chairman of the board of directors, which included "leaders of New York City's civic, cultural, and business communities."[38] The president of the new corporation was a real-estate attorney with "an active land development practice" who had served for six years as chairman of the City Planning Commission under Mayor John Lindsay. The vice president of marketing was previously a vice president of the Dreyfus Corporation who had been a director of the New York World's Fair and a consultant to the Montreal Expo and the San Antonio Hemisfair. The deputy executive director was an official at the Department of Housing and Urban Development who recently had served in the Urban Investment Initiatives Department at Equitable.

By the time the new group submitted its formal proposal to the City Planning Commission in August 1979, it had evolved considerably from the amusement-park plan originally offered by the Ford Foundation and the Forty-second Street LDC.[39] It still included a mid-block entertainment complex that combined exhibits and multimedia displays with theater, cinema, and retail facilities. Five of the nine theaters would be restored to their original uses as legitimate Broadway stages; the facades of three other theaters would be retained, although the interiors would be converted for a variety of entertainment-related uses; and one theater would be demolished. As explained in the promotional materials:

> The exhibit experiences will examine life in the City from a variety of perspectives using developments in media technology that are finding increasing application in both the cinema and theater. These methods are particularly suited to the creation of unique attractions for large numbers of people which has led to their application in world's fairs and theme parks. But their potential as a medium of sophisticated popular culture will be more fully developed here.[40]

Among the contemplated attractions were a "museum of museums" displaying samples from the city's stock of museums, a high-tech IMAX theater providing "a unique trip around the world," a "Slice of the Apple" ride simulating movement from subterranean New York City to the top of a skyscraper, a vertical theater offering "a balloon rider's view of public celebrations in great public spaces around the world," a cone-shaped theater whose interior would resemble that of the Guggenheim Museum, and a fifteen-story indoor Ferris wheel.[41] Another element—significant as a symbol of the connection of the *New York Times* to the redevelopment efforts—was a walkway joining the entertainment complex to the *Times*'s headquarters on Forty-third Street, which would enable visitors to see how "all the news that's fit to print" gets produced.

But, in addition, the project area had been expanded to cover three and a half city blocks in order to accommodate new commercial development on a scale that dwarfed the entertainment complex. Following a proposal made by one of the world's largest developers, Toronto-based Olympia & York, project sponsors included the construction of three large office towers totaling about 3 million square feet of floor space around the intersection of Forty-second Street, Broadway, and Seventh Avenue. Indicative of the switch from entertainment-based to office-based development, the Times Tower at One Times Square—the site of New Year's Eve celebrations and other public gatherings that was long considered the historic focal point of the square—was to be demolished to accommodate the visual coherence of the three new towers. This change was also made at the request of Olympia & York, which had signed on to build the towers. In response to a proposal by major New York developer Harry Helmsley, project planners also included a massive, 2-million-square-foot wholesale apparel mart spanning the western end of two city blocks across from the Port Authority Bus Terminal. Helmsley-Spear and Rockefeller Center, Inc., were prepared to build the mart. Financing for the project reportedly was made available by Equitable, which was an active participant in planning the project, and other life insurance companies.[42]

As a result of the participation by powerful real estate interests in the planning process, the project had mushroomed from 750,000 to nearly 6 million square feet of new construction.[43] This vast amount of new development exceeded even that of the original Rockefeller Center project in New York City. The price tag blossomed accordingly. The total cost was now estimated at more than $600 million. But project planners had eliminated any direct financial contribution from the city. Instead, a mere $40 million in federal funds, not otherwise available to the city, would leverage more than $600 million in private funding. Federal money to cover the cost of acquiring sites and demolishing existing buildings was anticipated primarily from the Urban Development Action Grant and Community Development Block Grant programs. Project sponsors also expected assistance from the National Endowment for the Arts and the National Endowment for the Humanities to support "cultural and artistic activities" in the project.[44]

Nevertheless, the project depended on certain key actions by the city. As the private sponsors insisted, "We are convinced that a continuation of the existing conditions on these blocks will make orderly and successful growth of midtown Manhattan impossible and that private action without government intervention cannot succeed."[45] Most important, they asked the city to designate more than three blocks as an urban renewal area so that the properties could be acquired for the private developers from owners holding out for windfall profits. The developers of the office towers and the merchandise mart would pay for the acquisition of their own sites, while The City at 42nd Street, Inc., would pay for the acquisition of the remaining area with a combination of federal money and private loans. Technically, the city would own all the condemned properties and lease them to The City at 42nd Street, which would, in turn, sublease the sites for the office towers and the merchandise mart. The City at 42nd Street would also lease development rights from above its mid-block sites to the office and mart developers in order to generate revenue for the restoration of the theaters and the construction of the entertainment complex.

Accordingly, the city was expected to approve several zoning amendments to allow for the transfer of development rights from above the mid-block sites of the historic theaters to the avenue blockfronts where the towers and the merchandise mart would be built. At the same time, the city would have to waive bulk restrictions limiting the size of these developments. In effect, the entire area would be treated as one lot for zoning purposes, so that despite the shift in density among sites, the level of development in the area as a whole would be less than the combined total of the allowable bulk for all the individual sites.

For its part, the city would receive a payment-in-lieu-of-taxes (PILOT) that would begin at an amount equal to 50 percent of the total tax liability for the area and increase to a full tax payment in ten years. In effect, then, the city would be providing the equivalent of a ten-year tax abatement. It would also receive all profits generated by the nonprofit organization The City at 42nd Street, Inc., from the entertainment complex. This would amount to the difference between the revenues—from the lease of development rights, contributions from exhibit sponsors, and admissions prices—and the expenses of operations and debt service. Project sponsors anticipated that, in the first full year of operation, the city would share profits of $4.2 million in addition to the PILOT payments of $3 million.[46]

DEFENDING THE PUBLIC INTEREST

The plan for The City at 42nd Street was presented to city officials for approval in August 1979. At that point, it began its journey through New York's standard process for land-use decision making known as the Uniform Land Use Review Procedure (ULURP).[47] According to ULURP in the 1980s, a proposal first was submitted to the seven-member City Planning Commission (CPC), which was assisted by the professional planning staff of the Department of City Planning (DCP), to make an initial determination that it was complete. Once the CPC certified the plan, it was forwarded to the relevant community board (out of the fifty-nine in the city) that represented the affected neighborhood—in this case, Community Board 5. The community board had sixty days to review and comment on the proposal before sending it back to the CPC with the community's recommendations. The CPC then prepared and issued a formal report. In the last step of the process, the Board of Estimate (BoE) held a public hearing and voted on a final determination regarding the plan.

The process was a long and frustrating one that was dreaded and loathed by anxious developers. The community boards were particularly vexing because their interests were often at odds with large-scale development and their recommendations were given considerable weight.[48] Ultimately, however, the support of the mayor was crucial to the success of a major development project, given his influence over the CPC, his position on the Board of Estimate, and his role as the primary representative of the city. This was especially true under Ed Koch, who established a firm grip on the CPC and BoE.[49]

Once the proposal for The City at 42nd Street was ushered off into the morass of ULURP, its sponsors, including some of the world's most powerful developers and corporations, sat back and waited for the city's blessing. But it never came. In late May 1980, Herbert Sturz, chairman of the CPC, refused to approve the plan; in fact, after more than six months had passed, CPC had not even forwarded the plan to Community Board 5 for review. The community board was outraged that the CPC was sabotaging the ULURP process because, in this case, it was actually eager for developers to clean up the mess in their neighborhood.[50] But the CPC had fundamental objections to the proposal, especially the vast size of the area slated for condemnation, the demolition of the popular Times Tower (described as "unnecessary nonsense" in the *New York Times*[51]), and the destruction—through demolition or conversion—of too many of the Forty-second Street theaters. The commission's objections centered on what architecture critic Ada Louise Huxtable had described as the plan's "unhappy resemblance to a discredited tradition of urban renewal."[52] In important respects, the proposal failed to recognize the changing context of urban development in which historic preservation and the arts were replacing the traditional urban renewal approach.

As it became clear that the city might withhold support for the plan, prominent businesspeople and planners involved in The City at 42nd Street launched what city officials called a "campaign of pressure" to secure the backing of the Koch administration.[53] Among other lobbying tactics, Coy G. Ecklund, the president of Equitable, wrote personally to Koch requesting a meeting to try to revive the proposal. Project sponsors charged publicly that the city had encouraged them to develop the plan, even providing staff assistance, guidance, and funding. Then, after the sponsors had invested roughly two years and $1.2 million into planning the project, city officials were backing out.[54] As Ecklund put it, "After working on it so hard and so long we thought we had the full cooperation of the city."[55]

Still, Mayor Koch withheld his approval. His resistance stemmed from two politically relevant considerations. First, Koch already had expressed serious concerns about the nature of the cultural vision that would guide redevelopment of the area. Even when The City at 42nd Street was in its formative stages, Koch and other city officials had revealed their unease about what they regarded as excessive demolition and conversion of the historic Forty-second Street theaters. In response, the project sponsors had shifted the focus of the cultural complex somewhat, from amusement rides to the performing arts, as the design evolved.[56] Ultimately, though, the plan remained defined largely by its world's-fair character. It never fully shed the entertainment approach of the earlier Cityscape version, which was described in the *Wall Street Journal* as a combination of Florida's Disneyland and Chicago's Museum of Science and Industry.[57] For Koch, this was the heart of the problem. He did not, it seems, object to the concept of creating an urban theme park on Forty-second Street, but to the "Disneyland" character of the proposed entertainment complex. As Koch put it, "New York cannot and should not compete with Disneyland—that's for Florida. . . . We've got to make sure [visitors to Times Square] have seltzer instead of orange juice."[58]

In response to accusations that he had acted in bad faith, Koch introduced a second issue into the conflict, one that built on the notion of the public interest. He argued that it was wrong to award an exclusive contract to a predesignated group of private developers; instead, the development team for such a project should be chosen through a competitive bidding process. Oddly, Koch was defining his administration as an adversary of real-estate interests that would not allow the city to be put at the mercy of development "sharks."[59] To some extent, Koch would have been understandably wary of such an arrangement because of previous scandals involving exclusive city contracts. But there were other factors behind Koch's decision, and he hinted as much. In response to threats from the project's developers and financiers that they might refuse to participate if the city imposed new terms, Koch argued that where such valuable real estate was involved the city could certainly attract other developers, some of whom might even offer the city better proposals. As Koch astutely noted, "We are talking about millions of dollars to be made here and that is very valuable real estate."[60]

Indeed, there was already good reason to believe that Koch's assessment of interest in Forty-second Street was correct. When The City at 42nd Street plan first emerged, a number of prominent developers had been inspired by the concept of using the power of eminent domain to take and develop large areas around Times Square.[61] The development team DeMatteis and Shaw proposed using an urban renewal approach to redevelop four square blocks north of Forty-second Street, between Sixth Avenue and Broadway (just east of The City at 42nd Street area). The Open Space Institute suggested the Times Square South project, which called for an office tower with more than 1 million square feet of space and three hotels with a total of 2,000 rooms on the block bounded by Sixth Avenue and Broadway, and Forty-second and Forty-third Streets.[62] The Cadillac-Fairview Corporation, one of Canada's largest developers, even recommended combining the DeMatteis plan and The City at 42nd Street and redeveloping the entire area of almost eight square blocks.

In short, there was widespread interest in Times Square, and Mayor Koch had strong political ties to the development community. With the privilege of redeveloping Times Square such a widely coveted goal, it would clearly serve the mayor's political interests to have greater control over the process of awarding this prize. So armed with the confidence that private developers could be easily lured to a publicly sponsored redevelopment plan, Koch made his final decision to withhold approval for The City at 42nd Street. He made his view clear at a meeting in June 1980 with the project's sponsors, who shortly thereafter withdrew their plan from consideration. The self-appointed developers of Times Square, who had been waiting with wrecking balls poised to strike, were furious with the mayor. But one aspiring New York developer and Koch supporter was overjoyed that he had held out against The City at 42nd Street.

THE PUBLICLY SPONSORED PLAN: EMBRACING THE ARTS AND SERVING PRIVATE INTERESTS

In spite of his refusal to support the privately sponsored plan, Koch proclaimed that he was committed to the redevelopment of Times Square. He insisted, however, that city and state officials be in control of the planning process. Rather than inviting private developers to offer their own plans, city and state planners would draw up guidelines (with input from community groups and public agencies), issue a request-for-proposals (RFP), and select the most advantageous proposal through an evaluation of competitive bids. In this way, the public sector would be fulfilling the responsibilities invested in it; that is, public officials would consider a broader range of public and private objectives than would otherwise be addressed in a private plan. As Koch presented it, he was carrying out his duty to defend the public interest.

Less than a month after The City at 42nd Street was put to rest, city and state officials issued a statement of intent announcing a joint effort to redevelop Times Square. The project would combine the city's planning capabilities, through the involvement of the CPC and DPC, with the development expertise of the New York State Urban Development Corporation (UDC). The UDC (renamed the Empire State Development Corporation in 1995) was a quasi-public authority created to promote the development of low-income housing, but by the 1970s its role was redirected to encourage the construction of office space and middle- and upper-income housing in the urban core.[63] The UDC was not a property owner or builder; rather, it acted as "a catalyst for land development."[64] It acquired land, made initial investments, formulated plans, and then recruited private investors and developers to carry out the projects. The UDC also enjoyed unique powers, derived from its original mission of promoting scattered-site, low-income housing, that enabled it to override local zoning laws and bypass New York City's ULURP process.[65] Thus "top politicians [saw] the UDC as an indispensable tool in assembling land and making end runs around the political process."[66]

Although the city initially relied on its planning agencies, the CPC and DCP, in the joint redevelopment effort, it soon turned to its own quasi-public development authority, the New York City Public Development Corporation (PDC), as its lead agency. The PDC (since renamed the Economic Development Corporation) functioned as a land development tool for the city analogous to the way the UDC served the state.[67] It worked to encourage private investment that would contribute to new construction and job creation in the city. As a quasi-independent, nonprofit corporation, the PDC was exempt from the normal restrictions on city hiring and contracts; nonetheless, it was accountable to the mayor because he provided the funding and appointed the board members—for the most part, prominent businesspeople. Thus the PDC served the mayor as "a powerful public agency insulated from popular control with development as its sole mission."[68]

The shift from the City Planning Commission to the Public Development Corporation as the lead city agency in Times Square redevelopment reflected the general priorities of the Koch administration, under which the city abandoned any pretext of independent public planning and placed planning at the service of private development.[69] In light of the PDC's lead role, Koch's heroic statements about defending the public interest against development sharks rang hollow. Instead, the city–state effort to redevelop Times Square would fit the classic mold of public–private partnerships in the 1980s, when entrepreneurial public officials used quasi-public redevelopment authorities and financial inducements to facilitate major new downtown development.[70] Such partnerships were "firmly rooted in the historically unequal relationship between the public and private sectors . . . that [gave] rise to the uneven development" of postindustrial urban restructuring.[71] Thus with the UDC and PDC taking the lead, it was inevitable that private development goals would figure prominently in the revitalization of Times Square.

The announcement of the joint undertaking expressed the desire that Times Square be redeveloped through a public–private effort that would build on the area's traditional strengths: the theater district and the tourist trade. This agenda offered a clue to the new direction that planners intended the project to take and to the importance of the discourse on Times Square. In February 1981, city and state sponsors released a "discussion document" setting out general guidelines for the project.[72] The official design guidelines, prepared by the architecture and design firm Cooper Eckstut Associates—whose highly praised design for Battery Park City had just been selected by UDC sponsors—were distributed in June. The document was followed shortly afterward by a formal request for proposals.

The most notable feature of the city–state plan was its remarkable resemblance to The City at 42nd Street proposal, which Koch had rejected the previous summer. The project offered the same basic vision for Times Square: it covered nearly three city blocks, roughly bordered by Forty-first and Forty-third Streets from Broadway to Eighth Avenue; it provided for a group of office towers around the intersection of Forty-second Street, Broadway, and Seventh Avenue, at the eastern end of the project area; it included a low-rise, mid-block stretch of entertainment attractions centering on the historic theaters; and it proposed a massive merchandise mart and hotel at the Eighth Avenue end of the project area. Conceptually, the pattern of development involved the same shift of development rights from the mid-block to the avenue sites. But because of UDC sponsorship, local zoning restrictions did not apply, and so no formal transfer of development rights was needed. For the most part, the project would be privately funded; the public contribution would come in the form of tax breaks and the use of eminent domain to force the sale of the properties slated for redevelopment. The total development cost of the project was now estimated at greater than $1 billion.

The plan did differ from The City at 42nd Street, however, in two respects, both of which are important to understanding the politics of the project. The first involved the cultural character of the entertainment facilities that would be constructed. Whereas the earlier proposal had envisioned a forward-looking, world's fair–type complex employing the latest in entertainment technologies, the new plan looked back to the romanticized history of the area for its inspiration. The new project called for the restoration of all nine historic theaters and their return to use for the arts, instead of housing the incongruous high-tech attractions outlined in the earlier plan. Seven of the theaters would be legitimate stages, representing an increase of about 20 percent in the city's stock of Broadway theaters; the other two would be nonprofit theaters for other types of performances. With the emphasis on reconstructing a Broadway theater district, the project firmly embraced the vision of a revitalized Great White Way as its fundamental theme. In this respect, the planners showed a sophisticated appreciation of the importance of cultural production

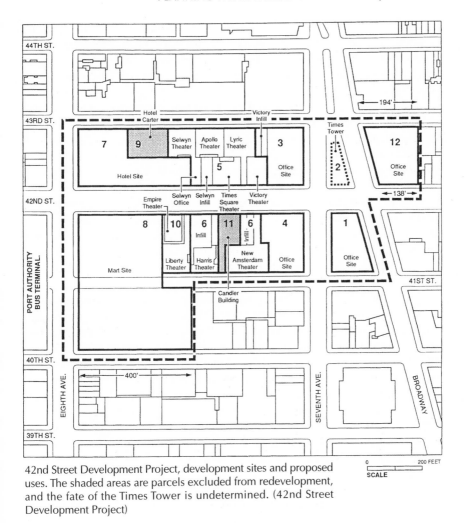

42nd Street Development Project, development sites and proposed uses. The shaded areas are parcels excluded from redevelopment, and the fate of the Times Tower is undetermined. (42nd Street Development Project)

to the politics of the project; following Koch's dictate, they proposed an entertainment district congruent with a glamorous image of the city as the historic center of theater and the arts.

Consistent with the focus on historic preservation, the planners called for the retention (and possible redesign) of the historic Times Tower. The guidelines even required the inclusion of bright lights and supersigns in the design of the new office towers, in a gesture of respect to the historic character of the area. (A zoning amendment pushed by the Municipal Art Society in 1987 imposed similar signage and lighting requirements on all new buildings in the greater Times Square area, thereby extending further this cultural project that *Times* reporter Mark McCain described as "a mandated comeback for the Great White Way."[73]) Thus, the project based its cultural strategy on a constructed history of place. True to his word, Koch was offering New York its seltzer, and it was packaged in the form of a sparkling Great White Way that higher-income New Yorkers could consume with pleasure.

The second difference between the new publicly sponsored proposal and its predecessor involved the extent of the commercial development. The city–state plan significantly expanded the already vast scale of new construction that had been proposed by The City at 42nd Street. Rather than three towers, the project now proposed four, representing an increase of roughly 1 million square feet of office space. The size of the merchandise mart, too, was increased by about 20 percent. And to complement the mart, the planners added a 550-room hotel at the western end of the project area. All together, the city–state plan provided for some 7 million square feet of new development, or the equivalent of about four Empire State Buildings. Thus the historic theaters would be elegantly dressed in the garb of the Great White Way to welcome the arrival of the midtown office district to Times Square.

The expanded city–state plan promised far greater profits to private developers than had the earlier proposal. Over time, it also became clear that the project would require vastly larger public subsidies. It is certainly no small irony that the publicly sponsored plan, offered in the public interest, contemplated a scale of construction that significantly exceeded that of the project generated by private developers. While the components of historic preservation were seemingly rooted in a conception of the public interest, they did not stand apart from the massive office and mart developments, which bespoke the influence of private interests over public ones. The integration of historic preservation and new construction epitomized the new cultural strategy of urban development that facilitates capital accumulation and the control of urban space.

HOW TO MAKE IT BIG IN NEW YORK CITY REAL ESTATE

In September 1981, the project sponsors received responses to the RFP. As Koch had predicted, there was genuine interest in participation among private developers. Sponsors received proposals from thirty developers who were interested in developing one or more of the ten project sites. The list of hopeful applicants ranged from local theater organizations to powerful international development corporations; prominent on the list were the Reichmann brothers (of Toronto-based Olympia & York) and Harry Helmsley, the designated developers of The City at 42nd Street whose money-making efforts had been frustrated by Koch's lack of cooperation. City and state officials spent the following months meeting with prospective developers to negotiate and formalize detailed proposals. In the spring of 1982, they finally made their conditional designation of the project developers. And the winner was . . . George Klein, whose company, Park Tower Realty, was designated to build the four office towers. George Klein? Here was a man, heir to the Barton's candy fortune, who had entered the real-estate field only in the mid-1970s.[74] His first shot at real-estate development in Manhattan began in 1978 with the acquisition of a small site on Park Avenue; his first building went up there only one year before he was designated for the Forty-second Street project. Yet, as a piece in *Forbes* put it, this "obscure candymaker" had landed "one of the great real estate plums in New York City history: four giant office towers around a reborn Times Square, in the heart of Manhattan, with 4.1 million square feet of office space and generous incentives from the city that could make him one of the richest men in America."[75]

How did Klein manage such a coup? After all, he was competing for the office sites against local developers such as Paul Milstein and Larry Silverstein, both of whom, according to *Forbes*, "were far more substantial and had been in real estate far longer than George Klein." An important clue to Klein's success was provided by Mayor Koch himself. In his book *Mayor,* Koch described Klein as "at the very top of my list of campaign contributors when I ran for reelection in 1981." This was the year that Klein first bid on the Times Square project. In case that was not sufficient, Koch also located Klein "at the top of my list of contributors in 1982 when I was running for governor."[76] The year 1982 was, of course, also the year that Klein was designated the top developer for the project.

This was not the only connection that Klein had to Koch. For some time, Klein had been an active spokesperson for Jewish and Israeli-American causes, and in this capacity he cultivated relationships with a conservative Jewish community in New York and with a variety of state and local politicians. He used these contacts to assist in fund-raising efforts for a number of national politicians, including Ronald Reagan in 1980. In the late 1970s, he earned the favor of Mayor Koch by lobbying his congressional contacts to support various programs of aid to New York City. In addition, Klein was considered highly skilled at marketing himself in particularly resonant ways. As one New York politician described Klein's technique, "He touches base with the do-gooders, like the Landmarks Commission and the Municipal Art Society."[77] Klein's retention of internationally acclaimed architect I. M. Pei to design his first building also boosted his reputation as a developer with a keen eye for aesthetics. In a project with roots in the arts community and an emphasis on cultural production, such credentials provided no small advantage.

It also appears that Klein's real-estate strategy benefited from techniques that were not entirely aboveboard. In the mid-1980s, he was implicated in a kickback scheme involving the procurement of leases for city offices.[78] Allegedly, Klein (among others) had paid off the city's former director of leasing operations, Alex Liberman, in return for the location of city offices in a largely vacant, dilapidated building that Klein owned in Brooklyn. The city's Human Resources Administration became the sole tenant of the building. Klein benefited from this lease deal to the tune of $6.5 million. While Liberman was ultimately sent to prison, Klein escaped prosecution as a result of the death of a primary witness. One law-enforcement official involved in the case described Klein as "the one that got away."

It might seem that in a competitive bidding process, such personal connections would be irrelevant. On the contrary, one insider described the procedure of round-by-round bidding orchestrated by UDC officials as "tailor-made for political games."[79] There were no sealed bids, and there was no means of public oversight. While perceptions obviously differ, the unsuccessful bidders for the office sites described a process that was loaded in Klein's favor from the outset. The critics pointed to a number of unexplained decisions made by the UDC that accommodated the selection of Klein. For example, the UDC inexplicably shifted away from its initial preference for a single developer capable of handling the entire project and sought a number of developers for the different sites; this weakened the position of Milstein, who was most capable of handling the entire project. According to him, UDC officials then encouraged the four developers competing for the office sites to form a consortium. Three of them—Milstein, Silverstein, and Rockrose Development Corporation—did so, but Klein remained confident of his own position and refused to join. Milstein maintains that his group was told that no final action would be taken for months; then, suddenly, he was informed that a final bid was due in five days. According to Milstein, his group then provided both a written and a verbal commitment to beat any price offered by Klein. The next thing he knew, however, Klein had been designated. Milstein's conclusion: "It was obviously a fix."

Although UDC officials were ostensibly free to select developers based on some objective standards, they had good reason to be responsive to Mayor Koch's interests. The deals negotiated between the UDC and the developers would ultimately have to be approved by the New York City Board of Estimate, and Koch exerted considerable influence over this body. Subsequent events lend additional credibility to the perception that Koch used his influence to secure Klein's participation in the project. In 1983, the Morse family, the developer originally designated to build the wholesale mart, dropped out because of financial problems. This triggered a burst of maneuvering among other developers interested in taking over the site. Two teams emerged at the center of the competition: one was led by Milstein and included A. Arthur Taubmann, a mall developer, and New York developer Alan Weller; the other was led by Klein and included Trammel Crow, one of the world's largest developers of wholesale marts, and Equitable.

The selection now rested with the 42nd Street Redevelopment Corporation (later renamed the 42nd Street Development Project, Inc.), a subsidiary of the UDC set up to carry out the city–state project.[80] (It should not be confused with the 42nd Street Development Corporation, the private local development corporation run by Fred Papert.) This corporation was governed by a five-member board; originally, the five members were to include two city officials, two state officials, and one impartial representative of the business community. But when Richard Stern, chairman of the UDC, named himself chairman of the new corporation, the state came to enjoy a three-to-two majority over city appointees. In Albany, Koch's archrival Democrat Mario Cuomo had succeeded Hugh Carey as governor, and Klein's base of support in the UDC had consequently been eroded. Although Koch insisted on the designation of Klein's development team, he lost on a vote of three to two. The 42nd Street Redevelopment Corporation chose the team of Milstein Taubmann Weller Associates instead.

In a startling display of pique, Koch singlehandedly abolished the development pact with the state, declaring that the city would complete the project on its own rather than be dominated by state officials. Stern would not budge, arguing that the city had relinquished its veto power with the creation of the 42nd Street Redevelopment Corporation. It was reportedly at the insistence of New York City's three major newspapers that Koch and Cuomo agreed to negotiate a resolution and salvage the project.[81] This behind-the-scenes pressure was backed up by an editorial in the *New York Times* gently coaxing the two to return to prudent cooperation.[82]

In a rare face-to-face meeting, the two political adversaries settled on a compromise by which a new developer, Tishman-Speyer Properties, would build the mart, Trammel Crow would operate it, Equitable would provide the bulk of the financing, and Milstein would be limited to a passive, minority interest (with a maximum 30 percent investment share). Klein would not be involved in the mart development. If it seems that Klein lost in this arrangement, *Forbes* argued that, to the contrary, Klein secured his primary interest by keeping the project out of the control of Milstein, who he feared would turn the space to office use and compete with Klein's own buildings.

Nor was Klein's selection for the project the only one to smack of political favoritism. The Brandt Organization leveled similar accusations against the UDC's decision to designate the Cambridge Investment Group as the developer of the Site 5 theaters, which were owned and operated by Brandt.[83] Cambridge was controlled by Michael J. Lazar, a former member of the City Council and head of the Taxi and Limousine Commission with no apparent background in the theater industry. Lazar was described by Brandt's attorneys as "a contributor of substantial sums to the political campaigns of most of the elected officials who must pass on the project, including his own conditional designation as developer of Site 5."

Lazar also happened to be the owner of the Candler Building on Forty-second Street, one of only two properties within the boundaries of the project area that were exempted, without explanation, from condemnation and redevelopment. This was somewhat peculiar, since the building was nearly half vacant (its only occupants included the Taxi and Limousine Commission and other quasi-public organizations) and in need of restoration. So Lazar not only would profit as the developer of the area theaters, but also would benefit greatly from soaring property values resulting from the redevelopment of all the properties surrounding his own. Ironically, Lazar was later dropped from the project after he was indicted for complicity in a scandal involving the city's Parking Violations Bureau. He was also implicated in the same scandal that Klein allegedly took part in, involving kickbacks for city leases.[84]

EMINENT DOMAIN: PUBLIC POWER IN THE PRIVATE INTEREST

The flip side of designating developers for the project sites was the process of condemning and taking area properties through eminent domain. Eminent domain is
the power of states (and certain localities) to acquire property unilaterally from a
private owner in the pursuit of a legitimate public purpose. The state must provide
"just compensation" for the taking; however, the fair price is determined, in effect,
by the buyer rather than the seller. In the case of the 42nd Street Development Project, the declared public purpose was the elimination of blight and the restoration
of a healthy social and economic environment to Times Square. The resolution
approving the Forty-second Street project passed by the Board of Estimate in 1984
elaborated this rationale in the following rambling clauses:

> The Project Area is marked by street crime, substandard and insanitary con-
> ditions, uses that inhibit the general public's use and enjoyment of the Project
> Area, and physical, economic and social blight which contribute to the growth
> of crime and delinquency and impair the sound growth of the Project Area and
> of the City as a whole; and . . .
>   The redevelopment of the Project Area is in the best interest of the City
> in that it will remove blight and physical, economic and social decay and
> replace them with a variety of new uses which will result in commercial and
> economic expansion, cultural and entertainment rejuvenation and improved
> public services and utilities, to the betterment of the Project Area in particu-
> lar and the City in general.[85]

As early as 1979, when the city was asked to condemn the project area for The
City at 42nd Street, critics had challenged the logic of this claim. Ada Louise
Huxtable, architecture critic of the *New York Times,* pointed out that the sites for
the office towers, particularly that of the Times Tower, were not blighted parcels
and thus the construction of the office towers would represent a "questionable use
of urban renewal."[86] But the most adamant objections came from owners of the
properties in the project area. Not only did they question the characterization of
their properties as blighted—buildings that were in use for legal purposes, and for
which all required taxes were paid—but they objected to the acquisition of their
properties for the enrichment of other private developers, when at least some of
the present owners expressed a willingness to upgrade their properties without public subsidy. The Brandt Organization, for example, had restored two of its theaters
to legitimate use in the early 1980s and proposed to restore the others at its own
expense as part of the redevelopment effort. In economic terms, the compensation
that the owners would receive from the state would be, by definition, below the
market price, since the sites would be acquired by judicial decree rather than
mutual agreement.

The exercise of eminent domain on Forty-second Street facilitated the transfer of property from one set of private owners to another in order to further the political and economic goals of the dominant pro-growth coalition in the city. The interests of local owners in realizing the maximum potential of their Forty-second Street properties had thwarted the westward expansion of the midtown office district, the goal shared by the Koch administration and the development community as a whole. The revitalization of Times Square promised to create development opportunities and restore an entertainment resource for higher-income New Yorkers, including the white professionals who were especially important to the mayor's political fortunes. Eminent domain served, therefore, as a trump card in the efforts of Koch's pro-growth coalition to promote its development agenda of postindustrial transformation. Yet private interests, rather than public ones, appeared to drive the process. Arguably, unblighted parcels were included in the project because they provided the most practical sites for profitable office development. But Lazar's Candler Building was exempted, although it was underutilized and in need of restoration.

The exercise of eminent domain thus split the business community into supporters and opponents of the project. On one side was a powerful pro-growth coalition, including major corporations and developers and top public officials, staging its bid to take over the area, redevelop and redefine it, and reap the political and economic rewards. On the other side were the existing property owners and business operators who profited from the status quo or held on to their buildings as speculative investments. The primary interests behind the latter group were the Brandt Organization and the Durst Organization, real-estate concerns with valuable holdings in the Times Square area, including some slated for condemnation. The relationship of these companies to the Forty-second Street redevelopment effort illustrates the conflicting development interests at stake in the area and the importance of public intervention.

The Brandt family had owned and operated theaters in the Times Square area since the 1930s, and in the early 1980s it still owned ten theaters, including seven of the historic theaters in the Forty-second Street project area. When city and state officials first solicited proposals from developers, all the parties assumed that Brandt would act as developer and operator of its own theaters.[87] But the UDC had included one Brandt theater on the south block in another project site that would be awarded to another developer. Brandt insisted that this theater be included with the five theaters on the north block under its control. Brandt wanted to retain ownership of all its theaters and develop them independently of the project. Negotiations broke down after several months, and the UDC requested bids from developers to restore and operate all the Brandt theaters. Instead of accommodating Brandt's proposal, which would have saved the city the millions of dollars it would cost to acquire the theaters and subsidize their operation, the sponsors awarded the Brandt theaters to Lazar's Cambridge group. Brandt opted to fight the condemnations in court.

The Durst family, which reportedly was worth $1 billion, was a "landbanker" with sixty-nine parcels in Manhattan at the end of the 1980s.[88] The Dursts objected to the redevelopment project because the construction of millions of square feet of subsidized office space would interfere with their own development efforts. In the 1960s, the Dursts were already planning to build as many as ten office towers in the area bounded by Sixth Avenue and Broadway, from Forty-second to Forty-seventh Street; but their plans fell apart with the real-estate bust of the mid-1970s. Still, the Dursts continued to pursue development opportunities while the Forty-second Street project was in the works; at the same time, they conducted a vigorous campaign to block the publicly sponsored project.

The Dursts were especially concerned about the block just east of the Forty-second Street project area (bordered by Forty-second and Forty-third Streets between Broadway and Sixth Avenue), where they owned more than half of the parcels. The block was ripe for new office development, but was also vulnerable to competition from the subsidized office towers of the Forty-second Street project. In the late 1980s, when the Forty-second Street project was losing momentum, the Dursts were almost successful in enticing Chemical Bank to a new twenty-eight-story, 1.2-million-square-foot office tower they would build at Forty-second Street and Sixth Avenue. Chemical had signed on as the prime office tenant for the 42nd Street Development Project, but was getting frustrated by the ongoing delays. Thus luring the bank to a new Durst tower would be a major moral, as well as economic, victory for the opponents of the project. The Dursts were thwarted, however, by other property owners with speculative investments on the block.

Ironically, after fighting the Forty-second Street project for almost fifteen years, the Dursts finally secured a dramatic place for themselves in the project: the first of the four office towers will be their creation.[89] For $75 million, they acquired the site on Broadway between Forty-second and Forty-third Streets (adjacent to their own properties) and are constructing a forty-eight-story office tower that will house the glamorous headquarters of Condé Nast Publications. George Klein reportedly was irate about giving up the right to build the tower—and "leave something in this world" akin to the pyramids in Egypt[90]—but did so at the insistence of the Prudential Insurance Company, his partner and financier after Equitable withdrew. (The team of Klein and Prudential operated under the name Times Square Center Associates.)

Ultimately, then, the Brandt and Durst cases exemplify the complex interests that divide the development community and the essential role that the public sector plays in shaping the opportunities for capital investment. Eminent domain made possible a reshuffling of real estate, and public subsidies substantially altered the structure of rewards for investment in the area. When the project was approved by the BoE in 1984, much was made of the public benefits that would accrue. Supporters emphasized that the developers would bear all the up-front costs of the project, including land acquisition and redevelopment, and even contribute $50 million or more to subsidize the renovations of the Times Square subway station and the historic theaters.[91] (The actual amounts were $33 million for the subway station and $14 million for the theaters, plus an adjustment for inflation that might raise the total contribution to as much as $60 million.) The substantial public subsidy, however, remained "one of the best kept secrets of the project."[92]

According to the original agreement, the developers would receive the equivalent of a fifteen-year tax abatement valued at more than $500 million. Since the UDC would technically retain ownership during this time, the developers would be making a payment-in-lieu-of-taxes (PILOT), which was set at $480 million over the fifteen-year period. Although this was significantly more than the $80 million or so that the city would receive if the area remained as it was (generating about $5.4 million a year), it was substantially less than the $1.13 billion that the redeveloped area would generate at the full rate of taxation. In effect, then, the developers received a tax break worth $650 million over fifteen years. The developers could, however, receive an additional reduction in their payments if the costs of land acquisition exceeded a cap set at $150 million. In other words, although the developers would pay all acquisition costs up front, the city would reimburse any amount above $150 million—with interest, at 1 percent above the prime rate—through additional reductions in their PILOT (or taxes, if they exercised their purchase option) after the fifteen-year abatement expired. It was this provision that created the potential for an explosive public subsidy.

Indeed, the $150 million limit on the developers' liability for acquisition costs proved to be "ridiculously low," as some critics argued.[93] The developer of the office sites was responsible for only $88 million in acquisition costs; but Klein's partner, Prudential, ultimately paid about $300 million, including tens of millions of dollars in soft costs that officials generously agreed to count toward acquisition costs. As a result, the public owed Prudential more than $200 million, plus interest payments that probably would amount to more than $10 million a year.[94] This would mean a lifetime of subsidy for the developer, who, after fifteen years, could purchase the land and buildings for a bargain-basement price of less than half a year's rent receipts.

Given the enormous stakes involved, it is not surprising that the conflict over the ownership of private property and the right to develop it became the primary issue of contention that threatened to derail the project. The public hearings and approval process offered a poor arena for any real political challenge to the plan. The legislative process served more as a public spectacle in which supporters of the project marshaled the Times Square discourse to mobilize widespread public approval; the BoE vote then provided a stamp of legitimacy on the project. Once the political process was cleared in 1984, however, the Brandts and the Dursts pursued what sponsors described as a "litigation conspiracy" aimed at halting the project.[95] Indeed, it was in the judicial rather than the political arena where other major projects in New York often faced their greatest challenges; for example, efforts to redevelop both the West Side Highway (Westway) and the site of the Coliseum at Columbus Circle were derailed in the courts. In the years following formal BoE approval, the Brandts and Dursts were involved in about three-quarters of the astounding forty-seven lawsuits that the project faced. For the most part, the lawsuits challenged the use of eminent domain on substantive and procedural grounds, although they also questioned the project on other procedural requirements. In 1989, in the midst of eminent domain proceedings, the Durst Organization even acquired seventy-year leases for seven of the Forty-second Street theaters and announced plans to clean them up; in this way, the company hoped to bolster its legal challenges by emphasizing the value of the properties and demonstrating the feasibility of private redevelopment.

Although their legal tactics seemed the most promising, the Brandts and Dursts also pursued a political strategy by joining forces with local grassroots opposition. Together with a coalition of residents and businesses fearing displacement, these organizations formed the Committee to Reclaim Times Square and waged a modest publicity campaign against the project. Their efforts included a demonstration in Times Square by residents, small-business owners, local politicians, and a Durst representative.[96] In effect, the large local property owners were trying to build a coalition among small businesses, residents, and users of the area to fend off the attempt by the dominant pro-growth coalition of corporations, developers, and public officials to control this space. But the latter group already had succeeded in mobilizing widespread support for its agenda through its ability to define and control the political discourse.

Although the project survived the lawsuits and other challenges, it faced costly delays that seriously threatened its viability. Officials did not win final legal approval to condemn properties until April 1990, more than five years after having secured political approval for the project. By that time, the project had begun to unravel. Chemical Bank had reneged on its commitment because of the delays, leaving the project without any major anchor tenant signed on for the vast new office space. The designated operator of the merchandise mart, Trammel Crow, had quit the project, as had the hotel developer; thus the redevelopment of the entire western end of the project area languished on indefinite hold. And, of course, the primary theater developer was bumped as a result of his involvement in two scandals. Consequently, once the state had authority to take the properties, it had a shaky reason to do so; and, initially, it condemned only the eastern two-thirds of the area, or about eight of the project's thirteen acres.[97]

No sooner did the state take these properties than warning signs began to appear questioning the prudence of adding millions of square feet of office space to an already glutted midtown market.[98] In the early 1990s, vacant office space on the West Side alone was estimated at 5 to 8 million square feet, or around one-quarter of the total available in west Midtown. The overdevelopment of West Side office space was the product of the new zoning incentives for the area that had been adopted in the early 1980s. Indeed, several of the imposing new office towers in the Times Square area filed for bankruptcy in the late 1980s, after remaining vacant for months or years.[99] Ironically, whereas the Forty-second Street project was originally conceived as a critical component of the new zoning strategy, by the late

1980s the development that had occurred as a result of the zoning incentives threatened the viability of the project itself. Indeed, given the soft market, the Forty-second Street project was the last thing that developers in the area wanted to see, especially since its subsidies would enable it to undercut the other buildings that were already struggling.

By the 1990, critics from all sides were challenging the economic rationale for the project. Although it had cleared the various political and legal hurdles, it was now foundering on a stubborn downturn in the economy. As the market for office space continued to deteriorate, even the development team of George Klein and Prudential realized the futility of building its monuments. For the third time in the century, the best laid plans were blocked by the unpredictable hidden hand of the marketplace itself. For the project's sponsors, it meant a return to the drawing board.

THE POLITICAL DEBATE OVER PUBLIC AND PRIVATE

The practice of taking and bestowing private property through eminent domain is interesting not only for the private interests that it serves and harms, but also for the justification in terms of its service to a public interest. The process derives its legal justification and public legitimacy from a conception of the public interest. Yet there is a fundamental ambivalence in the political efforts to define public and private action in urban development that is evident throughout the history of the 42nd Street Development Project.

The 42nd Street project had its origins in the initiatives of private interests that began in the late 1970s. When Koch rejected the private-sector plan, he did so largely because of his insistence on a greater public role. Koch suggested that public direction was needed to give the project the legitimacy of a public purpose. There was, however, little in the new publicly sponsored plan to suggest the assertion of some previously overlooked public interest. On the contrary, the new plan allowed a substantially larger scale of private commercial development and opened the way for a much greater level of public subsidy. The bidding process, too, appeared to work in favor of politically connected private interests rather than serving any additional public interest. Public officials even allowed Klein to violate their own design guidelines in his development plan for the office towers, although the guidelines were not negotiable.[100] Klein's towers exceeded bulk restrictions and disregarded signage requirements, and he also proposed to demolish the historic Times Tower, which was retained in the guidelines. (When the project received BoE approval, the fate of the Times Tower was put in the hands of an advisory committee that had yet to be named.) Koch justified the concession to Klein by declaring, "I for one have never felt it necessary to explain why we improve something."[101] Those who remained critical were derided by Koch as "idiots."

Still, the use of the power of eminent domain required a representation of the process as being publicly directed and serving the interest of the public. The resolution presented to the city's Board of Estimate, and the legal case made in the courts, both contributed to and depended on this characterization. Public officials emphasized the bounty of benefits that would accrue to the city and its residents, including tens of thousands of jobs, hundreds of millions of dollars in tax revenues, and improved public facilities.[102] Ironically, though, there was a simultaneous effort by officials to portray the project as essentially a private redevelopment effort in the public interest. They emphasized that no public dollars were being provided directly for the project, and they downplayed the public subsidy. At the BoE hearings in 1984, Governor Mario Cuomo could still describe the 42nd Street Development Project as "the greatest single private real estate development in the history of this great city, and state, and nation, and probably beyond."[103]

Thus when it came to the specific economics of the plan, there was a concerted effort by its supporters to represent it as a private project. This was a politically motivated strategy in response to critics' charges that the public was giving away too much. Nevertheless, the developers involved in the project remained strong advocates of government assistance. An article in the business publication *Barron's* noted the irony of the fact that the debate over the need for public subsidies had "transformed some builders and financiers who otherwise might be staunch supporters of the laissez-faire school of construction into advocates for an active government role."[104] In defining public and private roles, where one sits apparently determines where one stands.

The political debate, therefore, included a struggle between supporters and opponents over the definition of the public and private roles. Each side offered competing representations that were often plagued with contradictions and inconsistencies. Supporters sought to define the project as publicly sponsored in order to legitimize the pursuit of private interests. Yet they wanted to deflect attention from the public role as a source of enrichment for private developers; instead, they portrayed the project as a private effort from which public officials had exacted valuable concessions for city residents. Opponents described a process in which public officials were simply caving in to private interests. At the same time, they called on the same subservient officials to defend a vision of the public interest, thereby attributing to them the capability to do so. This debate over public and private interests and roles was an important component of the politics of the redevelopment of Times Square. The history of the project, however, exposes the limited usefulness of a rigid dichotomy between public and private in understanding local government and policy.[105]

THE POWER OF THE *TIMES* OVER THE AGENDA

The issue of representing public and private action was part of a more general concern about representing the redevelopment effort itself. The media is, of course, central to the process of representation. Newspapers, in particular, have historically played an important role in promoting urban development. Indeed, given their aura of objectivity and their ability to define issues and shape public opinion, they have been characterized as a central component in the traditional urban growth machine.[106] The media is a mechanism by which dominant economic interests shape political discourse to serve their investment strategies.

The Times Square case reveals the subtle ways that newspapers can mobilize public opinion in support of urban development. All the major daily newspapers in New York City contributed, in varying degrees, to a pro-development discourse that alternately bemoaned the horrors of Times Square and hailed the imminent return to the glory years of the Great White Way.[107] But the *New York Times,* because of its location at the border of the project area, played a particularly influential role in this respect: it simultaneously was the voice of a self-interested corporation striving to enhance its image and the value of its real estate, and a supposedly disinterested news organization reporting objectively on events concerning the Times Square area. As a result of its reputation for professionalism, the *Times* commanded a unique position of influence in the effort to define the debate over Times Square and to redevelop and culturally redefine the area.

In 1978, the New York Times Company was one of a dozen corporations that provided funds for a preliminary study of renewal possibilities for the Times Square area.[108] This was perhaps the first step in the evolution of the 42nd Street Development Project. For several years thereafter, the company continued to provide financial support for the redevelopment efforts of the 42nd Street Development Corporation and The City at 42nd Street, Inc. But the greatest contribution from the *Times* likely came in the form of its reporting on the area.

In general, from the point that its parent company began funding redevelopment initiatives, coverage in the *New York Times* followed a sort of manic oscillation between doom-and-gloom forecasts tied to inaction and a sunny optimism about the glorious entertainment district just waiting to be reborn. It was equivalent to a "good cop, bad cop" strategy of reporting that contrasted the benefits of cooperation and positive action with the dire consequences of obstructionism. This goading strategy served to highlight the cultural politics of the project, which argued for the replacement of a menacing street culture with a middle-class entertainment district derived from a romanticized past. Not all *Times* reporting on Times Square toed this discursive line; a succession of architecture critics—Ada Louise Huxtable, Paul Goldberger, and Herbert Muschamp—were notable for their critical analyses of the redevelopment project. Nevertheless, the reporting overall reflected a well-orchestrated pattern of support in the subjects and content of coverage.

In addition to the usual stories about crime, blight, and the dangers of Forty-second Street, with its troubled street population, the *Times* began in the late 1970s to run upbeat stories that cultivated and built on the imagery of the Great White Way. For example, in late 1978 it proclaimed that there was a " 'New' Times

Square Waiting in the Wings;"[109] real-estate values were up, the *Times* reported, as was tourism, with hotel occupancy and Broadway theater attendance at record high levels. There was, the *Times* claimed, an "ongoing resurgence" in the area driven by a "spate of individual development efforts." A few months later, an article in the *Times* announced that owners in the area were "finding new productive uses for Midtown properties" that were improving the atmosphere for further office development.[110] (The *Daily News*, with its headquarters on East Forty-second Street, also chronicled the many positive signs in an article with the showy title "East Side, West Side, 42nd Street Is Story."[111])

The *Times*'s respected architecture critic Ada Louise Huxtable pointed out that, in purely physical terms, Forty-second Street was "a fabulous street . . . with a magnificent assortment of superior structures and spaces, and what would ordinarily be considered an ideal urban mix."[112] She acknowledged that the block between Seventh and Eighth Avenues was "incredibly undervalued," but reminded readers that it still contained "a nearly continuous row of some of the world's most beautiful theaters built in the first decades of this century when Broadway was in its finest flower." Shortly thereafter, Paul Goldberger hailed "a new plan for West 42nd Street," called Cityscape, to which, he mentioned, the New York Times Company was contributing money for further planning.[113] By that summer, the "restoration of Times Square [was] moving closer to reality," and the *Times* boldly predicted that "1979 could be the turn-around year for the Great White Way."[114] And in early 1980, the *Times* introduced its readers to the "new Hell's Kitchen" beginning to thrive just west of Times Square.[115]

The *Times* consistently maintained high-profile coverage for the prospect of Times Square redevelopment. In December 1981, a lengthy article in the *New York Times Magazine* was devoted to serious consideration of a once unthinkable question: "A Times Square Revival?"[116] Several months later, the cover story of the Sunday "Metro" section asked, "Can 42d Street Regain Its Showbiz Glamour?"[117] The article began with an affirmative reply: "If all goes as planned, 42nd Street will be the glittering thoroughfare of marquees and restaurants it was in the early 1900s." The *Daily News* affirmed this prognosis. In "A Look at the Sunny Side of Times Square," the paper claimed that Times Square might again return to its "glory years" after serving for years as a symbol of "squalor and sleaze" and "the decline and fall" of urban America.[118]

Both the *Times* and the *Daily News* played important roles in defining the cultural politics of the redevelopment plan. This involved counterpoising articles about crime and decadence with a new type of story that evoked an image of the area in its "glory years" as the Great White Way. In this way, the stakes of the project were made clear. Times Square could remain "a breeding ground for prostitutes, pornographers, and drug pushers"—as the *Times* characterized it[119]—or could become the "glittering thoroughfare" of the Great White Way (sanitized of its crime and prostitution). Especially for the more affluent and educated readers of the *Times,* this choice represented no dilemma at all.

The *Times*'s role, however, went beyond simply defining a cultural-political agenda. When it mattered most, at crucial moments, the newspaper came through with an editorial strategy aimed at pressuring city officials into supporting the redevelopment of Times Square. In early 1980, when The City at 42nd Street was awaiting city approval, a *Times* editorial—"Times Square Stirs While Planning Sleeps"—took the city to task for being "inexplicably idle" as opportunities arose for Times Square redevelopment.[120] The editorial declared that "there is no shortage of plans or sponsors; what is missing is appropriate city action." The *Times* set forth its challenge: "The next move is up to the city and it is long overdue."

In June 1980, after Koch refused to support The City at 42nd Street, the *Times* ran an editorial lamenting the "painful, unpleasant lessons to be learned" from the failed redevelopment effort.[121] Specifically, it complained that "routine city planning broke down;" as a result, the city risked the "charge that developers can't do business in New York," certainly an accusation that no American city can afford. The editorial chastised the city for inexcusably "allowing sponsors [of The City at 42nd Street] to push their hopes and campaign so far." The *Times*'s parent company was, after all, one of those sponsors. To conclude, the *Times* offered some tempered hope that the city would atone for its failure by providing new life and direction for the redevelopment of Times Square. An editorial several weeks later again warned the city that empty gestures alone, such as the statement of intent by city and the state officials to redevelop Times Square, would not suffice.[122] The editorial even alerted city planners that they were now "on trial," and their performance in devising a new plan would be monitored and evaluated carefully. It did, however, conclude by grudgingly conceding that the apparent commitment to action represented "a good start."

Gradually, the *Times*'s editorial board overcame its disappointment about the failed City at 42nd Street plan and returned to optimistic support for the city–state proposal. In July 1980, it recognized that New Yorkers were understandably skeptical of the city's commitment to Times Square redevelopment, particularly after it gave such an impression of stalling on The City at 42nd Street.[123] The *Times* noted that members of the group pushing the project complained "with some justice" that they had been encouraged to proceed and then had been snubbed by the city. But the article granted, "It can now be seen, however, that the city does want to move with deliberate speed." Again, the *Times* laid down its public challenge to city officials, announcing that "the time has come for leadership to strike up the band." By the following summer, when the city had demonstrated its commitment to proceed with Times Square redevelopment, the *Times* became a cheerleader, chanting "seize the time for Times Square."[124] The editorial called the design guidelines of the 42nd Street Development Project "excellent" and argued that they demonstrated the "value of public leadership in development." It even went so far as to declare the plan superior to earlier private proposals, such as The City at 42nd Street. Apparently, city planners had passed their test and earned the *Times*'s seal of approval. When Koch threatened to terminate the city–state pact in 1983 because of a disagreement over the designation of developers and George Klein's role in the project, the *Times* counseled that "it would be in everyone's best interest for both parents to cooperate."[125]

The *Times* stepped in again with a timely editorial in the late 1980s when support for the publicly sponsored project seemed to be foundering as a result of lengthy delays and lingering aesthetic objections. At that time, the newspaper's reporting had to acknowledge that the withdrawal of the prime tenant for the project, Chemical Bank, was a "major blow."[126] Meanwhile, its own architecture critics continued to blast the project's aesthetics; indeed, they posed a continual challenge to the otherwise consistent message of support in the paper's articles and editorials. Still, the *Times*'s editorial board jumped in to rally support for the plan by offering "five reasons to transform 42nd Street."[127] All the reasons focused on the public, rather than private, benefits of the project. Specifically, the editorial emphasized that the project would "disinfect the 'Dangerous Deuce,' " reclaim the "magnificent theaters," upgrade the "seedy" subway station, generate millions of dollars in revenues for the city, and "conquer . . . [the] sour obstructionism" that had come to "strangle visions and stifle growth in New York City." The massive office construction was mentioned only in passing, as a source of funding for the vast public improvements. Most important, however, the *Times* reminded its readers that "the Great White Way dazzles . . . [and] that's what Times Square could look like."

Nor was the *Times* editorial board above using heavy-handed and moralistic appeals. Other editorials ordered critics to "Get Out of the Way on Times Square" and, with a missionary's zeal, confronted doubters with a choice: "Born Again or Porn Again."[128]

In hindsight, it is apparent that the *New York Times* applied direct public pressure on city officials at several critical junctures when it seemed that the efforts to redevelop Times Square might fail. Arguably, the opinion-making powers of the *Times* are a factor that cannot be taken lightly by astute politicians. The political endorsements of the *Times,* a respected news source for better-educated New Yorkers, carry a special value for most candidates. While it is difficult to prove the assertion that elected officials are reluctant to defy the *Times* on its most prized agenda items, and thus risk its editorial disfavor, there is anecdotal evidence to support this claim.

For example, in 1988, when the redevelopment project had cleared most of the legal and political hurdles it had to face, one important obstacle remained. It had to receive the unanimous approval of an obscure three-member fiscal review panel, the state's Public Authorities Control Board (PACB).[129] The newest member of the PACB was state assemblyman Mark Siegal of Manhattan, who had long been a vocal opponent of the Times Square project. Despite his previous objections, Siegal opted for a narrow reading of his authority—allowing him to scrutinize only the financial risk to the public—and cast his decisive vote in favor of the plan.

While many factors might explain such an about-face, it is in general politically easier to oppose a popular plan than to kill it. This is especially true if the proposal is backed by powerful vested interests. Predicting Siegal's favorable vote in advance, the *Village Voice* commented:

> Undoubtedly Siegal . . . recognizes that his vote against this project would earn for him the eternal editorial damnation of the *New York Times,* an unofficial chief sponsor of the project. For the *Times,* the project that bears its name is a long-awaited upgrading, at public expense, of the newspaper's own nest. Siegal would have to look no further than the *Times*'s editorial treatment of his colleagues [City Councilwoman Ruth] Messinger and [State Senator Franz] Leichter to get an object lesson on what would likely happen to him if he sank it.[130]

Again, this evidence is necessarily anecdotal. However, it is certainly credible that public officials will alter their behavior in important respects to maintain or win the favor of a powerful opinion maker such as the *New York Times.*

THE DEBATE OVER CULTURAL REDEFINITION

A preservation- and arts-based cultural strategy supported by, among others, the Municipal Art Society and the *New York Times,* became an important component of the economic revaluing of Forty-second Street and Times Square. But the two agendas, conventional economic development and high culture, were often at odds, pitting private real-estate developers against arts-oriented civic groups.

It is important to remember that, at heart, the 42nd Street Development Project was essentially for massive office construction. In terms of square footage, development costs, profits, jobs, or any other measure, the historic theaters and the performing arts accounted for a tiny fraction of the entire project. In the public representation, however, these elements were elevated to being the plan's principal focus, as a means of culturally redefining a dangerous and depraved area. The towers were justified on the grounds that they made the cultural project possible, by providing funds for theater preservation and other public improvements, and they concentrated office workers in the area in order to reclaim the turf from a dangerous minority street culture.

Even though they were united by the goal of taking back Times Square, the arts and development interests disagreed about the degree of commitment to the cultural revitalization that was the symbolic focus of the project. A particularly illustrative example of the division between arts groups and developers involved the design for the four office towers. The guidelines prepared by the firm of Cooper Eckstut for the project set forth detailed requirements governing the design of the towers. According to William Taylor, "What was most striking about these guidelines . . . was their recognition and evocation of the city's past."[131] Taylor argued that, by maintaining the "five-story building wall" along Forty-second Street, the guidelines emphasized a "horizontal monumentalism" associated with a civic and public purpose. Conversely, by keeping them back from the street wall, they deemphasized the vertical towers, which symbolized the power of corporate capitalism. In sum, the guidelines "made a strong statement for public values" over private ones.[132]

The UDC insisted that the guidelines were absolutely binding on the developers. When the actual designs were made public, however, in December 1983, it was apparent that they violated the guidelines in important respects. The primary discrepancy concerned the bulk of the buildings. The guidelines had called for frequent setbacks in the facades of taller but less massive towers. The planners were especially concerned about alleviating the impression of bulkiness, since these buildings would vastly exceed the densities normally permitted in the zoning laws; indeed, one tower would be more than double the density allowed under the special zoning incentives for west midtown development. Still, after months of wrangling, the UDC had given in to the wishes of George Klein on this issue.[133] Klein had argued that the smaller floors called for in the guidelines would make it difficult to lease them to corporate tenants, which wanted large contiguous floor spaces. According to the benevolent *Times,* the UDC may have conceded to Klein because of his impressive track record in development and his reputation as an architecturally conscious developer. In any case, the new towers would be among the bulkiest in the city. To cap it off, Klein's model also depicted an empty plaza in the place of the Times Tower, indicating his intention to demolish that structure despite the specific requirement that it be preserved.

Equally troublesome was the appearance of the skyscrapers, whose design sparked a protracted debate over the proper aesthetic for a rebuilt Times Square. At issue was the precise nature of the cultural redefinition of the area. The towers were designed by celebrity architects John Burgee and Philip Johnson. Johnson, in particular, has been among the most influential architects in the United States— first as a force in urban modernism, and then in postmodernism—since his emigration from Europe decades ago. Yet the design for the towers, providing for granite and limestone facades and European-style mansard roofs, reflected a return to a staid classical style of historical architecture. The design also disregarded the requirement that Broadway-style signage be incorporated into the facades. Johnson characterized the design as "similar in scope and symbolic significance to Rockefeller Center."[134] Contrary to the intentions of the design guidelines, the towers conveyed an impression of somber monuments to corporate power.

A variety of civic and professional organizations concerned with historic preservation, the arts, and urban design—including the Municipal Art Society— were strongly opposed to the bulk and design of the towers as an aesthetic betrayal of their vision for the new Times Square as a fashionably "honky-tonk" entertainment district. The opinions of these arts and culture organizations were especially important because they resonated with a more educated and affluent population that was important to Koch's pro-growth coalition.

Despite the ongoing effort of the *Times'* to mobilize support for the project, its architecture critics shared the objections to the design that were voiced by the rest of the arts community. Paul Goldberger initially offered rather muted criticism.[135] While he conceded that mansard roofs above Times Square "cannot but seem bizarre," he argued that the historical elements worked well and that the roofs would give a "lively profile" to the city's skyline. As he presented it, the architecture of Times Square had historically combined the "playful" and the "monumental," and he was perhaps alone among informed observers in considering the buildings compatible with a "glittery world of marquees and neon." Goldberger's reaction to the proposed demolition of the Times Tower was also surprisingly acquiescent; he argued that there was "little sense" in retaining it, since its historical significance had been lost with the recladding of the facade in 1966. His most serious criticism was still guardedly phrased: "It is difficult not to be concerned about the enormous size of these office towers particularly since their physical bulk violates [the] set of design guidelines."

Over subsequent years, however, Goldberger's appraisal became more and more harsh. While he accepted the public justification for the project—that the office towers, the mart, and the hotel were needed to fund the restoration of the "splendid stock of turn-of-the-century theaters"—he lamented that this purpose had been betrayed.[136] He complained that "everything about the design suggests that the priorities of real estate developers, and not the public, were put first." He described the design of the towers as something that came from a "cookie cutter" and argued that their "immense mass could not be worse" for the cityscape. As he saw it, even requiring the addition of lighted signs was irrelevant, since "lively lights on dull behemoths" would not solve the problem.

Ada Louise Huxtable voiced similar aesthetic objections with her ruthless criticism of the design and the planners who tolerated it.[137] She described the original design as "a set of mansard-roofed towers of blockbuster proportions, dubious historical antecedents, and consummate zoning overkill." She blasted the "failure of government" reflected in the sacrifice of the design guidelines to the interests of private developers.

Even the Committee to Reclaim Times Square, led by the Brandt and Durst Organizations, attempted to capitalize on this aesthetic debate as a way of derailing the project. In 1989, the group presented the results of a survey showing that four of five architects thought the project should go back to the drawing board.[138] But the local chapter of the American Institute of Architects, whose mailing list had been used for the poll, challenged the results as biased, claiming that the limited responses may not have actually come from New York City architects.

In this particular conflict, the development interests prevailed, and the towers were approved despite their violation of the design guidelines. Their mass and style were a visible testament to the dominance of corporate interests in the coalition supporting Times Square redevelopment. But as the project dragged on under the weight of lengthy delays, public enthusiasm began to wane while aesthetic objections mounted. Quietly, the architects were sent back to the drawing board. In the summer of 1989, the planners unexpectedly released a new set of designs for the office towers. In place of granite and limestone were glass and neon, with electric signs extending as much as twenty-seven stories in height; in place of the "authoritarian mansard roofs" was "a series of goofball asymmetries, angled roofs, turrets, fissures, and colored glass";[139] in place of an empty plaza was the revived Times Tower. In the *Times,* Goldberger described the new towers (each with a different design) as "brash, colorful buildings full of signs and lights and mirrors and jarring angles."[140] In defending the new designs, Koch quickly became a vocal proponent of the "importance of maintaining the vibrant spirit of Times Square" and keeping its honky-tonk character alive.[141]

Johnson, who had acted as consultant to Burgee on the new designs, maintained that the design was changed in response to the "revolution in architecture" that had occurred during the previous six years.[142] Apparently, postmodernism was out and "new modernism" was in. Critics, however, remained skeptical. Their main objection had always focused on the overwhelming bulk of the towers, which the new design failed to remedy. Consequently, Goldberger argued that, in spite of the laudable effort to create an entertainment aesthetic for Times Square, the new designs contained "merely token changes."[143] In general, the effort represented "less an architectural event than a marketing one" in face of a need to generate support for the project. For Goldberger, the dire prognosis for Times Square still called for "an office district with some theaters appended to it."

Huxtable was even more critical of the new plan, deriding it as nothing less than a "farce."[144] She argued that the new "Times Square look" of the towers was irrelevant; the abuses of zoning had simply been subsumed into a "ludicrous debate about a 'suitable style.'" The complex social and economic network that defined Times Square could not simply be pasted, like a veneer, onto an office district. In a biting summary, she declared that "this is not architecture at all. It is cosmetic window dressing."

The debate over the aesthetics of the office towers reveals the jockeying between the cultural and economic agendas of the project and the respective groups pursuing them. The development interests were able to impose their vision of a corporate office center, despite vocal opposition from arts and urban design groups. Yet when support for the project was waning, planners and developers returned to a cultural strategy to rally support. Without a willingness to concede on the bulk of the buildings, however, they were unable to ignite significant enthusiasm.

This case illustrates the role of cultural production as a basis for political exchanges in contemporary urban development. Preservation and the arts underlie a cultural politics that can generate public support for, or at least diffuse opposition to development, especially among higher-income residents. Therefore, arts and preservation groups can be united with development interests in the creation of a pro-growth coalition. In creating such an alliance, cultural organizations gain some leverage that enables them to pose a limited challenge to development interests. Thus cultural production engenders both support for and conflict in development. And, ultimately, it was a series of political accommodations that accounted for the nature of the 42nd Street Development Project.

5
Public Voices and Pro-Growth Politics

The plan represents a new model for urban development, one that leverages the rich and proud heritage of the Times Square area to motivate public action and private investment.
—New York City Regional Business Council (1984)

By the mid-1980s, Edward Koch was at the pinnacle of his reign as mayor of New York City.[1] First elected in 1977, Koch had so solidified his electoral and governing coalitions that he seemed unbeatable. On the electoral side, he had built a solid base of support among the city's middle-class white ethnic voters; at the same time, he was able to draw sizable support from among the city's diverse African-American and Latino populations. In terms of governing, Koch, whose roots were in the city's Democratic reform movement, reached an accommodation with the regular Democratic organizations that made him an extremely powerful mayor. By pursuing an aggressive pro-growth agenda that promoted the postindustrial transformation of New York, particularly Manhattan, Koch enjoyed enthusiastic support from elites in the business community. These relationships paid off in the form of millions of dollars in campaign contributions and generous treatment in the editorial pages of the city's leading newspapers.

Yet, in some important respects, the conservative coalition that backed Koch was an anomaly for its era in ways that would seemingly render it highly vulnerable. By the 1980s, the postindustrial transformation of large American cities worked against the white ethnic alliances that historically dominated city governments. The changes taking place in most large cities since before mid-century involved the loss of white ethnic residents and the growth of African-American and Latino populations. In those cities that were most successful in establishing an advanced service economy, there was also an increase in the number of white professionals who occupied positions in the upper tier of the polarized labor pool. These demographic shifts provided the raw material for African-Americans and Latinos to topple the traditional urban regimes constructed on alliances of white ethnics. In the late 1970s and the 1980s, African-Americans and Latinos were elected as mayors of many major cities by building successful coalitions of people of color and liberal whites, especially highly educated and affluent professionals.[2]

New York City was seemingly ripe for this type of political succession in the 1980s.[3] The postindustrial transformation of the city was far advanced; New York had matured into a "global city" that served as a center for international finance and corporate headquarters.[4] In the process, the city was transformed "from a relatively well off, white, blue-collar city into a more economically divided, multiracial, white-collar city."[5] The white population as a percentage of the city total declined from nearly two-thirds in 1970 to less than one-half in 1990. Non-Latino whites still remained a bare majority of the electorate into the 1990s, but it was age and citizenship status, not political apathy, that depressed participation among people of color.[6] In fact, African-Americans and Latinos had long histories of political mobilization and electoral accomplishments in New York City.[7] Moreover, these groups had potential allies in the city's large population of white liberals, especially among the politically influential Jewish community. Thus essential ingredients were present in New York City to facilitate the emergence of a dominant liberal coalition during the Koch era.

As early as the 1960s, it had appeared that such a coalition might take hold when the liberal white Republican John Lindsay was elected mayor with the support of African-Americans, Latinos, and white liberals. Lindsay's coalition did not, however, survive the racial tensions stirred up during the 1960s, and the fiscal crisis of the mid-1970s further eroded the basis for such a liberal alliance. Ed Koch then capitalized on the conservative backlash of the mid-1970s by embracing a pro-business agenda and appealing to racial fear and resentment among whites. But in the 1980s, the fallout from the crisis waned, and the city's minority populations grew; thus Koch's strategy seemed increasingly vulnerable. His implicitly racist appeals and harsh public exchanges with African-American leaders threatened to mobilize opposition not only from people of color, but also from white liberals. His pro-growth orientation and commitment to postindustrial restructuring also carried political risks: economic restructuring undermined the employment prospects of many African-Americans and Latinos who lacked advanced skills and education; gentrification drove up rents throughout the city; and office development threatened the livability of the upscale neighborhoods that housed white professionals.

Mayor Koch was defeated in 1989 when Manhattan Borough President David N. Dinkins finally succeeded in unifying an electoral coalition of African-Americans, Latinos, and white liberals to become the city's first African-American mayor. But Koch's durability as mayor of New York City for twelve years is testimony to his political savvy. Koch was remarkably effective in undermining a viable liberal challenge by siphoning off support from people of color and white liberals.[8] He cultivated ties with the city's regular Democratic organizations, thereby co-opting the support of African-American and Latino elected officials who could turn out votes from their communities. His conservative appeals won him significant backing from Latino and Jewish voters who otherwise might have joined with African-Americans on the basis of shared interests.[9] And Koch's fiscal conservatism and pro-business orientation—along with his background in the city's reform movement—also provided common ground with white professionals who held more liberal attitudes on social issues and race relations.

The effort to redevelop Times Square bears the unmistakable imprint of Mayor Koch's political strategy.[10] The 42nd Street Development Project, which Koch sponsored, served the political needs of his electoral and governing coalitions in a number of ways. Most obviously, the project promoted the interests of real-estate investors and developers by securing west Midtown as a focal point for postindustrial economic restructuring. At the same time, the project enhanced Koch's image as an entrepreneurial mayor who effectively tended to the economic health of the city by attracting investment that would create jobs and generate additional tax revenues. The ability to finally clean up Times Square would also serve the mayor's tough talk on maintaining law and order and making the city safe, once again, for the middle class.

The redevelopment plan worked on a more symbolic level, too, by sustaining a political discourse that helped secure Koch's pro-growth regime. Times Square was a symbolic focal point for anxieties among whites about racial transition in the city. As Robert Beauregard has demonstrated, the issue of urban decline is especially resonant among the dominant white population because of its synergy with issues of race and culture.[11] In the transition from the Great White Way to the Dangerous Deuce, whites saw the decline of their civilization and its subordination to an alien culture that threatened to displace them from the central areas of the city. Thus Times Square redevelopment fit well into Koch's strategy of playing on racial fears to consolidate a base of support among white voters. The African-Americans and Latinos who were a visible presence in Times Square—many of whom were middle class—provided the material for a constructed political enemy that could be defeated only through redevelopment. In much the same way, Koch had evoked the racist image of "poverty pimps" to legitimize the dismantling of social programs.

A particularly important political function of the Times Square plan was to generate support from white professionals. Because whites were a majority of the electorate, racially polarized voting worked to Koch's benefit. His greatest political danger, however, was that liberal whites would ally with African-Americans and Latinos to create an electoral majority, as they had done in other cities. Thus white liberals were the crucial swing bloc of voters in an electorate closely divided between white ethnics and people of color. Generally, it was whites with higher levels of education and income who were more likely to hold liberal attitudes, and this group included the white professionals of the postindustrial workforce. They had an ambivalent relationship to urban redevelopment: on the one hand, many were employed, housed, and entertained in the redeveloped areas of the city, especially in Manhattan; on the other hand, as residents, many were concerned about the impact of large-scale development on the livability of their inner-city neighborhoods. Indeed, opposition from white professionals defending historic neighborhoods and buildings had contributed to the demise of large-scale urban renewal by the 1970s. An ongoing concern for Mayor Koch, then, was preventing the defection of higher-income whites to a liberal coalition that would challenge his pro-growth regime.

The 42nd Street Development Project, with its focus on the preservation of the historic theaters and their use as Broadway stages, appealed to the cultural values of these white professionals. In effect, the return of the Great White Way promised a safe area of cultural resources that would contribute to the livability of the city. In this way, the discourse underlying Times Square redevelopment played on issues of race and culture to draw higher-income whites into the pro-growth alliance supporting the project and thereby pull them into Koch's pro-growth regime.

The Board of Estimate vote granting final political approval for the 42nd Street Development Project in 1984 was the central political event in the effort to redevelop Forty-second Street and Times Square. By the time the actual moment arrived the outcome of the BoE vote was a foregone conclusion. But the voices of supporters who testified at the public hearings that preceded the BoE vote illustrate the importance of political discourse as a unifying force in the pro-growth alliance. The hearings also provided one of the few public forums in which opposing voices could be heard exposing the fissures in the dominant discourse on Times Square. The public hearings reveal the links between political discourse, cultural politics, and political coalition-building.

THE POLITICAL INTERESTS AT THE PUBLIC HEARINGS

The success of the 42nd Street Development Project depended on legislative approval from the New York City Board of Estimate (BoE), which had primary authority over land-use decisions at the time.[12] Because the New York State Urban Development Corporation was sponsoring the plan, it was able to circumvent the usual checkpoints of the political process in the city; however, the BoE had to endorse the contracts that had been negotiated with the project's developers. The BoE was made up of three citywide officials—the mayor, the city council president, and the comptroller—with two votes each, and the five borough presidents with one vote each. The BoE held a public hearing on the project in October 1984, and then heard additional testimony at a second meeting in November. These were dramatic events that featured appearances by the state's top political figures and attracted raucous crowds. In the wee morning hours of November 9, 1984, after the second long day of testimony, the project was approved by a unanimous vote.

During the course of the hearings, nearly 300 witnesses registered their positions on the project (some 200 of whom provided spoken statements), with supporters outnumbering opponents by a margin of two to one.[13] The accompanying table provides a breakdown of all the witnesses who appeared to support or oppose the 42nd Street Development Project according to their interest affiliations (this includes those who testified and those who registered a position only, without providing oral testimony). This breakdown provides useful insight into the political contest over West Forty-second Street.

The table reveals a core triad of interests at the heart of the pro-growth alliance. Two of the three groups are traditional mainstays of the urban growth machine described by John Logan and Harvey Molotch: the business community and public officials.[14] But the third group was only just emerging as a primary participant in urban growth politics:[15] a collection of civic, professional, and business organizations concerned with historic preservation, the arts, and urban design. Additional support came from a unanimous construction industry, from a variety of social service organizations, and from religious leaders with congregations in the area.

Opposition to the project was centered around an antigrowth community coalition made up of residents of the adjacent Clinton neighborhood and their local political representatives, together with a collection of business and property owners from the project area who were facing condemnation and displacement. By examining the public positions of the various active interest groups, it is possible to develop a clearer understanding of the political strategy that supported the progrowth alliance.

The Business Community

In terms of sheer numbers alone, the business community formed the primary component of the pro-growth alliance. Some fifty witnesses registered in support of the project, almost three-quarters of whom spoke on its behalf. Within this group

Witnesses at Board of Estimate hearings, by interest classification and position

Interest Classification	Support N (%)	Oppose N (%)	Total N (%)
Business community	53 (18.2)	10 (3.4)	63 (21.6)
Public sector	28 (9.6)	13 (4.5)	41 (14.1)
Culture community	34 (11.7)	7 (2.4)	41 (14.1)
Construction industry	21 (7.2)	0 (0.0)	21 (7.2)
Social service sector	12 (4.1)	0 (0.0)	12 (4.1)
Religious sector	9 (3.1)	3 (1.0)	12 (4.1)
Clinton neighborhood	1 (0.3)	41 (14.1)	42 (14.4)
Housing/tenant/ neighborhood associations	1 (0.3)	6 (2.1)	7 (2.4)
Local institutions	1 (0.3)	1 (0.3)	2 (0.6)
Unknown/self	27 (9.3)	23 (7.9)	50 (17.2)
Total	187 (64.3)	104 (35.7)	291 (100.0)

Note: Representatives of the Broadway theater organizations designated to develop and operate theater sites in the Forty-second Street project were classified under business community rather than culture community. It was not possible to classify seven witnesses in terms of support or opposition; therefore, they were not included in this table. Percentages may not total due to rounding.

were three broad categories of business representatives. The largest included the designated developers of the Forty-second Street project sites and their professional consultants, such as architects and economists; together, they constituted the development team. Among the project developers was George Klein, the politically well-connected president of Park Tower Realty who had been chosen to build the four office towers; Trammel Crow, the nation's foremost developer of merchandise marts—described by a fellow developer at the hearings as "one of the greatest figures in the 20th Century in the development business"—who had been designated to operate the mart on Eighth Avenue; and Jerry Speyer of the prominent development firm Tishman-Speyer, which had been selected to build the mart. Representatives of the Nederlander and Jujamcyn organizations, prominent owners and operators of Broadway theaters that had been contracted to develop and operate theater sites, also appeared; so did representatives of Housing Innovations/Planning Innovations, a minority-owned firm from Boston that had been chosen as part of a consortium to build and run the hotel. Celebrity architects Philip Johnson and John Burgee also turned out to support the project and defend their much-maligned design for the monumental office towers.

In their brief public statements, the project developers stressed their enthusiasm about being part of a tremendous redevelopment effort that would lead to the social and economic revitalization of a tarnished Times Square.[16] Citing the millions of square feet of space he had created in merchandise marts in Dallas and elsewhere around the globe, Trammel Crow announced: "I will be more proud of [the Times Square project] than anything I've done." A partner in the hotel development compared the project with Rockefeller Center and the World Trade Center in terms of the positive impact it would have. Those involved in the theater restorations hailed the project as a "symbol of preservationism" that would "bring back the grandeur, the illusion if you will, and the mystique of Broadway . . . as it was known 50 years before." Philip Johnson proclaimed his own preservationist credentials as one who had fought to save Penn Station and Grand Central Terminal; consequently, he would have "no trouble keeping Times Square alive." John Burgee reassured the culture community that "it is not our intention to make [Times Square] so gentrified that it doesn't maintain some of that nostalgic character that everyone talks about, the Great White Way."

The second category of witnesses from the business community included a miscellaneous collection of individual business and real-estate owners and representatives of large corporations. For the most part, the owners who supported the project had a property or business located in the neighborhoods surrounding the project area and, therefore, stood to gain considerably from an increase in property values and upscale uses. Corporate representatives from Xerox and AT&T voiced their great enthusiasm for the potential of a high-tech trade mart where they could exhibit and market new computer technologies. Although representatives from a number of major financial institutions also appeared in support, none gave oral testimony specifying the basis of their position.

The third category of business support came from business and real-estate trade associations. The associations were organized on a variety of levels, from local groups representing businesses on Eighth Avenue, Ninth Avenue, and Forty-second Street, to state and regional business and real-estate associations. Considering the sheer number of businesses represented by these groups, it is possible to get a sense of the vast economic interests at stake. For example, the president of the Real Estate Board of New York, which had more than 5,200 members, emphasized that "rarely is there an issue [like the Forty-second Street project] that the membership can unanimously endorse. . . . [I]t is a first for the real estate industry, who have varied concepts of how development should be, to be supportive of one concept like this."

The associations and the interested businesspeople who appeared emphasized the economic benefits of the project—including the creation of jobs and tax revenues for the city and the growth of commercial real estate—and expressed their firm convictions that development would also lead to an improvement in the social conditions in and around the area. Thus the statements from the business community as a whole adhered closely to the planning philosophy articulated in the environmental-impact statement for the project, which held that because of the severity of the social problems in the Times Square area only massive economic redevelopment would succeed in effecting a positive transformation.[17]

A relatively small segment of the business community voiced opposition to the project. The opponents were owners of properties in the immediate project area who faced the condemnation and acquisition of their holdings for less than their full economic potential, as they saw it, and business owners who feared relocation without any assurance of adequate assistance.[18] As one local businessman noted, "[T]he project area is not restricted to the pornographic, to the movie-sex kind of businesses which the public relations people had led you to believe. [Other businesses] are going to be affected by the condemnation. They are going to be forced out." A property owner, bitter over the state's use of eminent domain, questioned why the developers did not "do it the American way . . . as most real estate deals are made, by going out and acquiring the property in the marketplace rather than utilizing the force of law." Proprietors of smaller businesses were concerned that commercial gentrification in Times Square would result in large increases in commercial rents because of rising property values and taxes and thus would force them to relocate. Nevertheless, the overwhelming sentiment of the business community, including some of the most powerful developers and corporations in the city, was solidly in support of the project.

The Public Sector

More than forty witnesses from the public sector at the BoE hearings held a public position on the 42nd Street Development Project from one side or the other. They included elected officials, from members of the City Council to a United States senator, and appointed officials, from the chairman of the New York City Public Development Corporation (PDC) to members of community boards. The most prominent elected officials in the city and state drew on the discourse of Times Square to marshal public support for the project. Mayor Koch hailed the plan to "restore the Crossroads of the World" because it would create jobs, restore theaters, and improve the subway station—all for a trifling public investment. Governor Mario Cuomo made an appearance—highly unusual, both because of the historical rarity of an appearance by a governor at a BoE hearing and because of the personal rivalry between the governor and the mayor stemming from two recent election contests—to laud one of the greatest redevelopment efforts in the history of the nation. In the eloquent words of the governor, the project would "clean away blight, and replace it with scintillating beauty . . . [and] wipe away pornography, and replace it with progress and an entertainment and culture our society can be proud of." Senator Daniel Patrick Moynihan, who was raised on the tough streets of Hell's Kitchen, lamented the fact that he had required an escort of four police officers to tour Times Square the previous day. Even two former mayors, Abraham Beame and Robert Wagner, Sr., were summoned to support the cause.

From the unanimous BoE vote, it is clear that the two other citywide officeholders, the comptroller and the city council president, also supported the project, as did the five borough presidents, even though none of them were registered as witnesses. If these seven members of the BoE are added to the numbers in the table, the overwhelming predominance of support from public officials is even more evident.

In addition, appointed officials—with the exception of community board members and district leaders with more local, representative roles—heavily favored the project. Some of them appeared on behalf of state and city planning and economic development agencies with narrow objectives and no direct representative role. Others testified on behalf of the Metropolitan Transportation Authority, the New York City Transit Authority, the Department of Housing, Preservation and Development, the Mayor's Office of Midtown Enforcement, and the New York Police Department. Each of these officials reiterated relevant aspects of the Times Square discourse and planning philosophy that formed the heart of the UDC's environmental-impact statement. For example, the director of the Mayor's Office of Midtown Enforcement declared that "42nd Street represents a unique combination of physical and social characteristics that foster criminal and anti-social behavior," creating "an environment that is now difficult if not impossible to control." He described a nightmarish urban street scene where

> drug pushers peddle their wares in broad daylight, attempting to force their goods on innocent bystanders and harassing them if they refuse to make a purchase. Groups of restless loiterers congregate under the marquees and on the street corners obstructing and menacing pedestrians. Derelicts high on drugs and cheap liquor sprawl across the pavement and wander aimlessly into the

streets, snarling traffic. Teenagers desperately in search of shelter and food become victims of prostitution and drugs.

According to the planning philosophy, it followed, then, that the magnitude of the social and physical problems required comprehensive state-sponsored intervention. The density of the office development was declared to be the minimum necessary to cover the cost of public improvements in the form of a restored theater district and a renovated subway station. Moreover, the displaced social pathologies of the area would not be replicated anywhere else because the social and physical environment of Times Square was unique. Clearly, an extensive city and state bureaucratic machinery was mobilized in support of the project and was well versed in the political discourse that served as its rationale.

While two-thirds of the public officials supported the plan, more than a dozen witnesses from the public sector opposed it. The opposition came primarily from the most local-level officials, with the smallest districts, who were inherently part of the community coalition that opposed the plan. These community representatives included members of the City Council, members of the New York State Assembly and Senate, and Congressman Ted Weiss, all of whose electoral districts were largely composed of the project area and/or the bordering areas of the Clinton neighborhood, the garment district, the theater district, the midtown office district, and the Upper West Side. Manhattan Community Boards 4 (representing Clinton) and 5 (representing Times Square) also registered opposition to the project, although they expressed some ambivalence given a choice between the proposed plan or no action at all.[19] (One community board member spoke in support of the project despite the official stand of opposition.)

The local representatives sought to chip away at the seductive simplicity of the dominant political discourse—with its narrative of decline and promise of renewal—by interjecting more complex issues into the debate. Their arguments highlighted the negative impacts that the project would have on the surrounding areas. They called attention to the inevitable displacement of lower-income residents and small businesses as a result of gentrification. They voiced concern that the massive project would "snuff out the lights and excitement of Times Square," overwhelm the local subway system, exacerbate problems of traffic congestion and air pollution, and displace pornography and illegal drug activities into the surrounding streets. State Assemblyman Jerrold Nadler even linked the project to larger issues stemming from the postindustrial transformation of New York, such as the replacement of manufacturing jobs with dead-end service-sector jobs for those with limited education and skills. Councilwoman Ruth Messinger summed up the concerns of the local representatives: "We are at risk of making the Great White Way great only for the size of its buildings, and white only for the people who can afford to live and work there."

Despite these efforts to add substance to the public debate, the local representatives were outgunned by more prominent officials who commanded the public's ear. The elected officials who supported the project had larger constituencies that insulated them from the overwhelming opposition of the nearby communities. They were widely recognized public figures with the ability to get their message out. In contrast, the local representatives enjoyed very limited exposure and influence over the public debate. As a result, the public sector overall formed an essential component of the pro-growth alliance. High-level elected officials and prominent technocrats combined to legitimize the redevelopment project.

The Urban Culture Community

While the business community and public officials are typically at the forefront of a pro-growth coalition, the third major group that supported the Forty-second Street project is an unexpected presence among the prominent players in the arena of development politics. This component of the alliance was formed by civic and professional organizations promoting historic preservation, the arts (especially Broadway theater), and urban planning and design. With more than thirty witnesses from this urban culture community registered at the hearings in support of the project, it was outnumbered only by representatives from the business community. This level of mobilization and visibility attests to the importance of the culture community to the pro-growth alliance.

Eleven organizations from the culture community were joined in a group called the Presidents' Council in order to speak out more effectively on planning issues, such as the 42nd Street Development Project.[20] The eleven members of the council were the Municipal Art Society, Architectural League, Cultural Assistance Center, Landmarks Conservancy, Parks Council, Public Art Fund, Regional Plan Association, Women's City Club of New York, and New York chapters of the American Institute of Architects, American Planning Association, and American Society of Landscape Architects. Because the New York City Public Development Corporation and New York State Urban Development Corporation (UDC) were essentially concerned with economic development objectives, the arts and culture organizations took on a leading role as the public's watchdog on aesthetic issues relating to preservation, planning, and design. The New York City Planning Commission (CPC) was officially responsible for evaluating the plans and designs for the Forty-second Street project in terms of public values, but the planning staff was not actively involved in the project.[21] Only Herbert Sturz, chairman of the CPC, was an active participant, but his planning credentials were dubious, and he was better known for his commitment to unfettered real-estate development than for his aesthetic judgment.[22]

In general, the Presidents' Council and its member organizations "subscribe[d] fully to the goals of the program that would eliminate blight, preserve theaters, reconstruct the subway, increase economic development, and complement the surrounding areas of the 42nd Street Development Project." Nevertheless, the representatives of the groups were very critical of certain aspects of the project. They

were distressed by the enormous bulk and somber design of the four office towers, which violated the design guidelines, and they called for tighter legal restrictions on future development above the theaters and on transfers of development
rights from these sites, to prevent even higher density development from occur-
ring later. The culture community was also concerned about inadequate provisions
for the historic theaters. Although the theaters were the symbolic focus of the redevelopment effort, their future remained highly uncertain: the money available for
their restoration was insufficient; the funding for their operation was nonexistent;
and there was no guarantee of their uses if they failed to be economically viable.
The possible demolition of the historic Times Tower was another cause of widespread concern, since the fate of the building that had helped define Times Square
was left up to an advisory council that had not yet been named.

Statements from members of the culture community revealed a gnawing sus-
picion about how "the project aims to eliminate much of the existing character and
replace it with something else." Representatives of a number of the organizations
decried the overall lack of input afforded them in general on planning and design
issues. Their "essential conclusion" was that "the 42nd Street project is an unfin-
ished proposal." They asked that the BoE approve only the general concept of the
plan, declaring that more specific approval should be granted in phases in order to
ensure continued public input and oversight.

Indeed, when the heads of the member organizations of the Presidents' Council testified, they were so critical of certain aspects of the plan, and so insistent that
aesthetic changes be made, that it was difficult to regard their testimony as support for the project. Yet with the exception of the Landmarks Conservancy, all the
members of the Presidents' Council went on record as supporters of the plan they
criticized. Several unaffiliated architects also offered support as design professionals in spite of similar aesthetic criticisms that they made.

On the business side of the arts, the League of Broadway Theaters and Producers as well as individual owners and producers formed a solid bloc of support
from the theater industry, with more than a dozen persons appearing on behalf of
the project. These witnesses supported the plan as a means to eliminate the blight
of the area and displace the threatening subcultures that allegedly deterred fearful
suburbanites from attending Broadway shows. As the chairman of the Shubert
Organization testified, legitimate theaters and the city as a whole "paid the price
for a deteriorated 42nd Street" because of its "notorious image which has inhib-
ited tourism . . . and menaces New York's stellar attraction, the legitimate theater."
There was, however, a notable absence of representation at the hearings from the
actors and stagehands affiliated with Broadway theater; the only speaker from
among these groups, a set designer, opposed the project.

Additional support from the arts community came from representatives of
several other cultural institutions and organizations. For example, Nat Leventhal,
the president of Lincoln Center for the Performing Arts (and a former deputy
mayor in the Koch administration), emphasized the parallel between that project

of high-cultural production—approved by the BoE nearly thirty years earlier, despite the extremely heavy burdens it imposed on the local community[23]—and the Forty-second Street project. He encouraged the BoE members to be equally bold in the face of strong community opposition, since history had proved the value of such culturally attuned development at Lincoln Center and would certainly do so again. He declared that "just as the creative proposal twenty-seven years ago to transfer a blighted West Side neighborhood into the world's foremost performing arts complex launched a renaissance in a large area of Manhattan, so will your proposal of the 42nd Street project in all likelihood have that result today." To encourage the BoE members further, he added: "You may never have a better chance to strike a blow for civilization." Indeed, Leventhal was astute in illuminating the similarities between the two projects: Lincoln Center is perhaps one of the earliest models of a major redevelopment project (still in the traditional urban renewal mode) aimed at redefining space through arts-based cultural production—a model adopted in the Forty-second Street redevelopment plan.

In the end, a group of prominent urban arts and culture organizations and professionals provided a significant bloc of support for the project in spite of some stinging criticism. Although the project did not satisfy the planning and design objectives that many in this group advocated for Times Square, the components of historic preservation and arts production were significant enough to secure its support. It is clear from the unaddressed concerns and the complaints about the lack of input that the urban culture community was a junior partner in the pro-growth alliance; indeed, no other supporter expressed such detailed criticism of the final plan. From another perspective, though, the outspokenness of the culture community reveals an awareness among its members of their political importance to the project.

The Construction Industry

More than twenty witnesses from the construction industry registered and provided rousing support for the 42nd Street Development Project. They included contractors, laborers, and representatives of the unions and building trades associations. The support from this group was unanimous and unequivocal, and, for the most part, it was framed as an openly stated desire for construction jobs. A representative from the carpenters' union laid it on the line: "We candidly declare our self-interest in the construction of this good project . . . which will represent a windfall of jobs to the 10,000 people in the construction industry . . . [a level] not seen since the construction of the World Trade Center." The president of the New York State and New York City Building and Construction Trades Council was equally direct: "The building and construction trades, of course, are selfish in [their] interests in the jobs [the Forty-second Street project] would create for our industry." He noted further that "labor is in full support . . . [and] to keep the peace here [at the hearing], we have another thousand [witnesses] downstairs we asked not to come up." The speaker did make a point of mentioning the broad benefits of the plan as well, including the permanent jobs, tax revenues, and subway station improvements that would accrue to the advantage of the public at large. Indeed, the appeal for jobs was often supplemented with descriptions of Times Square as a "cancer" on the body of the city that had to be removed to restore its economic health.

Yet, as critics from the Clinton neighborhood pointed out, construction jobs could be created as easily through any other type of large-scale construction project sponsored by the state, even low-income housing. The jobs did not depend on the nature of the plan, only on its magnitude. Moreover, residents accused the construction workers of residing outside the city and having little interest in the long-term impact of the project. In any event, the emphasis on jobs suggested that support from the construction industry had little connection to the specifics of the project. Nevertheless, representatives of the industry still drew on the Times Square discourse to legitimize their self-interests.

The Social Service Sector

A dozen witnesses registered in support of the Forty-second Street project on behalf of various social service organizations. Several of them represented job-training or other work programs and based their support on the need for the creation of construction jobs. Roughly half of the social service organizations provided aid to travelers, immigrants, crime victims, and the like, and operated out of offices located in the Times Square area. They were, therefore, closely tied to the tourist industry. The Travelers' Aid Services Program, for example, provides emergency assistance to "stranded travelers and tourists" and thus chose its Times Square location because of "the attraction Times Square has for many tourists" as well as its central location. The testimony of this organization had a certain contradictory quality: the group supported the project because it would reconstruct a dangerous Times Square, yet it served the mass of tourists who were drawn to the area as it was.

Religious Leaders

Religious leaders, most with congregations in and around the Times Square area, provided the moral firepower for the redevelopment plan. As one clergyman presented the issue, the depravity of Times Square surpassed even biblical proportions:

That the present conditions on 42nd Street even came into being and then proliferated is a heinous civic blot that makes Sodom and Gomorrah's offense seem mildly evil. I cannot believe there may be even one caring person who believes that such pervasively corrupting conditions should exist, conditions that consign human life in the Times Square and Clinton communities to such base levels that human beings have no value except as exploitable products, things to be used, bought and sold into a slavery of narcotics, and crime, and slime, and sleaze, in order to gratify the greed of merchants and property owners for whom human dignity is meaningless.

To sit by passively and allow such conditions to persist in Times Square was, in effect, a crime against God and humanity that could not be tolerated. Consequently, a vote for the project represented the only morally correct course of action.

Religious leaders had been at the forefront of moral crusades to clean up Times Square for more than a century, and their voices were prominent among the renewed calls for the redevelopment of the area during the 1970s. Their position of support thus reflected an inevitable choice given only two options: the Forty-second Street project versus no action. They were not evaluating the plan against other possible courses of action aimed at addressing the social conditions of the area. Another clergyman, representing the bishop of the Greek Orthodox Archdiocese, summed up the available alternatives: "If the price we must pay for ridding ourselves of that cesspool on 42nd Street is a line of office towers, I say so be it."

Still, a minority of the religious leaders opposed the plan on the grounds that it would contribute to housing problems and suffering among Clinton residents. For these leaders, including the executive director of Catholic Charities, it was essential to challenge all "public policies that directly or indirectly promote displacement or homelessness."

The Garment Industry

Several owners of garment-manufacturing firms testified in favor of the 42nd Street Development Project. In general, they anticipated benefits from the rejuvenation of the area at the northern boundary of the garment district. But, the Federation of Apparel Manufacturers (FAM)—with 5,500 member firms employing some 150,000 workers—opposed the project, as did the International Ladies' Garment Workers Union (ILGWU). Despite their general support for Times Square redevelopment, both groups expressed grave concerns about the displacement of jobs and businesses that might result from the conversion of manufacturing spaces. As the FAM director put it:

> [W]e are pleased with the prospect that the 42nd Street redevelopment project will bring a needed rebirth to the entire Times Square area. . . . We also wish to caution you as seriously as we can not to consider these benefits at the expense of the New York garment industry and the price we will pay if you were to proceed . . . without first creating indispensable legal instruments that will prevent such a [fashion merchandise] mart from shattering the viability of many in the industry.

The federation argued for expanded protection for the garment district as a condition of approval for the project. Specifically, FAM called for stricter limits on the conversion of manufacturing lofts to other uses and additional restrictions on the apparel-related uses of the merchandise mart. An informal agreement had been reached to convert the mart from primarily fashion to high-tech uses in response to studies, including the UDC's own data, showing its adverse effects on the garment industry. The author of one such study testified that there was no evidence supporting the need for an apparel mart; on the contrary, it would lead to job losses and no increase in buyers for the industry. Manufacturers, therefore, would fully support the project only when extensive protections for the garment industry were made legally binding.

With certain protections, then, this industry was prepared to join the larger business community in enthusiastic support of a project to clean up the nearby eyesore. Until then, they would remain allied in opposition with those local businesses that were most immediately threatened by the project.

Clinton Residents

At the hearings, opposition to the project was concentrated in a virtually unanimous group of some forty residents of the Clinton neighborhood (formerly known as Hell's Kitchen) who registered positions. Many of these opponents identified themselves as members of a loose organization called the Clinton Coalition of Concern, but others did not state an affiliation. All who spoke were vehemently opposed to the project on the grounds that it would lead to further gentrification of the neighborhood and extensive displacement of its low- and moderate-income residents, while providing an unwarranted "give-away" to wealthy developers and large corporations. Residents described the project variously as "a real estate ripoff," "the most outrageous land graft in the history of New York City," "one of the most insane and criminal land grab deals of the world," "voodoo economics . . . on 42nd Street," and the like. For the Clinton residents, the conflict was framed along class lines, and the project worked like traditional urban renewal by displacing the poor for the benefit of the wealthy.

Residents of the neighborhood had been prominent among the chorus of voices calling for the clean up of Times Square in the 1970s. Yet, as those most directly exposed to the area, they actually preferred the status quo to the project being presented for approval. Therefore, sponsors of the plan simply added insult to injury when they defined it as an effort to clean up Times Square for the benefit of neighborhood and city residents. As local residents saw it, those promoting the plan were disingenuous in drawing on negative images of Times Square to mobilize support for a project that masqueraded as a response to the concerns of the Clinton community, but in reality sacrificed their interests to huge real-estate profits. One resident declared, for example, that the project was actually "designed to remove us from our homes under the guise of getting rid of pornography."

Thus Clinton residents were aware, at least implicitly, of the importance of political discourse in mobilizing support for the project, and in their testimony they attempted to expose this aspect of the political spectacle taking place. But they had few allies in this effort, even among nonprofit organizations concerned with the dearth of affordable housing in New York. The director of one such organization joined Clinton residents in opposition, stating that "the proposal . . . will destroy the neighborhood of Clinton as one of the most economically, ethnically and racially diverse, vital and viable communities in our city" by unleashing "speculative forces the likes of which no neighborhood in this city has ever confronted, much less survived." In contrast, the director of another citizens' housing group uncritically reiterated the planning gospel: "We concur that only massive redevelopment, unpopular as it may be, can effectively dislodge the entrenched subculture that dominates this area."

A FURTHER LOOK AT POLITICAL INTERESTS

The survey of the interests represented and expressed at the public hearings on the 42nd Street Development Project provides a useful starting point for considering the nature of the political conflict over Times Square. It pitted a strong pro-growth alliance against a local community coalition with limited organizational resources. The pro-growth alliance centered on a trio of interests: the business community, public officials, and urban arts and culture organizations and enterprises. Each of these groups had a particular political or economic interest that was served by the project as it was specifically formulated: dominant politicians and their appointees would benefit politically from their part in fostering economic growth and reversing urban decay; the business community as a whole would profit from the economic opportunities opened up by the postindustrial transformation of Times Square; and the urban culture community would see the historic resources of Times Square restored. The objections from the culture community indicated, however, that it was a relatively disadvantaged partner in relation to the other two groups.

Additional support came from the construction industry, an assortment of social service organizations, and religious leaders. They formed a secondary layer of auxiliary supporters, since they had less direct interests in the specifics of the project, but were in favor of any plan that would create a large number of construction jobs or attempt to change the social dynamic of the Times Square area. This is evident from the testimony given by these secondary groups, which exhibited little concern for the details of the project (and indicated no direct involvement in their formulation) and focused instead on the importance of simply taking action. In contrast, the testimony from the core pro-growth groups dwelled more on the particular project components important to each respective group.

The considerable criticism of the plan from the culture community, based on aesthetic concerns, reflected the only fundamental line of division among the partners in the pro-growth alliance. The disagreement centered on the way in which, precisely, the new Times Square culture should be constructed. The arts and culture groups largely shared a concern that the project—with its emphasis on four stodgy, hulking office towers and its lack of provisions for the future of the theaters—failed to go far enough in re-creating the culture of a historic theater district. The conflict was one of economics versus aesthetics, and for the culture community the project sacrificed the latter to the former. At the UDC hearings on the environmental-impact statement in the spring of 1984, Brendan Gill, chairman of the Landmarks Conservancy and one of the most vocal opponents from among the Presidents' Council, had expressed the concerns shared by the civic groups:

> We are concerned about losing Times Square as we know it: as a lively and dazzling entrance to the theater district. We have seen no evidence . . . that the addition of four million square feet of conventionally dreary office space is necessary to achieve the stated goal of the project; on the contrary it will drastically affect the character of the area, not for the better but for the worse.[24]

In a sense, through its evocation of the symbolic imagery of the Great White Way, the culture community drew on the political discourse that supported the project to challenge its overemphasis on office construction.

Despite its criticisms, the culture community as a whole remained an important member of the pro-growth alliance because it regarded the preservation of the historic theaters and the construction of new Broadway stages as important accomplishments. These objectives would be difficult to achieve without being linked to the larger development agenda for Times Square. It was strategically important, therefore, that the culture community cultivate and maintain a cooperative working relationship with the dominant political and economic players in Koch's pro-growth regime. At the Municipal Art Society, for example, Fred Papert led the organization to support the Forty-second project despite widely shared aesthetic concerns by arguing that, because the MAS had helped engender the project, a stand in opposition would mark the group as an untrustworthy ally in development efforts.[25]

So although it had grave misgivings, the culture community realized it must join with the pro-growth coalition that was making things happen in Times Square. Indeed, the alliance of development supporters was well organized and powerful. It included some of the most prominent individuals and corporations in the field of commercial real-estate development and the most influential politicians in both New York City and New York State. And by the time of the hearings before the Board of Estimate, these groups were connected by years of negotiations and cooperative planning. Consequently, the pro-growth alliance combined the economic resources and political muscle to make redevelopment possible. Allies in the culture community, too, had cooperated and compromised with this coalition while initiating a redevelopment effort that satisfied their own goals.

Business and political support was, then, a necessary exchange for the project's attention to historic preservation and the arts.

There were, of course, divisions within the business community, within the public sector, and within the arts community about the desirability of the project; however, in each case, the more powerful faction continued to support the plan. Within the business community, only those with the most local investments in the Times Square area (the existing business and property owners) opposed the project, whereas nationally active real-estate developers and corporations, and state and local business associations, joined with major New York developers in supporting the project. Similarly, within the public sector, the divisions of support and opposition were based on district size, with opposition coming from the elected officials and community board members whose districts were smaller than the borough level and centered on the neighborhoods that bordered the project area. But the more powerful elected officials with larger districts, broader constituencies, and greater public visibility overwhelmingly supported the project. A mobilized bureaucracy also worked to promote the development agenda of the most powerful city and state political actors.

The Broadway theater industry was divided as well, although the division is barely discernible from the testimony of witnesses at the BoE hearings. In contrast to the unanimous support among theater operators, only one industry employee, a set designer, spoke against the project, warning that it would transform Times Square into a sort of Houston. But, in fact, the Actors' Equity Association, representing some 35,000 actors and stage managers, and its organizational offshoot dedicated to theater preservation, Save the Theaters, Inc., "jointly withheld approval of the plan."[26] These groups had become bitterly skeptical of city planners and their appreciation for the theater district after the city had allowed the demolition of two historic Broadway theaters, the Helen Hayes and the Morosco, in 1982 to make way for the construction of John Portman's heavily subsidized Times Square Marriott Hotel.[27] In light of other initiatives in the area—including the massive Westway highway project, the convention center, and the new high-density zoning district—it seemed to many in the theater industry that the city was launching a development assault on west Midtown that displayed callous disregard for the viability of the theater district.

To the Broadway employees, the Forty-second Street project failed to recognize the interests of the theater industry in a number of additional ways: by neglecting to designate the theaters on Forty-second Street as landmarks or to provide for their future operation; by failing to protect the many small theater-related businesses in Times Square (costume shops, musical instrument stores, dance studios, rehearsal spaces) from dislocation as a result of rising rents; by threatening to disperse a criminal population into the streets of the theater district; and by imposing an office-tower aesthetic in "near-total ignorance of the area in which [the towers] are to be built."[28] In essence, Actors' Equity and Save the Theaters felt that "although not asked to help develop the policy for the project the theatrical community was invited to ornament it" in an attempt to "legitimize the plan."[29]

Despite their lack of support, actors and stagehands were virtually invisible at the BoE public hearings and so were a weak source of public opposition. But a vocal bloc of Broadway theater owners and producers, constituting a more powerful economic interest group, formed an important component of the core pro-growth alliance. Thus, as with the divisions within the business community and the public sector, the more powerful segment of the theater industry firmly supported the Forty-second Street project.

In sharp contrast to the powerful pro-growth alliance, the community coalition consisted primarily of individuals from the Clinton neighborhood with few resources and little organizational backing. Most of the opponents who listed an affiliation appeared as members of the Clinton Coalition of Concern, a neighborhood group that was active on housing and related issues. Other witnesses appeared simply as individuals who reiterated the general neighborhood position. What is most notable about the opposition, therefore, is how localized and limited it was. There simply was no broad-based citizen opposition expressed or any opposition from a significant citywide organization.

The only significant resource for neighborhood opponents was the collection of responsive local public officials who accurately represented the community's position. Although they were not powerful citywide or statewide political figures, they were a vocal and united bloc and thus provided a source of valuable support for Clinton residents. There was a widespread feeling among community activists, community board members, and other observers that the public had been excluded from the planning process from the inception of the project through the hearings at the BoE, in spite of repeated calls for participation.[30] Only after the first hearing, when the depth of public opposition was able to achieve an added degree of visibility, did public officials make an effort to respond to neighborhood concerns. Then, as Susan Fainstein has noted, "the key intermediaries in translating outside pressure into concessions were the elected officials rather than the planners, who until this point had remained obdurate."[31]

In fact, the concessions to the Clinton community came directly from the elected officials and involved no modification of the Forty-second Street project as formulated by the planners and developers. Shortly before the second hearing, Governor Cuomo and Mayor Koch announced an agreement to provide $25 million in equal shares of city and state funds to support low- and moderate-income housing resources and other community services in the Clinton neighborhood. Most local residents and officials felt strongly that the housing money should come from the developers, who were receiving generous public subsidies, rather than from the public coffers, which must serve all city residents; indeed, this was the principal point of conflict in frantic last-minute negotiations among local legislators, representatives of Community Board 4, and the staffs of the mayor, the governor, and the BoE.[32] But in the end, the concession came from the public sector, not from the private developers.[33] Still, it is unlikely that there would have been any concessions at all without the efforts of a united band of local political representatives who were able to generate responsiveness from higher-level public officials. The local representatives played a valuable mediating role between the pro-growth alliance and neighborhood interests.

INVISIBLE INTERESTS

The data on the witnesses at the BoE hearings reveal much about the political battles surrounding the Forty-second Street project, but little about the underlying conflict of interests. Land-use decision making straddles the artificial lines among developmental, allocational, and redistributive types of policies because of the far-reaching costs and benefits that it creates. For this reason, land-use policy is a quintessentially political sphere, even if the full nature and extent of the costs and benefits often remain obscure. In studying development politics, therefore, it is important not to repeat the missteps of early theoretical and empirical pluralist studies, which assumed that all affected interests would be organized and visible.[34] Publicly articulated interests do not exhaust the entire range of those gaining or losing from a land-use decision. Other interests affected by the redevelopment of a particular urban place can and must be identified based on the patterns of actual public use, the existing economic activities, the sources of redevelopment initiatives, and so forth. Therefore, the records of the BoE hearings must be examined as much for the interests they do not reveal as for those they do.

It is clear, for example, from the UDC's environmental-impact statement, from the CUNY street studies, and from direct observation that the Times Square area was a primary entertainment district for the city's lower-income residents, especially African-Americans and Latinos, through the 1980s.[35] According to the findings of street studies, the number of low-income people who used the area for legitimate entertainment purposes may have even rivaled or surpassed the entire population of Clinton. Indeed, Times Square was probably a relatively safe entertainment district for residents of low-income neighborhoods that were plagued by crime and drugs and lacked basic attractions, such as movie theaters. Clearly, the loss of such a unique and important resource for so many people constitutes a significant redistributional impact.

Yet whereas more than forty witnesses turned out from the Clinton community to oppose the project on the record, only one unaffiliated witness spoke on behalf of the city's low-income minority populations that stood to lose an easily accessible, centrally located district of inexpensive fast-food outlets and discount first-run movie houses. He pointed out that

> forty-five percent of this city is minority, and . . . they are in the lowest economic status. 42nd Street to them is an outlet for their entertainment with pictures that are at $2.50, $3.00 top admission, the same pictures that are playing on Broadway for $5.00, in addition to which on 42nd Street you are getting a

double feature. . . . There is no way for the people who are coming to 42nd Street . . . [who] only have minimum money . . . to pay the forty and forty-five dollars that it takes to go into a legitimate theater. . . . I want to know what is going to happen with the minorities. . . . I have heard about nothing about what their pleasures are and what is going to exist for them. . . . Forty-five percent, I repeat, we represent in this city. . . . And we feel now, particularly now, justified in having some kind of recourse and some kind of input to anything of this nature in this city which we feel is as much ours as anybody else's.

The invisibility of low-income people of color at the public hearings can be explained in more convincing ways than a simple disavowal of any legitimate political interest on the part of those who depended on the entertainment resources of Times Square. For example, Mancur Olson demonstrated that the "logic of collective action" favors small groups over large ones.[36] The group of low-income patrons of Times Square, drawn from throughout the city, was unmanageably large and diffuse; therefore, it was by nature a difficult one to organize for political action. Individuals in this group had little incentive to expend their resources on political action when their own contribution would have little impact on the group's chances of success. Moreover, as a lower-income group, organization was likely hindered by a more limited sense of political efficacy among its members.

And yet the residents of the Clinton neighborhood were also a large, lower-income group that seemingly should have faced similar barriers to collective action; nevertheless, they were a prominent presence at the public hearings. The difference in the level of political mobilization between Clinton residents and low-income patrons of Times Square further illuminates the importance of political discourse in the study of development politics. These two groups stood in stark contrast to each other in terms of their position in the dominant discourse on Times Square. Local residents were widely recognized as victims of Times Square decay; indeed, the plight of families living just around the corner from the place that defined moral turpitude was used as a justification for the redevelopment effort. Consequently, they enjoyed some political leverage, since they were in a position to make the case that they should not be victimized a second time by the impact of the redevelopment project on their neighborhood. In contrast, the low-income African-American and Latino patrons of Times Square had been identified in the discourse as a source and symbol of the area's (and city's) decline. As a result, they faced the overwhelming challenge of generating widespread sympathy for their interest in maintaining the inexpensive resources of Times Square.

The Times Square discourse had a similar impact on the political position of the adult-entertainment industry. Given the economic value of this industry, considerable opposition to redevelopment from the owners and even patrons of sex-related establishments in the area would be expected. Their failure to mobilize publicly reflects the dubious neutrality of the pluralist process as a result of the role that political discourse plays in shaping political participation. The business of sex-related entertainment, legal and illegal alike, was already vilified in public discourse as both source and symbol of decay in the Times Square area; indeed, a central stated objective of the entire Forty-second Street project was the clean up of this industry. As a result, legal sex-entertainment businesses had little to gain from mobilizing as an interest group in the public arena, in spite of their vast economic resources; in this arena, they were already denied the status of legitimate participants through the dominant political discourse. The adult-entertainment industry, it appears, must compete for urban space through the raw power of the purse alone. It exists where it is the highest bidder, paying top-dollar rents to commercial landlords who own undervalued properties in advantageous locations.

It is hardly a coincidence that the two groups most notably absent from the hearings were already labeled as contributors to the area's demise in the dominant discourse on Times Square. Regardless of its veracity, this discourse—as defined by politicians, investors, planners, and the media—played an important role in structuring the political conflict and the relative status of various interests. By denying legitimate interests to the low-income patrons of action movies and fast-food outlets, and to the adult-entertainment industry and its middle-class patrons, backers of the project furthered their goal of manufacturing widespread public support for the redevelopment project.

Aside from these unrepresented opponents of the project, a number of major institutions in the city with substantial economic interests in its completion failed to appear in support at the hearings. Among them were the New York Times Company and the Ford Foundation as well as corporations such as the National Broadcasting Company and American Express. While these companies' may not have had a direct interest in the project, they had provided funding and organizational support for street studies and/or proposals for the revitalization of Times Square. Representatives of NBC, AMEX, Salomon Brothers, the Dreyfus Corporation, and other corporations and law firms had been members of the board of The City at 42nd Street, Inc., the nongovernmental organization whose plan for the redevelopment of Forty-second Street grew out of efforts by the Municipal Art Society and the Ford Foundation and provided the prototype for the 42nd Street Development Project. Nevertheless, none of these companies attended the hearings to voice support for the final proposal. Even those representatives of major financial institutions who did appear—Chemical Bank, American Savings Bank, and Goldman, Sachs—did not provide oral testimony indicating the basis for their support. In this way, they limited their publicly stated interest in and connection to the project.

It is not entirely clear why corporations that expended resources to promote a redevelopment project would fail to appear publicly on its behalf. Suffice it to say that these companies have alternative methods of pursuing their interests. By providing funding for studies, formulating proposals, and serving on the boards of nonprofit development corporations, these institutions can ensure that their interests are accommodated early in the process. They possess the resources that enable them to initiate action aimed at achieving their objectives; in this way, they obviate the need for participation at such a late stage in the process, when final public approval for a project is decided. Major economic interests can establish the choices that form the basis of successive decisions, which finally culminate in the simple yes or no decision made in a public legislative body. In short, these institutions enjoy the power to set the agenda on such development issues.[37]

Thus an important deficiency of traditional pluralist theory evident in the Times Square case was its failure to recognize the sequential nature of public decision making and the entrance of some players into the process much earlier than others. Pluralism assumed that all participants articulated their interests more or less simultaneously; competing interest groups exerted pressure on government, and the articulated interests could then be metamorphosed into a compromise outcome. As the Times Square case demonstrates, however, power comes into play by determining the point at which a player can enter the decision-making process and attempt to shape the further sequence of alternatives. The foundation of the Forty-second Street plan began with the initiatives from the culture and business communities, culminating in The City at 42nd Street; then, when government approval and backing were needed, city and state officials and planners worked within the contours of this proposal and modified it to better suit the political and economic objectives of the pro-growth coalition.

At the BoE hearings, the culture organizations and, especially, the Clinton residents and their representatives all spoke about their exclusion from the planning process despite repeated requests for participation. The relative weakness of the neighborhood residents in particular was apparent from their having to rely on this public forum to make appeals for changes in the project, at a time when the alternatives were essentially reduced to a yes or no vote on the plan as presented. For all the purposes that such hearings might serve, they were a poor forum for negotiating substantial changes in the project. The attention to the concerns of Clinton residents that arose at the BoE hearings did contribute to the establishment of a community housing fund, but this money represented less a change in the plan than compensation for its detrimental impacts.

In the end, there was something pitiable about the emotional local residents who stood at the podium pleading for attention to their plight from BoE officials who had long since left the hearing in the hands of their proxies. As one Clinton resident expressed it: "It's painful for me to note that the mayor is not here and the media is gone. No one is here to listen to our protest. I hardly know who I'm talking to." The signal being sent was that the decision was a foregone conclusion. That the neighborhood residents had to rely on the BoE hearings for an opportunity to influence the project was a stark indication that they did not have the political or economic resources needed to shape it at an earlier stage in the planning process.

When the BoE voted unanimously to approve the Forty-second Street plan, it seemed that the outcome had been predetermined. Despite two days of hearings at which its merits were contested and debated, the project still represented years of planning and cooperation between the public and private sectors. The vote understandably reflected the active government involvement in the project, the support from major elements of the business and culture communities, and the absence of any broad-based public opposition. In this sense, the BoE action was a reasonable reflection of observable societal interests. But it can be argued that the hearings were an extremely limited part of the actual decision-making process. All the important decisions relating to the project had been made during the planning process, when economic goals were balanced with political needs in the process of constructing a pro-growth alliance. The decision of the BoE was effectively reduced to a yes or no, thereby precluding genuine public debate over alternative plans for the area. Thus the hearing served more as a legitimating event than a decision-making one. It provided a public forum for reiterating and reinforcing the dominant discourse on Times Square, and thereby mobilizing public sentiment behind the redevelopment effort.

The hearings before the Board of Estimate on the 42nd Street Development Project illustrate a number of biases in the articulation and recognition of interests in a pluralistic, public decision-making process. Some groups may be denied the status required for effective participation, while others enjoy an advantageous position by the symbolic imagery of political discourse. Some groups possess sufficient political or economic resources to initiate and define the alternatives from the start, while others are left to struggle for modest palliatives when the final deal is being sealed. The key to a group's success, then, is possessing some political or economic resources that make it a desirable partner in the governing coalition and that can be used as leverage to ensure that the coalition is responsive to the group's interests. Valued resources include tangible assets, such as money and influence in government, and less tangible opportunities, such as the role a group can play in shaping political discourse and thereby altering the status and alignment of various interests. In the end, successful political coalitions must recognize and cultivate both the material and the symbolic side of politics.

CONSTRUCTING SUPPORT IN THE BOARD OF ESTIMATE

The unanimous vote by the Board of Estimate in support of the 42nd Street Development Project may have been a foregone conclusion, but BoE support for a Times Square redevelopment project was not inevitable. It is important to recognize the need to construct political support among the various members of the BoE. By the mid-1980s, Mayor Koch had established vast influence over the BoE through his skill in reaching accommodations with the regular Democratic organizations throughout the city.[38] Nevertheless, the potential for opposition was there. The BoE often had been the source of political rivals who could use their citywide exposure to challenge sitting mayors; indeed, David Dinkins was the Manhattan borough president when he successfully ousted Koch in 1989. Several issues, too, might have threatened the unanimity of support had Koch's political strategy been less effective.

It is easy to assume, for example, that the city's top elected officials would be unified in their support of the postindustrial economic restructuring that would establish New York as a preeminent global city. But, in fact, the postindustrial transformation under Koch had a widely disparate impact on the city's five boroughs. Investment in commercial and residential development was heavily concentrated in Manhattan, with few direct benefits for the outer boroughs. Brooklyn, Queens, and the Bronx had large populations of African-Americans and Latinos, many of whom would lose out in the transition from a manufacturing to a service-based economy. A statement read at the hearings on behalf of Brooklyn Borough President Howard Golden noted, therefore, his record of voting against many development efforts for Manhattan, including the special midtown zoning amendment and the Times Square Marriott Hotel. But the statement went on to declare: "He finds it difficult at this point to stand in the way of a lot of people's dreams to see 42nd Street become a place which is admired rather than one that is disdained." His position reflected, therefore, the power of the dominant discourse to shape public sentiment and circumscribe the range of options open to prominent city officials.

The issue of the Clinton neighborhood was also a concern, especially for Manhattan Borough President Andrew Stein and City Council President Carol Bellamy. The assistant to the mayor reiterated the compromise proposal offered by the mayor and the governor to provide $25 million to the Clinton community for housing assistance. The council president and the Manhattan borough president applauded this plan, which they felt provided the necessary protection for neighborhood residents and therefore enabled them to support the project. The $25 million thus provided sufficient political cover for their support, even though Clinton residents and their representatives continued to oppose the project after the announcement of this community fund.

Stein and Bellamy also asked for final assurances that the resolution authorizing the project would preclude the possibility of future transfers of air rights or demolition involving the historic theaters in the project area. Because the project was sponsored by the New York State UDC, it was not bound by the New York City zoning code, and thus an official transfer of development rights was technically never needed. (The project involved a transfer of development rights only as a design concept, shifting bulk from the mid-block sites of the theaters to the corner sites of the office towers.) Land-use determinations were made by the UDC according to the authorization set forth in the BoE resolution. For the theater sites as well as the other sites, any proposed major changes—such as the demolition of theaters—would require the approval of both the UDC and the BoE, according to testimony from the city's corporation counsel.

The components of the project relating to historic preservation and the re-creation of a theater district were central to its widespread political support. As the comments of the members of the BoE indicated, they were concerned about the degree of commitment among project planners to the cultural task of reproducing the historic theater district. In this way, they were attentive to the culture community and the issues that it raised. They remained actively concerned about these issues up to the last minute, demanding assurances that the UDC would not be able to deviate from the plan of cultural production. As a result, the final BoE resolution was modified to mandate only theater uses for specified sites and to prevent the construction of additions above theater structures, or the transfer of air rights, for the ninety-nine-year term of the UDC lease. That these stipulations were made in spite of their legal redundancy, according to the city's corporation counsel, attests to the political saliency of the arts and preservation goals and the voices of the culture community. In the end, BoE officials, too, were heavily swayed by the dominant discourse on Times Square as a justification for redevelopment.

REDEFINING THE POLITICS OF URBAN DEVELOPMENT

This analysis of the political contest and contestants surrounding the 42nd Street Development Project, as revealed and obscured in public hearings, has yielded useful insights into the importance of culture and discourse in pro-growth politics. The insights drawn from this case are suggestive of new ways of thinking about the politics of urban development. It seems particularly relevant that a community of urban culture groups—including civic, professional, and business organizations involved in historic preservation, the arts, and urban design—has become an important participant in the paradigmatic urban growth machine. Historic preservation and the arts certainly have been important forces in the redevelopment of undervalued neighborhoods in New York City, such as SoHo and the East Village. But J. Allen Whitt has documented widespread participation by an "arts coalition" in urban growth machines.[39] The alliance of the arts and business communities is revealed in urban development projects throughout the United States and even in the overlapping memberships of the boards of corporate and cultural organizations.[40] It remains to be shown, however, precisely how and why this new pattern exists. The Times Square case suggests that the integration of the culture community into the pro-growth alliance is valuable because of the way this can alter the nature of political conflict and debate about urban redevelopment.

The culture community has been drawn into the urban growth machine by the inclusion of preservation- and arts-based components in development projects in ways that clearly advance its causes.[41] The involvement of the culture community appears to have a very practical political benefit for pro-growth forces. Even though aesthetic debates are not eliminated from development politics, they are confined to being resolved by project supporters, rather than being a source of conflict between supporters and opponents of development. As a result, aesthetic objections do not serve as a mobilizing issue for an antigrowth opposition. This is certainly evident in the Times Square case, where aesthetic issues were a major point of contention, but never threatened to derail the project because the debate was largely contained within the pro-growth alliance.

The culture community is especially important because it speaks to and for a larger constituency of high-income, well-educated urban residents who are often crucial to a pro-growth regime; indeed, this population had helped block traditional urban renewal agendas. The strategy of including preservation- and arts-based components in redevelopment projects not only secures the support of the culture community, but also allows for a new language of development—in contrast to the cold rationality of modernist urban renewal—that speaks to the cultural sensibilities of affluent city residents. The cultural redefinition of an area is made the central and explicit focus of redevelopment in political discourse in such a way as to generate support from higher-income residents. Simply put, high culture is offered as an alternative to symbols of urban decline, such as threatening subcultures of African-American and Latino youths or obsolete industrial districts and waterfronts. In this way, the redevelopment of Times Square promised Pavarotti instead of Public Enemy, high heels instead of high-tops, champagne flutes instead of malt liquor forties, and chorus lines instead of police line-ups.

By representing redevelopment in this way, the pro-growth coalition can take control of the political debate and undermine the effectiveness of antigrowth arguments. In development politics, environmental concerns—such as traffic congestion, air quality, sewage treatment, even endangered species—often threaten to pit better-educated, higher-income urban residents against the growth machine. By introducing preservation and the arts into development projects as alternatives to social and physical decay, the environmental debate is recast along social and cultural lines. In other words, the environment is defined as a social rather than an ecological system, and what becomes relevant in development politics is the focus on improving the social environment rather than protecting the ecological environment. The result is a realignment of environmentally concerned segments of the public as a higher-income, politically active constituency is relocated, by the nature of the debate, from the antigrowth to the pro-growth side.

This phenomenon was clearly evident in the politics of Times Square redevelopment. The pro-growth forces framed the debate as the reconstruction of a historic theater district versus the continued dominance of crime, drugs, pornography, and young African-American and Latino males; in this way, they defined the environment in social and aesthetic terms. In a city chronically afoul of the Clean Air Act, there was remarkably little public concern about the impact on air quality of the increased traffic congestion that would inevitably accompany 7 million square feet of new commercial construction in the heart of Manhattan. Several witnesses at the hearings, including a traffic consultant, argued that the environmental-impact statement seriously underestimated the adverse effects of the project on air quality, but the issue never became politically salient. Even the Clean Air Campaign, a citizens' group active on planning issues that had fought and defeated the Westway highway proposal, was absent as a public voice on the Forty-second Street project. The environmental debate had been defined on social terms, and, as evidenced by the absence of broad citizen-based opposition, the attentive public was solidly behind the social and cultural project of restoring a theater district.

The Times Square case makes a useful contribution to the ongoing debates in urban research, particularly those centering on the role of politics in urban development. On the one hand, the BoE hearings reveal that there was no consensus in support of the 42nd Street Development Project in a literal sense, in spite of the promise of thousands of new jobs and millions of dollars in new tax revenue that would accrue to the "unitary interest" of city residents.[42] There was opposition not only from unanimous local residents, but also from members of the business community and the public sector, groups that usually are assumed to be the most unified supporters of growth. As earlier regime studies discovered elsewhere, there was meaningful political conflict over the project stemming from the widely varied costs and benefits it created.

The overwhelming predominance of support, on the other hand, might reasonably approximate the kind of broad-based support for development described by Paul Peterson.[43] But it did not result simply from the abstract operation of an economic imperative. Rather, it was politically constructed by means of a coalition strategy that centered on cultural politics. Mayor Koch used the symbolism of the Great White Way to entice a crucial constituency of higher-income professionals into his pro-growth regime. Thus the Times Square case suggests that the new pattern of urban development, involving preservation- and arts-based cultural production, deflects opposition by incorporating the culture community into the pro-growth coalition and recasting the political debate in a way that predisposes higher-income urban residents to support redevelopment.

Successful economic development requires more than just political support, however. The real-estate market, with its wily twists and turns, also sets the parameters for what is possible and when. Officials of the 42nd Street Development Project discovered this when the market for their office towers turned sour. They would need a new strategy to realize their vision for Times Square in the face of changing economic and political realities. A little luck would help, too, and it arrived in the form of Disney's Magic Kingdom.

The redevelopment effort was intended to rid Times Square of undesirable people and activities. (Photograph by Michael Ackerman)

Forty-second Street exhibited an eery desolation after the existing businesses had been evicted and before redevelopment began later in the 1990s. (Photograph by Michael Ackerman)

Robert A. M. Stern Architects and M & Co. drew on a historic image of Times Square as a place of popular entertainment and visual excitement in their proposal for the interim development plan: 42nd Street Now! (Photograph by Robert A. M. Stern Architects)

The Forty-second Street Art Project brought Dr. Seuss's Cat in the Hat and other art instal-
lations to a desolate Forty-second Street awaiting redevelopment. (Photograph by Michael
Ackerman)

The Walt Disney Company was lured to the Forty-second Street project by the opportunity to restore the elegant New Amsterdam Theater, shown around 1910, as a venue for its live stage productions. (Photograph, *New Amsterdam Theatre, c. 1910, Hall: Interior.* Museum of the City of New York, Theatre Collection)

Disney will operate a vacation club in the "E Walk" entertainment, retail, and hotel complex, whose design suggests a comet falling to earth. (Photograph by Tishman Realty and Construction Co., Inc.)

The restored historic theaters on Forty-second Street serve as a cultural code that designates the area as a place of consumption for middle- and upper-income people. (Photograph by Philip Greenberg)

The Disney Store on Forty-second Street at Seventh Avenue epitomizes the transformation of Time Square from a national symbol of urban decline to a symbol of urban renaissance in the 1990s. (Photograph by Philip Greenberg)

6

Fin-de-Siècle Forty-second Street: Disneyspace for the Twenty-first Century

The renewed 42nd Street will be an enhanced version of itself—not a gentrified theme park or festival market.
—Robert A. M. Stern Architects and M & Co. (1993)

Times Square Land! It's safe, it's full of new theme stores and it's absolutely packed with tourists.
—Paul Tharp, "Times Square Land!" *New York Post* (1996)

In March 1993, more than a decade after city and state officials first presented their redevelopment plan for Times Square, a stroll down Forty-second Street between Seventh and Eighth Avenues revealed some familiar sights. Blazing theater marquees lined both sides of the block, beckoning passers-by with titles like *Hot Blood* and *Screaming Mimi* that combined images of sex and violence, trademark symbols of Times Square. Storefronts featured a perplexing array of sexual toys and novelty items, martial arts weaponry, drug paraphernalia, and discount electronics. Street peddlers hawked a variety of mysterious unguents and incenses from makeshift display counters set up under the low-hanging marquees. People of all types crowded the sidewalks: some looked frightening, others frightened; some hurried purposefully, others loitered about with no apparent purpose. West Forty-second Street looked much as it had during its reputed nadir in the 1970s.

Appearances, however, can be misleading. Much had changed on West Forty-second Street since the late 1980s. In April 1990, the New York State Urban Development Corporation had received final approval from the courts for its plan to condemn properties in the project area. Over the next few years, state officials proceeded to condemn 34 buildings, forcing out some 240 commercial tenants and closing down movie theaters, offices, sex-related businesses, fast-food outlets, delicatessens, game arcades, and an assortment of retail outlets featuring everything from T-shirts and souvenirs to discount electronics and scuba gear. Along the notorious block between Seventh and Eighth Avenues, storefront businesses were boarded up, the prominent marquees were somber and dark, and the pedestrian population had dwindled. By the summer of 1992, the eastern two-thirds of the project area displayed the aura of a ghost town in the middle of Manhattan.[1]

The disturbing appearance of West Forty-second Street in March 1993 was only an illusion. An art director had created the false facade for the filming of *The Last Action Hero,* a movie starring the muscle-bound Republican superhero Arnold Schwarzenegger. For a brief moment in 1993, West Forty-second Street was reconstructed in the image of its prior incarnation. Despite the distressing hint of déjà vu, the appropriation of the street as a film set signified that it was poised to emerge as the star attraction in the symbolic economy of New York City. The menacing ambience of Forty-second Street had been transformed from a setting for the genuine and unsettling dramas of urban life to a setting for the constructed and nonthreatening dramas of the entertainment industry. Rather than office towers leading the way for cultural change on West Forty-second Street—the formula that project planners had long sworn by—it would be the manipulation of culture through new entertainment uses that would lead to the preeminence of Times Square in the postindustrial economy of New York City at the millennium.

THE FORTY-SECOND STREET DEVELOPMENT PROJECT BREAKS DOWN

The Forty-second Street Development Project reached a turning point in the early 1990s. By the time that state officials were finally able to begin condemning and vacating properties in preparation for redevelopment, momentum for the project had reached a low point and was steadily sinking. Years of legal challenges and other setbacks had seriously hobbled the project. The developers of the merchandise mart and the hotel had quit the project altogether, leaving no firm plan or funding in place for the entire western end of the redevelopment area (about one-third of the total project area). As a result, state officials were prevented from condemning the properties near Eighth Avenue and displacing the undesirable businesses that operated there.

One potential bright spot was the unwavering commitment to the office development by Times Square Center Associates (TSCA), the team of Park Tower Realty and the Prudential Insurance Company. Prudential even increased the stakes when it put up a $241 million letter of credit in 1990 to cover the anticipated costs of acquiring the eastern two-thirds of the project area. But after Chemical Bank backed out of its agreement to locate in the new towers, the developers were left without a single major committed tenant for more than 4 million square feet of planned office space. This did not bode well.

The culture community had also become increasingly vocal and critical of the project during the latter half of the 1980s, threatening to shift important segments of public opinion against it. In 1989, Paul Goldberger, architecture critic of the *New York Times,* publicly lamented the "truly depressing prospect" of following through with the Forty-second Street project, whose "priorities [had] come to look more like those of any other commercial venture" than one with a genuine public purpose.[2] After officials unveiled funky new designs for the office towers later that year, hoping to generate a spark of enthusiasm for the flagging plan, the response from the culture community was renewed ridicule. Critics blasted the new designs as a crass marketing event that attempted to mask hulking behemoths in a "suitable style" for Times Square.[3]

In addition, the Municipal Art Society had come to regret its earlier positions on the city's planning efforts for Times Square, especially its support for the Forty-second Street project and the special midtown zoning amendment adopted in the early 1980s to stimulate development in the area.[4] The MAS came to realize that these two initiatives would unleash massive overbuilding and destroy Times Square as an entertainment district. So from the time of the public hearings in 1984, the MAS was engaged in a public campaign to protect the area from becoming another staid office district. The group helped orchestrate a half-hour blackout of the electric signs in Times Square to demonstrate their value to the area;[5] it sponsored an open design competition for the endangered Times Tower; it led a successful campaign to have several dozen Broadway theaters designated as historic landmarks; and it helped establish new contextual zoning guidelines that mandated setbacks and lighted signs on new buildings in Times Square. In order to dramatize the need for contextual zoning requirements, the MAS produced a sobering film that simulated a future pedestrian's view of Times Square if development continued to proceed unchecked.

Through its campaign, the MAS succeeded in constructing a new identity for Times Square as a valued "entertainment district" that, despite some acknowledged problems, possessed distinctive characteristics and uses deserving of protection. Gradually, even city planners began to think of the area in these terms, endorsing such measures as contextual zoning for Times Square. This new identity was, however, seemingly at odds with the massive office development envisioned in the Forty-second Street project. Implicitly, at least, the fundamental premises of the redevelopment effort were being called into question as the 1980s came to a close.

The end of the 1980s also marked the demise of Ed Koch—if not the Koch coalition—in New York City politics.[6] He was finally ousted from office by a liberal electoral coalition constructed by David N. Dinkins.[7] Although Dinkins, then the city clerk, had voted for the 42nd Street Development Project as a UDC board member in 1984, he had done so "with a heavy heart" because of his concerns about the displacement of lower-income residents of Clinton.[8] For a time, it appeared that Mayor Dinkins might preside over a progressive coalition with a development agenda less oriented to the postindustrial transformation of the city and more responsive to neighborhood interests and people of color. That turned out not to be the case.[9] Dinkins was constrained by lingering economic recession, federal retrenchment, and budget deficits. Nevertheless, even with a more progressive mayor in charge of City Hall, there was little he could do to forestall the project at this point. It had succeeded in clearing the political process, and it continued to rack up victories in the courts. So it was unlikely that waning political support alone would lead the project's sponsors and developers to revise their plan.

The most serious obstacle to confront the project in the early 1990s came, therefore, not from political or legal challenges, but from a fickle real-estate market that refused, most stubbornly, to cooperate with the development goals of the plan. As state officials were taking title to the existing buildings and preparing them for the wrecking ball, the market for office space that had appeared so limitless in the early 1980s collapsed. The combined impact of the stock market crash in 1987, forcing large-scale cutbacks in the financial services industries, and the building boom of the 1980s left the city with a glut of office space. The problem was particularly severe in the Times Square area, where special zoning incentives had produced such overbuilding in the 1980s that several brand-new office towers stood vacant, or nearly so, at the end of the decade. These grim, lifeless monoliths virtually taunted George Klein to "make my day": go ahead, build, take your final, fatal shot. But neither Klein nor his partners at Prudential were feeling that lucky. By late 1991, they were "getting cold feet"[10] and asking state officials to delay the project, even though they had spent nearly $200 million in site acquisition costs.[11]

State officials were no more eager to proceed with a doomed project whose failure would be impossible to conceal. According to the terms of the existing agreement, the developers were required to begin construction on their first tower within one year of receiving the vacated site. So state officials began to postpone the final evictions, maintaining the operation of entire buildings for a few holdout tenants, in order to avoid triggering the clock that would count down to the construction start date.[12] By mid-1992, the project had perhaps reached its lowest point: West Forty-second Street had been transformed into an urban wasteland, and yet there was no hope of redevelopment in sight. The prospects for the area seemed so grim that Prudential itself was unwilling to commit to relocating even its own employees to a new Times Square tower when its current lease expired in 1994.[13]

A NEW STRATEGY FOR FORTY-SECOND STREET

In August 1992, the developers and the officials of the 42nd Street Development Project bowed to the realities of the marketplace and formally agreed to delay the construction of the office towers indefinitely. The move was a tacit acknowledgment that, after more than a decade in the works, the grand plan for the transformation of Times Square had failed—at least for the time being. The postindustrial vision of Times Square as the western node of the midtown office district would have to be set aside for the foreseeable future. The time had come to rethink the most fundamental premises of the project and formulate a new image for Times Square. This was what critics of the project had been demanding for years; now, finally, the real-estate market provided the leverage needed to reshape the project that political opponents had lacked.

While reluctantly conceding a momentary defeat on the office construction,

project sponsors already were announcing the preparation of an interim development plan—optimistically named 42nd Street Now!—for the vacated properties
in the project area. The office developers agreed, in principle, to fund the redevelopment of existing buildings for temporary entertainment uses in exchange for the
right to build their towers at a later date when the market permitted. The new
goal—as described with unintended irony by Rebecca Robertson, president of the
42nd Street Development Project—was "to create an environment that is lively
and exciting but that will only be there for a certain amount of time."[14] The strategy of the interim plan would be to build on the resources of Times Square as an
entertainment district, an identity that was by now widely accepted.

To that end, UDC officials selected architect Robert A. M. Stern, who combined an extensive knowledge of New York's architectural history with experience
working for the Walt Disney Company, to lead the design team for the interim plan.
The design guidelines that Stern produced (with Tibor Kalman's M & Co.) were
released in the fall of 1993.[15] The plan sought to create, within the existing fabric
of the street, a jumble of entertainment uses in a dazzling visual atmosphere of
kinetic lights and signs. Existing buildings would be redeveloped for use as retail
stores, restaurants, nightclubs, and a range of other entertainment attractions. The
historic theaters would be restored not only as Broadway stages, but for cabaret,
dinner theater, comedy clubs, and even movies. The backdrop to the street would
be formed by a rooftop "billboard park," while building facades would radiate with
layers of vibrant lights and signs.[16]

In the New York Times, David Dunlap characterized the plan as paying homage
to both Florenz Ziegfeld, whose "Follies" defined popular Forty-second Street
entertainment in the early twentieth century, and Jane Jacobs, whose assault on
modernism propelled new planning principles that emphasized the preservation of
older buildings and their adaptation for diverse uses.[17] Herbert Muschamp, architecture critic of the New York Times, wrote that the plan could be called "Learning
from 42nd Street" because it worked within, rather than against, the context of the
street.[18] In doing so, it followed the principles of Learning from Las Vegas, the book
by Robert Venturi, Denise Scott Brown, and David Izenour that helped tear down
the modernist orthodoxy in architecture and establish a postmodern style that drew
inspiration from the everyday language of commercial architecture.[19]

Indeed, the new design guidelines were hailed for their sensitivity to the history of Forty-second Street, especially by influential voices in the culture community. For many critics of the original project and its office-tower aesthetic, the
interim plan represented a far more genuine effort to redevelop Forty-second Street
by building on its historic strengths. It was not an attempt to create a sterile Great
White Way of upscale theaters on a stuffy street of office towers. Gone were the
offensive towers, or at least so it seemed at the time; and, significantly, the requirement that the restored theaters be dedicated to the production of Broadway shows
had been quietly dropped. The emphasis was rather on more popular entertainment
forms within the existing fabric of small-scale buildings. This new focus suggested

a less glamorous, and perhaps less romanticized, representation of the history of Forty-second Street and Times Square.

Yet another year passed before the project officials reached a formal agreement with the office developers on the precise terms of the interim plan in August 1994.[20] According to the deal, the team of Prudential and Park Tower agreed to provide $20 million to redevelop about thirteen buildings in the project area (including those on the future office sites) for entertainment uses, and another $2.6 million for decorative lighting and street improvements. The developers would pay New York State a base annual rent for the redeveloped sites of $3.3 million, with an inflation factor, while collecting rent of their own from the new tenants. These obligations came on top of the more than $270 million that the developers had spent on acquiring properties in the project area, and the $18.2 million they had committed to the restoration of historic theaters.

Although the new agreement required Prudential to pump additional money into a project from which it had yet to derive any benefits, the renegotiated deal was not a bad one for the developers. With the office towers on indefinite hold, the restoration plan for the Times Square subway station was severed from the Forty-second Street project and the developers were released from their obligation to provide $91 million for improvements to the station. They also were allowed to increase the floor-to-ceiling heights in the towers, and thus the overall building heights (but not floor area), to accommodate additional computer and telecommunications lines and thereby make the office towers more marketable to the most prized tenants. And while paying the state an annual rent in the range of $3.5 million for the redeveloped sites, the developers could expect to collect between $8.5 million and $10 million a year in rent from tenants in the restored buildings.[21]

In a more fundamental sense, project officials cushioned the developers against losses arising from their own miscalculation of the marketplace. By agreeing to release the developers from their contractual obligation to build and by renegotiating the deal, UDC officials allowed the developers to avoid the kind of enormous losses that plagued other private development efforts in the Times Square area.[22] For example, the developers of an office tower at Broadway and Forty-seventh Street in the late 1980s were hemorrhaging almost $2 million a month by 1991, with only one tenant in a building of nearly 1.35 million square feet.[23] And a development group led by Ian Bruce Eichner lost a whopping $200 million on a doomed forty-four-story office tower built in the late 1980s at Broadway and Forty-fifth Street in Times Square.[24]

In contrast to these failing investments, the $300 million that Prudential had sunk in the Forty-second Street project still promised a sizable return. Nearly $200 million in site acquisition costs—the amount that exceeded the $88 million cap for which the developers were responsible—would be returned to the developers with interest through future tax abatements on the office towers. Although the developers and project officials agreed to suspend the interest accruals until construction started on the towers, they also settled on a new rate slightly higher than the generous prime-plus-one-percent previously agreed on.[25] In 1994, critics were warning that "the subsidies go off the chart," with the developers potentially receiving between $1.5 billion and $4.2 billion in forgiven taxes over a period of as long as ninety-nine years.[26] Although Prudential and Park Tower were undoubtedly uneasy about being in so deep, it was only the cooperation of public officials that enabled them to salvage a soured real-estate investment. As part of the publicly sponsored redevelopment effort, the developers were able to play in the big leagues without facing the risk of losing badly because of their own errors.

NEW PLAN, NEW POLITICS

Abandoning the project of office development at Forty-second Street and Times Square, even temporarily, and replacing it with a modest plan of building restorations for entertainment uses was a delicate political maneuver. After all, the new strategy signaled a confession of sorts by project sponsors that their original planning philosophy had been a sham. The planners always had been adamant in maintaining that office development was essential to pave the way for desirable entertainment venues on West Forty-second Street; yet they were now proposing to skip the towers and redevelop the street directly for entertainment uses. They were acknowledging—even asserting with confidence—that the street could be revitalized through the preservation and restoration of existing structures without the construction of office buildings. This strategy had been explicitly and unequivocally rejected a decade earlier in the project's environmental-impact statement, with hundreds of pages of data analysis documenting the intractable social ills of West Forty-second Street.[27] Thus adopting the new plan for Times Square suggested disingenuousness, if not duplicity, on the part of project sponsors; the change in plan implied that the original proposal had been driven more by the real-estate euphoria of the 1980s than by sound public planning. In this respect, the shift in strategy had the potential to ignite renewed public debate on the project and enhance the political position of critics who were challenging its basic premises.

By this time, of course, the project had moved beyond the immediate realm of mayoral politics and was under the control of economic development officials of the New York State UDC. Nevertheless, a project so central to New York City, literally and symbolically, was not immune to public opinion. Thus the success of the revised plan depended in part on how well it fit into the pro-growth politics of the city. Although Dinkins had replaced Koch in City Hall, he never really altered the nature of development politics in New York. Major downtown development interests continued to drive the development agenda; and they still depended on the support, or at least the acquiescence, of middle- and higher-income city residents. Therefore, the new plan would have to satisfy important opinion leaders in the culture community, who were increasingly at odds with the project, or risk triggering an opposition movement from among the politically potent group of white-collar professionals.

At the same time, the new redevelopment strategy carried significant economic risks, since it went counter to the assumption that a viable upscale entertainment market would only follow massive redevelopment. Project sponsors and developers had reiterated so often the necessity of office development that potential investors largely accepted this formula as gospel. Thus the shift to a new plan that would begin with entertainment uses required an entirely different representation of West Forty-second Street from that conveyed in the dominant Times Square discourse of the 1980s. The original proposal of large-scale redevelopment was supported by simple symbolic imagery: it promised to restore the Great White Way to the Dangerous Deuce through the mechanism of office construction and theater restoration. This representation of the project effectively mobilized important segments of public opinion behind the redevelopment effort. But it also dictated one viable strategy for successful economic revitalization of the area: only massive redevelopment could dislodge the entrenched decadence of the Deuce. In this way, the discourse not only supported the original development plan, but also shaped perceptions of what was economically feasible for the area. Political discourse operated as both product and producer of economic objectives; consequently, redefining the development agenda involved reshaping the nature of political discourse.

In an enthusiastic analysis of the interim redevelopment plan, Herbert Muschamp addressed head on the role of symbolic politics in the evolving efforts to redevelop West Forty-second Street:

> The goal of the [interim] plan is not so much to overhaul the street physically as to reconstruct people's perception of it. And don't think that goal doesn't call for engineering every bit as elaborate as would be needed to rebuild the street from top to bottom. A lot of time, money and public relations have gone into constructing the image of 42d Street as a squalid corridor of horrors that can only be redeemed by ripping it apart. Of course, that image is not unconnected to reality. . . . Still, even in its most blighted state the street continued to draw people who came to enjoy the bright lights, crowds and budget movie tickets. And it has never been clear that real estate development is the ideal deterrent to squalor or crime. But a deal had been signed.[28]

By revealing the importance of political discourse in defining and legitimating the redevelopment project, Muschamp highlighted the need for a new symbolic representation of Forty-second Street to facilitate the fundamental change in the development agenda.

In light of the political and economic challenges posed by the new development strategy, a new discourse was crucial to the continued survival of the project. Its sponsors had to secure public support for, or at least minimize public opposition to, the interim plan, which required mobilizing the support of influential opinion leaders, including those in the culture community. They also had to secure the cooperation of the business community, including the project developers and other potential investors in the area, in order to accomplish the revised agenda for Forty-second Street. Both the political and the economic support would depend, in turn, on the way in which the plan was represented. A redefined discourse was essential to gaining support for the renegotiated plan, which ultimately would allow for the major redevelopment of West Forty-second Street envisioned in the original proposal. But public discourse is not so easily controlled, and project sponsors and supporters faced a difficult challenge in devising a new plan that would satisfy the political and economic interests of the pro-growth coalition. Once again, they would utilize a cultural strategy to mobilize political support for the redevelopment effort.

REPACKAGING THE PAST AND FUTURE OF FORTY-SECOND STREET

As project sponsors were formulating an interim plan of entertainment-oriented redevelopment to secure West Forty-second Street for later office development, they were simultaneously constructing a new discursive framework to support their new agenda. In embarking on the task of preparing design guidelines for the interim project, Robert A. M. Stern set out the key principle of the new vision for the area: "On 42nd Street, the lesson is the good time."[29] Instead of office towers, the vital components of the area would be restaurants, stores, and theaters bedecked in brilliant lights and signs. Stern was aiming to create a "dazzling place," but he "[did not] want to make it so gentrified that there is no sleaze or sensationalism." As if to clear up any confusion arising from his previous affiliation with Disney, Stern declared: "We're not doing Disney. You have to have a little sense of threat, excitement, derring-do—a sense of adventure."

Stern's imagery hints at a crucial change in the discourse on Times Square, a change that is evident, too, in the language of other prominent supporters of the project during 1992. The imagery of the Dangerous Deuce, which dominated public discourse during the 1980s, was quietly dropped from the lexicon of project supporters—even though the objectionable uses associated with West Forty-second Street continued to thrive, and even multiply, at the Eighth Avenue end of the project area. In its place, prominent voices from government, business, and media circles were now reconstructing the image of Times Square as an "entertainment mecca." Thus they were drawing on the language and vision of the culture community to facilitate a new development agenda for the area.

True to form, the *New York Times* provided a timely editorial that put a positive spin on the redirected development efforts and assisted in the process of redefining the public discourse.[30] Although confessing a sense of disappointment and "loss" at the delay in the office development, the *Times* bravely hailed "a new opening for

Times Square." In language that might have been perplexing only a few years earlier, the paper noted the enormous potential of an area that "remains a mecca for New Yorkers and visitors from every corner of planet earth." The stodgy *Times* even welcomed the opportunity for "faster restoration of the street-level hurly-burly" of West Forty-second Street. A series of upbeat headlines accompanying news of the project's delay hinted further at the new twist in public discourse: "Times Square's Future May Be Found Back at Its Roots";[31] "For Times Square, a Reprieve and Hope of a Livelier Day";[32] "New Times Square Plan: Lights! Signs! Adventure! Dancing! Hold the Offices";[33] and "Time to Reset the Clock in Times Square."[34] At *New York Newsday,* too, editorials were welcoming the "Decorous 'Deuce'"[35] and hailing a "Glad Reprieve for Times Square."[36]

As the sponsors of the project formulated an interim plan, they did not have to reject historicity as a legitimizing vision. They were now more free to draw on the historic role of Forty-second Street than they had been when trapped in their own romanticized vision of the Great White Way. Indeed, this image of the Great White Way, which had defined the project for nearly a decade, also vanished from public discourse. In the new plan, history would again be used to establish the vision that would guide redevelopment; it was necessary only to redefine and repackage the history of the street.

When the design team headed by Stern unveiled its guidelines for the interim plan in 1993, the new discursive themes were clearly evident. In contrast to the formula of office towers and Broadway theaters set out in the 42nd Street Development Project, the new proposal celebrated and embraced the "honky-tonk" image of West Forty-second Street. It emphasized the historic diversity of popular entertainment forms that had made Forty-second Street "a living symbol of American culture and democracy."[37] The redefined vision for Forty-second Street was described in the following terms:

> 42nd Street Now! calls for the restoration of New York's quintessential entertainment district, our most democratic good-time place. The renewed 42nd Street will be an enhanced version of itself—not a gentrified theme park or festival market. The focus of the renewed 42nd Street will be theaters and all that goes with them: restaurants and retail establishments related to entertainment and tourism. Once again 42nd Street will be able to take its rightful place among the world's great urban entertainment destinations.[38]

West Forty-second Street was no longer defined in terms of the glamorous Great White Way, but as a "democratic good-time place" offering entertainment for everyone. Thus the new plan promised a revitalized Forty-second Street fit for popular consumption. Whether the new Forty-second Street would defy the theme-park label remained to be seen, but the plan clearly imagined a sanitized version of the street's more recent honky-tonk incarnations. Certainly, Stern's flashy design sketches omitted the ubiquitous "XXX" that had dotted the landscape of West Forty-second Street.

Despite his best intentions to make Forty-second Street an "unplanned" and "enhanced version of itself," Stern was still offering a marketable revision of history. Politically, the approach had distinct advantages. The cultural imagery of good, clean, honky-tonk fun—Times Square à la 1950s Americana—promised to foster broad public support. The cultural project was, moreover, firmly grounded in the image of Times Square as a popular entertainment district that was shaped by the culture community, including the Municipal Art Society. Economically, the shift from Broadway theater to popular attractions opened up the possibility of a twenty-four-hour entertainment district with an unlimited clientele, a prospect that could inspire interest among the biggest names in the entertainment industry. The interim plan, then, offered a new formula of symbolic politics to accompany a new strategy of economic development. This time, however, the cultural project would pave the way for the office development.

The interim plan succeeded in generating enthusiasm from the culture community, whose members were thrilled that the redevelopment effort would finally shift from office towers to entertainment venues. Their only objection was that the agreement allowed the developers to discard these interim uses and construct their office buildings whenever the market dictated. The Municipal Art Society, in particular, became a vocal opponent of continuing the subsidy for future office development.[39] Kent Barwick, president of the society, pointed out that the vision motivating the interim plan implicitly acknowledged that office development was not necessary for revitalization. Just before the interim plan was formally approved in August 1994, the MAS released a report that was highly critical of the public subsidies, which would extend into billions of dollars. It argued that the city should simply reimburse the developers for their expenses and allow them to build without a subsidy if the plan still made sense. The MAS even contemplated a legal challenge to block the terms of the interim plan, a strategy that it had used successfully in forcing the redesign of the Coliseum project at Columbus Circle in the 1980s.[40]

The increasingly confrontational stance adopted by the MAS since it had supported the 42nd Street Development Project a decade earlier reflected its enhanced bargaining position in development politics.[41] The society had been integrated into the pro-growth coalition over the previous twenty years because of its ability to influence opinion among important constituencies. Articulating values of historic preservation, the arts, and urban design, the MAS contributed to a development agenda and discourse that resonated with a wide range of white-collar professionals who constituted a powerful bloc of political support. In this way, the MAS had become a significant player on development issues during the 1980s, contributing to the redesign of such major projects as the Coliseum site and Donald Trump's Riverside South. The same group that had gone along with office development in the early 1980s in order to achieve its goal of theater preservation on Forty-second Street no longer saw its options so clearly constrained in the 1990s.

By the early 1990s, the MAS had helped redefine the discourse on Forty-second Street, establishing an identity for the street as part of a Times Square entertainment district that should be cultivated and protected against an invasion of office towers. As it became clear that the market for office space was failing, sponsors of the project embraced this entertainment-based strategy and discourse. Thus they were able to capitalize on ready-made political support for a revised plan. As for the office towers, officials pleaded that their hands were tied; they were legally and morally bound to honor their deal with the developers whose money was making possible the transformation of Forty-second Street. Once again, they would count on the culture community preferring compromise to obstruction. The important thing for the redevelopment effort was to make the entertainment strategy a success, and on this all parties could agree.

PREPARING THE WAY FOR POPULAR ENTERTAINMENT

The process of reconstructing a vision for West Forty-second Street already was taking place on other fronts, too, as project sponsors were formulating their revised plan. By the time the original proposal collapsed in 1992, officials of the 42nd Street Development Project were pointing to a number of positive developments in the Times Square area that would provide the groundwork for a revised strategy focusing on entertainment uses.[42] Aside from the recent overdevelopment of office space in Times Square, the area's entertainment economy had benefited from investment in new hotels (3,000 new rooms), restaurants, and nightspots. Broadway theater was enjoying a big season, with the number of shows up by nearly a third over the previous season and record-setting attendance levels and box-office receipts.[43] The number of adult-entertainment businesses in Times Square had decreased by nearly half over the preceding decade, from seventy-two in 1981 to thirty-eight in 1991. Crime, too, had declined, dropping 12 percent since the mid-1980s. Times Square literally glowed with greater intensity, as the number of super-signs increased to thirty-nine from twenty-two a decade earlier—due to the new zoning requirements pushed through by preservationists.

On New Year's Day 1992, the Times Square Business Improvement District (BID) came to life, sweeping away the refuse of the previous night's celebration in a dramatic announcement that there was a new sheriff in town. The BID provided a mechanism by which property owners in Times Square[44] could pool their resources, through a special tax assessment, "to make the 'Crossroads of the World' clean, safe, and friendly."[45] Toward that end, the BID deployed a crew of more than fifty sanitation workers—outfitted in snazzy red jumpsuits fashioned by a Broadway theater costume designer—and a team of forty public-safety officers, "unarmed but fully trained" and linked by radio to the police department. In addition, the BID launched a vast array of other initiatives, including street and sidewalk improvement projects; a visitor center (at the corner of Forty-second Street and Seventh Avenue) and information kiosks; a homeless outreach team and other social programs coordinated with social service providers; and such promotional efforts as ad campaigns ("Times Square—everything you want in a neighbor-hood"), restaurant and business guides, New Year's Eve festivities, an annual "Broadway on Broadway" outdoor musical extravaganza, and a weekly "behind the scenes walking tour" of Times Square.[46]

The creation of the Times Square BID illustrates the trend toward the parcel-ing of cities into privately controlled public spaces (and neglected or abandoned public spaces), especially in areas deemed most desirable for the postindustrial economy by the city's economic elites.[47] The Times Square BID was initiated at the prodding of influential business and civic leaders, and its board of directors included "some of the most powerful property owners in the city."[48] Arthur Ochs Sulzberger, the publisher of the New York Times, became its chairman after actively working for the creation of the BID. The BID operated on a substantial $4.5 mil-lion annual fund collected from about 800 area property owners, the largest of which were assessed as much as $1,000 a day for the BID's services.[49] In this way, dominant economic interests in the area were able to target their resources directly to accomplish their own goals for Times Square. They were free from the need to tangle with the political process or to see their resources redirected to improve con-ditions elsewhere in the city. Mayor Dinkins, characteristically responsive to the business community, signed the law that ceded authority over the Times Square area to the private board of the BID.

As the BID was working to enhance the environment and culture of the larger Times Square area, officials of the 42nd Street Development Project were work-ing to prepare West Forty-second Street for its role in a newly polished entertain-ment district. Public safety was of paramount concern, and in May 1992 officials of the New York State UDC announced that since they had taken over the eastern two-thirds of the project area crime along Forty-second Street had declined by "a staggering 54 percent."[50] A new property management team was working to improve the condition of vacated buildings.[51] Several historic theaters were already being used intermittently as venues for plays, concerts, readings, and movies.

In February 1992, the UDC approved a lease with The New 42nd Street, Inc. ("The New 42"), a nonprofit organization created to oversee the restoration of six historic theaters in the project area. This cleared the way for implementing con-crete redevelopment plans for the theaters, to be paid for with money committed by the office developers as part of the original deal. Quietly, in September 1991, state officials had approved changes that allowed the historic theaters to be used for a variety of "lively entertainment activities."[52] This change significantly broad-ened the potential of Forty-second Street as a popular entertainment district.

The arts continued to be central to the new strategy for West Forty-second Street, as they had been in the redevelopment efforts of the 1970s and 1980s. In the summer of 1993, and again in the summer of 1994, officials of the 42nd Street Development Project transformed Forty-second Street into an outdoor public art exhibit between Broadway and Eighth Avenue.[53] They commissioned several dozen artists, designers, and architects—including Jenny Holzer, Tibor Kalman, and Liz

Diller and Ric Scofidio—to produce works that were integrated into the streetscape of vacated storefronts. Many of the pieces drew on, and made palatable, the once-disturbing images of Forty-second Street: *Soft Sell* consisted of a pair of large, sensuous red lips projected by video onto the entrance of a historic theater, seducing passers-by with such phrases as "Hey you, want to buy a place in heaven?" Mannequins in a shop window for the faux boutique "American She-Male" modeled outfits made entirely of condom packages, while the message on the display window read: "MAKE A STATEMENT!! WEAR CONDOMS!!" The statuary of *History Lesson* brought the nude body to Forty-second Street in its classical cultural forms, for a change. Graffiti art—of the commissioned sort—brightened the iron security gates covering vacant storefronts. The theater marquees that once boasted the best porn in town now featured Jenny Holzer's "Truism" and "Survival" messages, such as "MEN DON'T PROTECT YOU ANYMORE" and "SAVOR KINDNESS BECAUSE CRUELTY IS ALWAYS POSSIBLE LATER." The overall theme was conveyed prominently in a billboard-style piece featuring the word "EVERYBODY" in black letters on a yellow background, located at the base of Times Square.

The artworks thus were part of the larger process of repackaging West Forty-second Street for consumption by a more desirable crowd of tourists and higher-income city residents. The art transformed and tamed the same troubling images of the street that had been emphasized to justify redevelopment. Symbols of hard-core commercial sex and African-American hip-hop culture were recast from deterrents to attractions for "everybody" through the medium of an art exhibition. West Forty-second Street was transformed into a museum for the display of images and relics captured from its own recent past. Put under glass, as it were, the raw stuff of West Forty-second Street became material for the symbolic economy—much as photographs of gruesome accident scenes became art under the direction of Andy Warhol or violent medieval weaponry is the object of detached contemplation at the Metropolitan Museum. And analogous to the thrill of viewing wild animals in natural-habitat displays at a zoo (designed for the benefit of captive or viewer?), the Forty-second Street experience was enhanced by the faint thrill of danger conjured from the undesirable activities and populations that still lingered nearby. The street's new cultural status was affirmed by a telling headline in the *New York Times:* "42d Street Says Move over SoHo."[54]

Project sponsors were especially eager to integrate families into the entertainment economy of a renewed Forty-second Street. Officials of The New 42nd Street, Inc., announced in the fall of 1993 that the first of the historic theaters to be restored on the street—indeed, the first tangible redevelopment of any kind—would be dedicated for use as a children's theater.[55] The organization's president, Cora Cahan, made explicit its goal: "The replacement of X-rated films with family fare within a single theater will communicate a message of hope up and down the block." As another welcoming gesture to families, the art exhibition on Forty-second Street in 1994 featured a multistory mural of Dr. Seuss's Cat in the Hat smiling and waving his gangly arms. Certainly, the arrival of the Cat in the Hat on Forty-second Street was an aggressive statement that things had changed. Nevertheless, the image of West Forty-second Street as an area fit for family entertainment would not be officially established until the arrival of the Walt Disney Company.

DISNEY LANDS ON FORTY-SECOND STREET

In 1993, the Walt Disney Company began negotiating with officials of the 42nd Street Development Project about the landmark New Amsterdam Theater on Forty-second Street just west of Seventh Avenue.[56] Disney had begun presenting live stage versions of its blockbuster movies in 1992, with a production of *Beauty and the Beast,* and Chairman Michael Eisner was interested in acquiring a theater as a showcase for additional productions. Robert A. M. Stern, who was both an architect on the Forty-second Street project and a board member of the Disney company, coaxed Eisner into considering the New Amsterdam. Although the ten-story Art Nouveau theater was in derelict condition after years of neglect, it had been a magnificent creation when completed in 1903 and had continued to stand out among even the most elegant Broadway theaters. In 1994, the chairwoman of the city's Landmarks Preservation Commission described it as "the crown jewel of all the theaters in the city."[57]

For officials of the 42nd Street Development Project, the possibility of luring Disney into the redevelopment effort was an extraordinary opportunity to resuscitate a project that had sputtered along on life support for more than a decade. Other entertainment companies were interested in the New Amsterdam, but none offered the symbolic might of Disney. With its sparkling image of wholesome Americana, Disney's presence alone would symbolize the conquest of Forty-second Street by the forces of good over evil. Although the entertainment economy of greater Times Square was thriving, project officials continued to be frustrated in their efforts to generate the same enthusiasm for the Forty-second Street theaters. Negative perceptions of the street—inspired in part by the discursive imagery of decline that officials themselves had freely employed in public statements until recently—still threatened to obstruct the interim plan. Cora Cahan, in charge of redeveloping historic theaters on the block, later recalled that "we were getting inquiries from mud-wrestling operators, and those were the better ones."[58] With Disney in place, widespread interest in the rest of the block would certainly follow, thereby sealing the new image of West Forty-second Street as an area of popular entertainment. In sum, Disney represented nothing less than a major public-relations coup for the project.

Project officials therefore coveted Disney's participation. Rebecca Robertson, president of the 42nd Street Development Project, later revealed her perception that "Disney brought to the table, all by themselves, the possibility that the project would get done, and that it would be done by the most important entertainment company in the world."[59] This attitude gave Disney no small advantage at the bargaining table. Despite its carefully polished, warm-and-fuzzy image, Disney did not hesitate to play hardball in order to wrest concessions from public officials. The entertainment giant haggled relentlessly and even set a "drop-dead date" by which its conditions must be met, or else.[60] At least once, negotiators for Disney left the bargaining table in a fit of pique—declaring "We're finished"—when their demands were not met.[61] In the end, Disney's heavy-handed tactics paid off, and the company extracted a deal from project officials that went well beyond what other developers received.

When, after two years of negotiations, Disney officials formally sealed the deal on the New Amsterdam in July 1995, they had considerable reason to be optimistic about the move to Forty-second Street.[62] Not only did project officials foot the bill of $250,000 for acquiring the site, but they also agreed to subsidize the restoration of the theater with city-financed low-interest loans that covered about 75 percent of the estimated $34 million cost.[63] (When other Broadway theater operators objected to the subsidy, on the grounds that it gave Disney an unfair competitive advantage, Governor Mario Cuomo co-opted their support by establishing a state-financed loan program for the upkeep of Broadway theaters.[64]) Disney itself faced an up-front investment of about $10 million, the equivalent of pocket change for such a large company. In return, it would have a magnificent showcase theater to facilitate its savvy move into live stage productions; *Beauty and the Beast* was already proving enormously successful in its run at a nearby Broadway theater, and those box-office receipts certainly helped seal Disney's interest in Times Square.

In a more fundamental sense, Disney found a way to test its magic in the increasingly strong market of urban entertainment while risking relatively little.[65] Generous public subsidies made the numbers work; the only other major concern was the character of the street itself. The Disney formula depended heavily on a controlled environment for the success of its entertainment venues. Disney therefore sought assurances about the other uses allowed on its Forty-second Street block. Plans already were in place to restore the first of the historic theaters; by the end of 1995, the New Victory Theater would be presenting children's fare across the street from the New Amsterdam. But the redevelopment of other properties remained uncertain.

The Disney negotiators originally demanded a right of first refusal regarding all the other properties on the block, allowing Disney to preempt any deal that project officials might make with a competing offer of its own.[66] The officials successfully resisted this demand on the grounds that it would undermine negotiations with other companies. The compromise, then, was the requirement that two more entertainment companies satisfactory to Disney be committed to the street before Disney's drop-dead date of mid-July 1995. So when the deal was done, the announcement came that Disney would be joined in its move to Forty-second Street by American Multi-Cinemas (AMC) and Madame Tussaud's of London.[67] American Multi-Cinemas planned the city's largest multiplex movie theater, with twenty-five screens and seating for 5,000; Tussaud's planned a high-tech wax museum modeled after its successful attraction in London.

By the time the deal with Disney was finalized, concern about the rest of the block was effectively moot. Word that Disney was likely to join the Forty-second Street project sparked widespread interest in the street among prominent entertainment companies. By the end of 1994, Frank Rich of the *New York Times* reported that "virtually every 42d Street parcel has become the subject of active negotiation."[68] During 1995 and 1996, there flowed a stream of reports announcing deals for new entertainment attractions and themed restaurants, bars, and cafés.[69]

Nor did Disney limit its presence on the street to the New Amsterdam. Amid the renewed excitement, project officials reopened bidding on the hotel site at the northeast corner of Forty-second Street and Eighth Avenue. Disney was part of a development team that submitted a proposal for a hotel and entertainment/retail complex on the site.[70] Specifically, their plan called for Tishman Realty and Construction Company to build and run the hotel, while Disney would operate 100 time-share apartments under the Disney Vacation Club. The competition pitted Disney's team against high-powered hoteliers Marriott and Hilton, and matched celebrity architects and their exciting designs: Disney's Architectonica, Marriott's Michael Graves, and Hilton's Zaha Hadid.[71] The Disney team won, despite Marriott's having financing in place and being prepared to start the project immediately. A disappointed Marriott official declared, "We feel that the Disney name was most important to the people who were making the decision."[72]

Thus Disney developments would serve as sentinels at both ends of Forty-second Street between Seventh and Eighth Avenues. The Disney anchor at the western end, called E-walk, will include a forty-seven-story hotel, itself a visual spectacle.[73] Through a play of streaking light and colored glass, the tower will simulate a meteor crashing to earth. At its base, a visual explosion of video monitors and postcard images will mark the facade of the ten-story retail/entertainment area and vacation club. Periodic bursts of "pixie dust" will further highlight an event of planetary significance. At the eastern end of the block, a Disney superstore opened at the corner of Seventh Avenue and Forty-second Street in 1996, followed shortly by the inauguration of the magnificently restored New Amsterdam Theater next door.

West Forty-second Street was emerging as a multifaceted venue for the dissemination of Disney culture. Disney was positioned to present live stage shows, market its vast line of merchandise, and house vacationers all on one block of Forty-second Street. In addition, the AMC movie chain, as one of the biggest Disney distributors, would provide an outlet for Disney movies in its twenty-five-screen multiplex. The Disney-owned ABC television network, too, had negotiated in 1997 for use of the Times Square Theater on Forty-second Street as a location for its *Good Morning America* show, but the plan fell through. Network officials had hoped to use the Forty-second Street backdrop to re-create the success enjoyed by the NBC *Today* show, with its curbside studio in Rockefeller Center—a clear indication of how much things had changed on the street.[74] In a dramatic event symbolizing Disney's conquest of Times Square, courtesy of a gracious Mayor

Rudolph Giuliani, even the public space of the Forty-second Street itself became a Disney Main Street, with a spectacular parade marking the premiere of the movie *Hercules* at the recently opened New Amsterdam Theater.[75]

While public officials gave up much to accommodate Disney, it was an investment that clearly produced enormous dividends. More than any other single factor, Disney was responsible for sparking the transformation of West Forty-second Street. Within a few years after signing Disney, arrangements for the remaining sites had fallen into place. West Forty-second Street was full of entertainment attractions and sharing in the booming tourist economy of Times Square.[76] Restoration projects were in place for all nine historic theaters: the New Amsterdam was Disney's stage; the New Victory was presenting live entertainment for children; the Apollo (Academy) and Lyric were combined by the Livent Company of Toronto into the Ford Center for the Performing Arts (named after its corporate sponsor), a house suitable for major Broadway musicals that opened in January 1998 with a production of *Ragtime;* Livent also won the right to operate the Times Square as a 500-seat theater with a restaurant and office space (beating out a more lucrative proposal from the World Wrestling Federation); the Liberty, Empire, and Harris were being redeveloped by Forest City Ratner for the AMC and Tussaud's projects; and the Selwyn was designated the new home of the Roundabout Theater Company, with a ten-story building of glass and light going up above to provide rehearsal spaces.

Other major pieces of the original development plan were coming to life as well. In 1997, project officials finally resolved the issue of the site, a parking lot on Eighth Avenue across from the Port Authority Bus Terminal, originally slated for a merchandise mart. It was acquired by the Milstein brothers in 1983 in an attempt to get in on the imminent redevelopment project.[77] When the Milsteins were passed over, repeatedly, in the selection of developers, they fought the project in an epic legal battle. In 1996, they were the last holdouts against condemnation from among the 280 businesses and property owners once located in the project area. The value of the lot had soared from the $5 million that the Milsteins paid in 1983—shortly after city officials passed on an option to buy the land for $1 million—to perhaps $35 million in the mid-1990s. Because this revaluation made site acquisition costs prohibitive, project officials finally settled on a deal by which the Milsteins will develop a thirty-five-story budget-rate hotel. Thus the last piece of the Forty-second Street puzzle was in place.

By the latter half of the 1990s, even the office towers were beginning to stir from the subterranean depths to which they had sunk only a few years earlier. The Prudential Insurance Company, eager to begin recouping some return on the hundreds of millions of dollars it had invested in the project, began offering to sell its development rights—and tax breaks—to developers prepared to build.[78] In 1996, Douglas Durst, a longtime foe of the project with his own development interests in the area, acquired the right to build the tower at the northeast corner of Broadway and Forty-second Street for about $75 million. He combined the site with adjacent parcels of his own and began construction in 1996 on a forty-eight-story tower with just shy of 1.5 million square feet of space. With the help of $10.75 million in tax breaks, Durst lured Condé Nast, the nation's largest magazine empire, as an anchor tenant for the new tower.[79] Deals for the remaining sites were expected "to fall like dominos."[80] By 1998, a deal was in place for a second office tower, the thirty-two-story Reuters Building, at the northwest corner of Forty-second Street and Seventh Avenue. According to plan, the area was now fit for corporate headquarters.

Disney effectively resolved the political and economic challenges that accompanied the revised plan. In terms of economics, Disney transformed Forty-second Street into a safe, even desirable, area for investment by entertainment companies and office developers. Under Disney's tutelage, West Forty-second Street was finally integrated into the postindustrial economy of the city. Politically, the Disney name ensured widespread popular support for the revised development agenda. Disney epitomized the popular entertainment that officials had emphasized in their new vision for Forty-second Street. Even the culture community was silenced by Disney's power to transform the street. Of course, it became impossible to escape the theme-park label that sponsors had hoped to eschew, and references to a honky-tonk atmosphere were notably absent from accounts of the street's renaissance. In this respect, the transformation taking place was at odds with the discursive theme that had rationalized the interim plan a few years earlier. But Disney had redefined the discourse on Forty-second Street. Indeed, given its hegemonic position in popular culture, Disney was its own justification. Aside from an odd assortment of eggheads and social critics, few commentators were challenging the transformation from the Dangerous Deuce to a Disney Deuceland. In this way, the Disney name acted as insulation from any broad-based political challenge.

Although Disney proved to be a godsend in terms of political and economic goals, its effect on the public life of Forty-second Street is still an open question. As the beachhead of Disney's foray into the urban entertainment market, Forty-second Street provides an important case for understanding the impact of so-called Disneyfication on contemporary cities.

7

Learning from Forty-second Street

Bring back the porno
42nd Street bellows
Mickey denies us
—Patricia M. Murphy, quoted in Christopher Reynolds, "Times Square Now
a Reason to Be in a New York State of Mind," *Kansas City Star* (1997)

The effort to reclaim the city is the struggle of democracy itself.
—Michael Sorkin, *Variations on a Theme Park* (1992)

In the redevelopment of Forty-second Street and Times Square taking place during the 1990s, many of the processes at work in cities throughout the United States are evident in magnified form. Cities have attempted to revitalize central districts characterized by urban decline in similar ways: creating spectacular spaces of consumption and entertainment, often through the adaptive reuse of historic buildings, and constructing new places of work, such as office towers, appropriate for an advanced service-based economy. Times Square is nothing if not a unique place, but in some important respects, it differs from other central urban areas more in degree than in kind. Thus from the exaggerated features of the Times Square case we can identify important lessons about the nature of urban development at the end of the twentieth century.

The lessons from Times Square fall into two broad categories. First, the case offers insight into the political processes that drive contemporary urban development. Who is behind the construction of new urban places, and how are they able to succeed in mobilizing political support for such transformations? We can draw on the Times Square case to theorize inductively about the operation of political power in cities, and thereby enhance our understanding of urban political economy. Second, the case raises important questions about the nature and impact of contemporary urban development. How does development affect the social life of cities, and are these social consequences good and desirable? We turn now to the tasks of making sense of, and making normative judgments regarding, the transformation of 42nd Street and Times Square.

*　*　*

TIMES SQUARE AND URBAN THEORY

The Times Square case illustrates that the politics of urban development can operate on several levels. At the most basic level, political and economic elites interested in the redevelopment of Times Square had to construct a political coalition in support of their effort. Mayor Ed Koch presided over a stable regime built around a conservative social agenda that favored middle-class white ethnic voters and a conservative economic agenda that served major downtown business and development interests. The redevelopment of Times Square fit squarely into the goal of postindustrial transformation that Koch shared with the city's economic elites, but the process had significant political risks as well.

Economic restructuring threatened to mobilize opposition from the city's African-American and Latino residents—who were close to a majority of the city's population during the 1980s—who often bore the brunt of the changes through displacement and higher living costs while benefiting relatively less by the shift from an industrial to a service-based economy. At the same time, restructuring generated uncertain responses from the growing population of white-collar professionals. Although many in this group might be expected to support development projects that accommodated them with places of work, residence, and entertainment, they were also potential opponents of development projects that imposed quality-of-life costs on their Manhattan neighborhoods. During the 1980s, for example, a number of conflicts on the Upper West Side pitted higher-income residents against developers.

The greatest political danger confronting Koch was a potential alliance among African-Americans, Latinos, and white liberals (often drawn from professional sectors). Indeed, in many other cities, such liberal coalitions recently had succeeded in wresting power from traditional white-ethnic alliances. Koch was effective in gaining some support from African-Americans and Latinos through his control over appointments and social spending, and through his accommodations with the regular Democratic organizations. But his racially charged rhetoric, used to fire up his own political base, left him vulnerable to a strong liberal challenger.

An ongoing political objective of the mayor was, therefore, drawing white professionals into his pro-growth regime. Not only did he hope to undermine a liberal electoral challenge, but he sought to weaken the kind of mobilized antigrowth community movements that had shown political savvy in obstructing development projects. Key ingredients of the postindustrial vision for Manhattan had been thwarted by such opposition—most notably the Westway plan for a new West Side Highway—and Koch was eager to avoid similar challenges to future development initiatives. Major restructuring of Forty-second Street and Times Square was a crucial ingredient in the recipe for a postindustrial Manhattan, but the effort would certainly ignite political opposition. Thus the redevelopment plan had to be carefully tailored to maximize political support.

Looking back to 1984, when the 42nd Street Development Project received final approval from the political process, it is remarkable how widespread public support was for the redevelopment effort. After all, the scale of the proposed construction—involving four massive office towers, an enormous merchandise mart, and a large hotel—bore a troubling resemblance to the discredited urban renewal tactics that provoked so much opposition a decade earlier. Yet what stands out is the way in which political support was linked to a particular symbolic representation of the redevelopment effort. Because the plan also provided for the restoration of historic theaters as Broadway stages, the project had come to be portrayed as a return of the Great White Way to an area that symbolized urban decline. Perhaps more than anything, this political discourse, promising an escape from harsh urban realities and a return to the imagined glamour of New York past, served to mobilize broad support for the project. With this symbolic representation, progrowth forces avoided the kind of political opposition that had stymied traditional urban renewal efforts.

The Forty-second Street case, therefore, opens up additional levels of analysis relevant to understanding how urban regimes are constructed and maintained. It points to the importance of political discourse in the process of forging political coalitions. Regimes are built on more than material exchanges and tangible benefits; they depend also on a shared vision that defines and justifies an urban policy agenda. The importance of a structuring discourse has been recognized, at least implicitly, in a variety of urban studies. Clarence Stone, for example, noted that a vision of Atlanta as "the city too busy to hate" was used to unify a biracial coalition behind an agenda of racial moderation and postindustrial economic growth.[1] Michael Pagano and Ann Bowman have even made the "vision" of city leaders the central concept in their analysis of development politics: "Local officials pursue development as a means of reaching an ideal, reflecting an image they hold collectively of what their city ought to be."[2] Leaders formulate and pursue particular visions for their city "for reasons that include its history, its place in the hierarchy of cities, and its aspirations to change."[3] Pagano and Bowman point to Times Square as an example of the kind of symbolic place that can serve to define a city's vision.

This attention to "vision" begins to capture the importance of political discourse and its relevance to regime studies. But the Times Square case suggests that the significance of political discourse may go deeper, to a more complex level of symbolic politics. At this level, the potency of political discourse is derived from the interplay of cultural images and symbols; in effect, political discourse may tap into an arena of cultural politics in ways that lend legitimacy to a particular urban agenda. Urban scholars have discovered the importance of these political realms: Sharon Zukin has identified cultural production as a driving force in urban restructuring,[4] and Robert Beauregard has illuminated the structuring power of political discourse in shaping the urban policy agenda.[5] The conceptual tools are available, therefore, for addressing directly the roles of culture and discourse in development politics.

These analytical approaches can be integrated into the regime framework for a richer understanding of urban development politics. In the Forty-second Street case, the preservation of historic theaters was a relatively minor component of the project, but it provided the necessary political capital that traditional urban renewal projects lacked. In part, this can be explained in terms of a standard regime analysis: the theater restorations operated as tangible selective incentives drawing into the pro-growth alliance important constituencies that had opposed traditional urban renewal efforts. The restored theaters were a primary objective of various civic and professional groups concerned with historic preservation, the arts, and urban design; and they represented new cultural resources for higher-income New Yorkers. In this way, the project provided tangible benefits to the affluent white professionals who were so important to the Koch regime.

But the elements of preservation and the arts served the regime's interests on another level as well, by facilitating a political discourse that represented the project as an effort to reclaim part of the city's glorious past. Prominent pro-growth voices juxtaposed a romanticized Great White Way against unsettling images of urban decline, especially images of racial transition, and thus constructed a political discourse that tapped into deep-seated anxieties among whites about the loss of their status, culture, and security. Because it resonated with potent cultural symbolism, this discourse was salient among whites of all income levels, who formed the electoral foundation of the Koch regime, even though the majority of them might benefit little from new Broadway theaters charging as much as $75 or more for "da noise and da funk" of an earlier Times Square.[6] In effect, cultural politics formed the basis of a political discourse that contributed to the construction of a broad pro-growth alliance in support of the regime's agenda. This analysis illustrates how the concepts of culture, discourse, and regime can be nested together to form a coherent analytical framework.

Although Mayor Koch was ousted from office before the 42nd Street Development Project produced any results, the Koch regime—built on the support of white ethnic voters and downtown development interests—was never dismantled. David Dinkins failed to solidify an alternative regime during his single term, and Rudolph Giuliani came into office on what was, in effect, a reconstituted Koch regime. Thus there was considerable continuity in the nature of pro-growth politics in New York City during the 1980s and 1990s. Development policy reflected the agenda of major downtown development interests, but preservationists and others in the culture community played an important role in shaping development projects and patterns of support among an all-important constituency of white professionals.

Although the Forty-second Street project had moved by the 1990s from the arena of mayoral politics to the more insulated domain of state development officials, it remained closely tied to the reality of development politics in New York. So when a temperamental real-estate market forced sponsors to delay the planned office development, they turned to an interim plan that continued to build on the theme of historic preservation. This proposal involved restoring the entire physical fabric of Forty-second Street for entertainment uses. Again, historic imagery was mobilized to smooth the way, but the history of the area was redefined to construct an image of Forty-second Street as a "democratic good-time place." By altering the political discourse in this way, pro-growth forces could mobilize broad support for a more popular entertainment district. The Disney name then secured this new development strategy and new discourse. Throughout the life of the project, then, historic preservation has served as the essential ingredient in the political discourse and cultural politics; and, therefore, patterns of political support have been fairly consistent as well. Thus despite having done little to bring about the redevelopment of Forty-second Street, Mayor Giuliani has sought to reap political rewards from a project that was custom-designed by Koch for the same regime interests.

Attention to the role of historic preservation in shaping political discourse may help explain the frequent appearance of broad public support for contemporary development projects. Paul Peterson's thesis that the imperative of local economic growth produces widespread public support for urban development appeared to fit well with the pro-growth orientation of cities that emerged in the late 1970s.[7] But this economic determinism failed to account for different patterns of development politics, most notably the political conflict that had increasingly overwhelmed earlier urban renewal efforts. It also did not acknowledge important differences in the political and economic interests of urban residents. Indeed, what rankled urban scholars was a nagging sense that Peterson's neat analysis was as much a contribution to the pro-growth discourse of the Reagan era as an explanation of observable political phenomena.

Rather than being based on purely economic incentives, the pro-growth consensus common in contemporary urban politics may be grounded in the shift from modernist urban renewal to preservation- and arts-based development strategies. Middle- and upper-income urban residents had increasingly become a source of opposition to urban renewal efforts in the 1960s and 1970s. They objected both to the widespread "creative destruction" of the built environment and to the severe modernist aesthetic that guided the redevelopment of the city. While the austere International Style appealed to architects and planners as an expression of rationality in the urban form, it frustrated the middle-class population that was denied its prized cultural resources. In this context, preservation-based development emerged as a revitalization approach that appealed to the cultural tastes of middle- and upper-income groups. They could embrace massive development as long as it was linked to new cultural resources in the form of historic districts and arts facilities. Times Square and the South Street Seaport in New York City are good examples of such mixed-use areas.

And, as the Times Square case illustrates, historic preservation and the arts can have a powerful political effect by making it possible to recast the terms of public debate over urban development through the mobilization of cultural symbolism. Historic preservation allows pro-growth forces to depict development as a means to restore romanticized images of the good ol' days, whether the glorified past is packaged in the form of an elegant theater district, a lively place of popu-lar entertainment, a bustling waterfront market, a friendly main street, or some other reassuring symbolic place.[8] By evoking historic imagery, pro-growth inter-ests can frame the debate over development in terms of a social agenda of reclaim-ing an idealized past, thereby deflecting attention away from such issues as the biological or physical environment, quality of life, public subsidies, and economic restructuring that often ignite antigrowth movements. Preservation-based devel-opment offers a historic theme park as an alternative to the places that symbolize urban decline, including obsolete industrial districts of factories and warehouses, underutilized waterfront docks, and blighted older residential neighborhoods. The imagery is particularly salient when development can play on racial anxieties, as in the case of Times Square, by capitalizing on the fear of racial transition in cen-tral cities that is associated with urban decline.

Thus while economic imperatives do indeed dictate the need for urban devel-opment, political considerations still determine the way development can be suc-cessfully achieved. The Times Square case demonstrates that historic preservation and the arts can generate political support for development projects. Of course, it is important to acknowledge the limitations of generalizing from this case alone about development politics. It might be tempting, for example, to hypothesize that development projects that include elements of historic preservation and the arts will enjoy greater political support than those that do not, the key to consensual development being the creation of places of consumption that appeal to the cul-tural values of middle- and upper-income groups. But as the regime studies of the past decade have demonstrated, the methods by which pro-growth alliances are constructed and maintained vary according to the particular political contexts of different places and times. It pays to be cautious, therefore, in generalizing about urban development politics from the example of Times Square.

Indeed, a cursory look at the role of historic preservation in American cities other than New York reveals great differences in its impact on urban development.[9] Historic preservation has had virtually no effect on the development agenda in Atlanta because it lacks relevance to the main groups that form the city's biracial regime.[10] Business leaders have opposed any values that interfere with unrestrained "investor prerogative," and African-Americans have found little worth preserving in a history defined by their own oppression. But both groups have enjoyed con-crete benefits spinning off from "full throttle development." Since a stable regime has been constructed around these selective incentives—and the related vision of a forward-looking southern city—preservationists have had little of political or eco-nomic value to offer the regime.

Historic preservation has been important in New Orleans.[11] That city was one of the first in the nation to protect its historic buildings, adopting a preservation ordinance in the 1930s for the historic Vieux Carré, or French Quarter. Through subsequent decades, historic preservation fit well with a caretaker regime that was content to forgo an activist development agenda while maintaining the traditional social order.[12] In the 1960s, preservationists were able to defeat a highway plan promoted by a nascent growth coalition that would have destroyed the riverfront border of the French Quarter.[13] Thus historic preservation served as a restraint on pro-growth forces. By the 1980s, however, the city's historic resources had become the basis for an aggressive tourist-oriented growth agenda.[14] This shift reflected the process of regime change that occurred in the city.[15]

Still, historic preservation has become ubiquitous in the downtown redevelopment efforts of cities throughout the United States, just as clean-sweep urban renewal reshaped the nation's urban terrain in previous decades. And relatively little has been said about the specifically political basis for this phenomenon, which emerged as a response to the political failure of traditional urban renewal. The Times Square case may, therefore, yield valuable insights into the political significance of a preservation-based development approach. New York City has often provided a magnified picture of urban development trends that occur elsewhere, and so it is an appropriate starting point for theorizing about changes in the urban form. To the extent that historic preservation is linked in other cities to pro-growth regimes pursuing an agenda of economic restructuring, the lessons from Times Square can prove enlightening. How well these observations hold up more generally remains to be determined through the study of other urban spaces.

Although an analysis of the redevelopment of Times Square can suggest new ways of thinking about the political significance of historic preservation, the argument presented here does not depend on generalizing about preservation per se. The purpose is, rather, to document the importance of political discourse to the process of coalition building in the Times Square case, and so demonstrate that political discourse can be a valuable conceptual tool in the framework of regime analysis. In Times Square, historic preservation provided the cultural symbolism that framed the development discourse and helped unify the pro-growth alliance. Historic preservation does not necessarily serve a pro-growth agenda, as is evident in Atlanta, but all coalitions and regimes are built around a unifying political discourse, which may be constructed around historic imagery.

Based on the analysis of the redevelopment of Times Square, four theoretical propositions can be made about the nature and impact of public discourse in the urban arena.

1. Public discourse must be recognized as an instrument of politics. The way in which cities and urban spaces are represented in public debate will shape patterns of political activity. Thus the power to define political discourse is the power to promote a given agenda.

2. Political discourse reflects dominant political and economic interests. This is especially true in city politics because political and economic elites are more able to define the nature of public debate in the limited confines of the urban arena than on the larger state or national stage. The dominant discourse can be found, therefore, in the public voices of public officials, businesspeople, and the media—the voices that are most prominent in public debate. There may be cracks in the dominant discourse, and there will be competing voices, but local elites enjoy the greatest opportunity to construct the narratives that define the local agenda. The extent to which they are successful in constructing an effective discourse will vary, depending on their unity and savvy.

3. Effective political discourse draws on symbolic imagery to promote political and economic interests. Facts do not speak for themselves, and the function of political discourse is to establish a symbolic representation capable of mobilizing public sentiment behind a particular agenda. The imagery may be cultural, racial, and historic, as in Times Square. Or it may be visionary, promising a break with the past and the creation of a new and better future, or progressive, promoting ideals like equality and social justice. The themes of a dominant discourse will vary, depending on the makeup and agenda of the governing regime.

4. Although political discourse is grounded in material interests, it also shapes the pursuit of material interests. Political discourse establishes a framework for interpreting reality and thus both defines and limits what is desirable and possible. As a political instrument, discourse unifies coalition partners behind a given agenda; in so doing, it circumscribes the range of acceptable alternatives and necessitates certain benefits. In Times Square, for example, the developers were forced to pay for historic restorations and elaborate lighted signs, despite their resistance to these amenities, because the pro-growth alliance was unified around a discourse that emphasized historic symbolism.

These four propositions point the way to a new approach to the study of urban regimes and urban political economy. In analyzing how support is generated for urban development efforts—and, relatedly, how enduring coalitions, or regimes, are constructed—we must pay close attention to the way in which the policy agenda is represented in public debate. Media coverage and the statements of public officials and economic elites do not simply offer an objective representation of the development agenda. Rather, we must look for the narrative themes, often constructed around symbolic imagery, that predominate in public debate and structure the way in which the public will interpret and evaluate public policy. We must, in turn, think critically about how the dominant discourse serves political and economic interests as a mechanism by which pro-growth forces can mobilize public support. Finally, we must consider how political discourse also shapes the pursuit of material interests. Through this type of analysis, we can gain better insight into the nature of urban regimes and the way in which their agendas are defined and their coalitions are formed.

POWER, CULTURE, AND PLACE

The redevelopment of Times Square is a prime example of the importance of culture in urban development. Numerous scholars have drawn attention to the interconnections among power, culture, and place in the urban arena.[16] From a variety of perspectives, they have recognized that the urban terrain is composed of different systems of cultural signification that reflect underlying social relations of power and control. The fortified walls and Gothic cathedrals of the medieval city, the palaces and boulevards of the Baroque city, the factories and slums of the industrial city, the office towers of the modern megalopolis, and the gentrified theme parks of the postindustrial city all reveal much about the political and economic arrangements that produced them. Urban places are the concrete products of economic and political power, and the redevelopment of Times Square is the most prominent modern example.

Increasingly, though, urban scholars have been discovering a system of feedback at work in the interaction of power, culture, and place.[17] In other words, urban landscapes not only reflect power relations, but also reinforce them by shaping what is possible in the social life of cities. From this perspective, the urban form is both product and producer of the social order. For example, the cultural symbols inscribed in the urban form serve to establish and demarcate control over urban spaces. The visible characteristics of a block, street, or neighborhood contain important information about the social groups that control the area. Excessive graffiti suggests the unsettling presence of young African-Americans or Latinos associated with hip-hop subcultures or even street gangs; public art is a reassuring sign that an area is safe for middle- and upper-income groups. Race and class are fundamental characteristics expressed in these cultural codes.

Urban residents are remarkably adept at deciphering these codes and interpreting the language of the built environment as they traverse the public spaces of the city. For this reason, cultural forms and symbols take on special significance in the process of establishing control over urban spaces. They reinforce patterns of control over space by intimidating outsiders and "others." Wealthy residents are certain to eschew the graffiti-tagged streets of low-income neighborhoods, and hip-hoppers are scarce at festival marketplaces like the South Street Seaport.[18] The nightly news and other popular media regularly alert different social groups to the prices that are paid for failing to follow the codes of the urban terrain. Tom Wolfe's *Bonfire of the Vanities* was a warning that even the "masters of the universe" can be brought down by one careless mistake in navigating balkanized city turfs.[19]

Cultural symbols can, therefore, be manipulated to alter perceptions and bring about changes in the patterns of control over urban places. In the late 1980s, for example, New York City transit officials conducted a major offensive to eradicate the trademark graffiti from the subways and thereby reassure the middle class that this underground terrain had not been ceded to roving bands of brown-skinned youths in large sneakers. By the early 1990s, graffiti had been effectively replaced with "Art En Route" and "Poetry in Motion" to create a cultural ambience better suited to the refined aesthetic tastes of more upscale subway riders. Where unsettling cultural symbols are not as easily eradicated, they may be mobilized to transform a place into a marketable commodity. Such was the case with Manhattan's East Village, where the same forces of rebellion that thwarted conventional gentrification became the material for a trendy countercultural cachet.[20]

The revitalization of Times Square clearly illustrates the importance of cultural symbols as a mechanism of control over urban spaces. The culture of West Forty-second Street during the 1970s embodied popular images of urban decline in the form of physical decay, pornography, and the prominent presence of young African-American and Latino males. The perception that the area was controlled by dangerous populations was sufficiently powerful to deter the westward migration of the midtown office district, in spite of the enormous economic and political might behind that agenda. The 42nd Street Development Project was an effort to wipe out these troubling cultural images in one concerted assault and thereby open the way for economic development that would expand the boundaries of the midtown office and entertainment districts. The new office towers and Broadway theaters would redefine the culture of lower Times Square from an area taken over by African-Americans and Latinos to an area serving the employment and entertainment activities of higher-income groups.

The Times Square case exemplifies the political significance of historic preservation and the arts in the use of cultural symbols to alter patterns of control over urban space. According to the original plan for Forty-second Street, new office towers would draw whiter and wealthier people to the street by day, and the restored historic theaters would entice them there at night. The physical presence of the magnificent Broadway theaters would thus constitute a cultural code—aptly defined as a Great White Way—demarcating the street as an area for upscale users. When the sponsors of the project were forced to put the office towers on hold, they returned to a theme-park strategy that adapted the entire physical environment of the Forty-second Street project area for entertainment uses. The historic theaters were joined by themed restaurants, superstores, and mass-market retailers to form a unified cultural code of mainstream consumption. When the Disney name went up on Forty-second Street, this cultural code was complete. In the meantime, to ease the transformation of Forty-second Street, the frightening cultural images of the street were transformed, through outdoor art exhibits, into something safe for mass consumption.

By emphasizing the political significance of images of urban decline, this analysis of the redevelopment of Times Square might appear to support the writings of conservative scholars like Lawrence Mead who regard anxiety about urban disorders, such as crime and poverty, as central to contemporary American politics.[21] Certainly, concerns about social disorder on West Forty-second Street were at the forefront of the political debate over redevelopment. In this respect, the redevelopment plan seems linked to and driven by efforts at social control in the city. It offered a means of restoring order in an area of disorder. Indeed, this was precisely the message conveyed by the project's sponsors.

But the redevelopment of Forty-second Street was not simply a response to urban disorder. If it were, a compelling case could be made that areas of the South

Bronx or central Brooklyn were more deserving of revitalization than Times Square. And it is difficult to accept the proposition that economic development is intended to cure—rather than displace—social problems, which was offered half-heartedly in defense of the 42nd Street plan.

Rather, the desire to redevelop Times Square was ultimately driven by the recognition of the enormous profits that could be made from real-estate development on West Forty-second Street. The irony is that at the same time that Forty-second Street from Seventh to Eighth Avenues was decried as the worst block in town in terms of its social ills, it was extremely valuable real estate. As John Logan and Harvey Molotch have argued, the value of a parcel of property is determined less by the workings of a free market than by the uses of surrounding properties.[22] Thus the possibilities for a place, and consequently its value, are defined by the larger geographic context in which it exists.

The location of West Forty-second Street at the nexus of office, theater, and fashion districts in midtown Manhattan made it critical to completing the postindustrial transformation of the city. Of primary interest to political and economic elites was that the area offered the most logical outlet for the expansion of the overbuilt midtown office district. Planners recognized this and established it as a goal by the late 1970s. But investors were aware of the possibilities much earlier, and real-estate speculation was well under way at least by the 1960s. It is this economic potential for West Forty-second Street that explains the persistence of redevelopment efforts. It also explains why owners had to be forced, through eminent domain, to part with property on the worst block in town; they saw the price of their holdings in terms of their potential for office development rather than in terms of their present uses (which were still tolerably profitable because of the adult-entertainment industry).

Economic interests thus provided the underlying motivation for the redevelopment of Forty-second Street. Concerns about social order were used to support the economic project by representing it as an effort to reclaim an area of urban decline for respectable uses. Since hulking office towers and other enormous new construction threatened to spark the antipathy that increasingly confronted traditional urban renewal, these buildings were linked to a project of cultural production centered on historic preservation—or, more accurately, on a marketable · packaging (and repackaging) of history. The Forty-second Street plan was, at heart, an economic project framed as an effort to replace a menacing street culture with the cultural symbols of a glamorous New York past. In this respect, it was an economic endeavor that proceeded under the guise of social and cultural renewal.[23]

This is not to argue that concerns about urban disorders are purely political constructs that lack any objective basis. Clearly, there are serious problems of crime and poverty in contemporary cities, and they constitute a genuine source of public concern. This was certainly true of West Forty-second Street in the 1970s. But careful analysis undermines the claim that the social conditions of the street necessitated wholesale redevelopment. On the one hand, few would argue seriously that economic redevelopment would solve, rather than merely displace, the problems concentrated on West Forty-second Street. On the other hand, street studies conducted at the time revealed fundamental misconceptions about the social life of West Forty-second Street that were influenced in part by the political discourse concerning the area. Aside from its social problems, West Forty-second Street served as the central entertainment district for lower-income New Yorkers; massive redevelopment would destroy this positive function too, while possibly driving the social problems into other areas of the city.

The public has long been concerned about so-called urban problems.[24] Yet the way in which these concerns play into development politics has undergone an important change with the shift from urban renewal to preservation-based development. Traditional urban renewal was up front about its racial agenda in combating urban decline. Urban renewal projects specifically sought to relocate African-Americans away from central business districts, and in this respect they were more overtly racist. Contemporary development continues to have serious racial impacts, often promoting the displacement of African-American and Latino communities through large-scale redevelopment projects and gentrification while confining lower-income groups to areas of neglect and abandonment. But historic preservation makes it possible to play on concerns about urban decline through the manipulation of cultural symbolism. Anxieties about racial transition, in particular, may operate as a concealed subtext in a discourse that emphasizes the effort to reclaim a lost golden age of the past. Consequently, contemporary urban development can proceed without widespread public concern about its impact on racial minorities and poor residents of cities.

In the redevelopment of Times Square, historic preservation became a mechanism by which to reclaim urban space for a higher-income, whiter population by facilitating a political discourse that deflected attention from the project's detrimental effects on people of color. There was little public concern about how the project would dispossess African-Americans and Latinos of a valuable entertainment district and accelerate the displacement of lower-income residents of Clinton. This case indicates that while race continues to be a powerful factor in urban development politics, it now operates more insidiously through the cultural symbolism of political discourse. This may help explain public tolerance for the formation of "dual cities" that are increasingly divided into areas of upscale consumption and concentrated poverty.

DISNEYSPACE AND THE CITY

The emergence of the Walt Disney Company as a major force in the revised development agenda for Times Square both redefined and reinforced the patterns of political discourse and cultural politics that had supported the project in its earlier incarnations. In an important sense, the Disney name came to define the discourse on Times Square redevelopment in the 1990s. Disney's presence meant an end to the trope of the Great White Way as the discursive image supporting redevelopment. Instead, Disney promised to restore Times Square to its preeminent position in mass commercial culture. But this agenda, too, allowed the sponsors of the project to play on nostalgia for another romanticized golden age of Times Square past. Disney's position as the dominant force in family-oriented popular culture made it the definitive antidote to urban decline; thus the symbolic power of the Disney name substituted nicely for the Great White Way as a discursive image justifying the redevelopment of an area that symbolized urban decline.

Disney's impact on West Forty-second Street is not limited to the realm of discourse, however. Disney increasingly permeates the physical, commercial, social, and cultural activities of the street. Disney itself is presented on stage and screen and is sold over the counter, and soon it will be a vacation resort for visitors. At a more fundamental level, though, Forty-second Street has come to embody the Disney model of public space as an orderly, controlled, and themed environment.[25] Private security and sanitation teams of the Times Square Business Improvement District (BID) supplement city services to create an enhanced sense of cleanliness, safety, and order. Public officials of the 42nd Street Development Project, in close cooperation with powerful developers and corporate investors—including Disney—determine which commercial and cultural products will have access to the street, and how they may present themselves visually.

These top decision makers have pursued a vision of Times Square as a fantastic entertainment mecca for family-friendly commercial culture. In the process, they have accommodated an array of upscale entertainment resources, including live theater and movies, themed restaurants and bars, chain retailers, and the latest in high-tech amusements, all within a physical environment characterized by such trademark Times Square features as historic theaters and dazzling lights and signs. As new office towers and hotels take West Forty-second Street to new heights, these skyscrapers also will reinforce the Times Square theme with their funky designs and dramatic lighted signs. More and more, Forty-second Street and Times Square are Disneyspace.

What difference does it make if Disney controls the culture of West Forty-second Street? People like Disney, and the revitalized West Forty-second Street is now packed with throngs of enthusiastic visitors. Close to 25 million tourists stroll West Forty-second Street each year on the block that was, not long ago, decried as the worst in the city.[26] By this measure, the Disneyfication of the street has been a resounding success.

Among a crotchety intellectual elite, however, the Disney name is considerably less well received. Many social commentators harbor a visceral dislike for Disney and its impact on public life. These critics regard the Disney theme parks as contrived, false places that preclude genuine social interaction, enforce conformity and stifle diversity, and deflect attention from meaningful social concerns.[27] They express a more general fear among urbanists that this theme-park phenomenon is being replicated in the revitalized urban places of today—the trendy historic districts, festival marketplaces, and gentrified neighborhoods—with the result that truly democratic social life is increasingly out of reach.[28] From this perspective, the transformation of West Forty-second Street represents a tragic loss of a genuinely diverse public place central to the social life of the city.

Susan Fainstein has provided an insightful analysis of this "post-structuralist" line of argument—so named because it emphasizes the power of the urban form to shape social interaction, rather than focusing on the underlying socioeconomic structure that shapes the urban form.[29] Fainstein identifies two suspect assumptions behind criticisms of urban theme-park places as unauthentic and antidemocratic: "(1) that the city once nurtured diversity more than it does now, and (2) that a desirable city would be more authentic than the one currently being created."[30] In challenging these assumptions, she correctly notes that the segregation of urban space by class and race has always been a feature of American cities and probably was even more pronounced in the past than it is today. Moreover, democratic (majoritarian) processes continue to reinforce such segregation (within some legally prescribed limits), suggesting that most people want to remain among those similar to themselves.

With regard to authenticity, Fainstein points out that "bastardized historical recreation" has been a prominent architectural feature of Western cities for centuries. Nor have critics identified what an authentic urban form should look like in the high-tech postindustrial era of the late twentieth century. Perhaps Disneyland is an authentic form after all in a society that operates in the realm of virtual reality. As Fainstein sees it, then, contemporary cultural critics are in "the same uncomfortable position as their modernist predecessors. They justify their ideas in the name of democracy but speak for an intellectual elite, which seems to be as unanimous in its distaste for the new projects as the popular media are concerted in their praise."[31]

Certainly, Fainstein raises important questions for critics of Disneyesque places. But her astute challenges should not lead us to drop our concerns about democracy and authenticity in urban life. It is still possible to defend these ideals as valid (and interrelated) principles for judging urban development. That segregated spaces have always been a feature of American cities should not dissuade us from pursuing integration as a goal. We have not yet abandoned completely the effort to integrate social and economic institutions, and we should likewise consider this a desirable goal for premiere public spaces—especially those, like Times Square, that have been places of diversity. Nor should we hesitate to challenge majority opinion on this issue as something sacred and immutable. Most people were never allowed a real choice to "vote with their feet" in favor of integrated places. Enduring patterns of segregation did not just occur naturally, but reflect a complex web of past and present policies among public and private institutions that have shaped patterns of urbanization and suburbanization.[32] Public attitudes about segregation are learned responses shaped by biased public policies; as such, they can also be unlearned with the implementation of more enlightened policies.

In our concern for diverse, democratic places we must also consider how that goal is related to the principle of authenticity. This is more than simply an issue of physical forms and facades. After all, the contest over what and who would be accommodated on 42nd Street has largely occurred within the same basic physical framework: The ornate, fantastical historic theaters served Broadway shows, live burlesque, "XXX" films, and action movies all equally well before being absorbed into Disney's magic kingdom.

The issue of authenticity involves a more complex interaction of form and content. Following an "Olmsteadian vision of public space" as a place of class mixing,[33] the ideal authentic public space is one where the physical environment supports a diversity of uses and users, thus creating an area for genuine, or relatively unrestricted, social interaction. Here Jane Jacobs's insights are still relevant: diversity in the physical environment—for example, in terms of building sizes, styles, ages, conditions—can aid in promoting diversity in the social sphere.[34] But where a dictatorial planning power spends seemingly unlimited amounts of money to reshape an area, healthy diversity is precluded. A necessary, if not sufficient, condition for authentic places, then, is the absence of overriding control imposed from above on the physical form and its contents.

The importance of pursuing democracy and authenticity in urban development can be observed in the redevelopment of Forty-second Street, which has proceeded with disregard for these principles. Before its redevelopment, the Times Square area, although an imperfect place, was a public space of genuine diversity that served a wide range of racial, ethnic, and income groups. West Forty-second Street anchored a lower-income entertainment district that coexisted, albeit uneasily, with the more upscale activities of the Broadway theater district. The resulting diversity was remarkable in the heart of money-making Manhattan. The wholesale redevelopment of West Forty-second Street destroyed an essential basis for this diversity and thus furthered the postindustrial transformation of Manhattan into an exclusive area of work, rest, and play for a higher-income, whiter population.

It may be that, as Marshall Berman has suggested, the centrality and accessibility of Times Square will provide "a critical mass [of people] that limits how much damage any developer can inflict."[35] But this seems optimistic, since there is more than the isolated impact of one developer shaping the new face of West Forty-second Street. The entire area between Forty-first and Forty-third Streets from the east side of Broadway to Eighth Avenue is under the control of one authority that was created to implement the agenda of public and private elites. This fact alone reveals an orchestration of form and content in a way that precludes a genuine diversity of uses and users. If an authentic place depends on the absence of such omnipotent control over the possibilities of everyday life, then the new Forty-second Street fails on this score. Instead, the ingredients are there for a theme-park area whose theme, in part, is the reassurance of a relatively homogeneous population in terms of class and race.

Some of the primary players behind the transformation of West Forty-second Street have gone to great pains to avoid the theme-park label.[36] This is particularly true of the officials who head the organizations most overtly controlling the new Forty-second Street: Rebecca Robertson of the 42nd Street Development Project, the subsidiary of the Empire State Development Corporation (the new operating name of the Urban Development Corporation) that is in charge of the redevelopment effort; Cora Cahan of The New 42nd Street, Inc., the organization that oversees the redevelopment and operation of eight historic theaters in the project area; and Gretchen Dykstra of the Times Square BID, which employs the resources of area businesses and property owners to promote order and economic growth in the area. These three women—and it is perhaps fitting that women should administer the redevelopment of a street once known for its exploitation of women—vehemently deny that they are managing a theme park; rather, they maintain that they are simply nurturing the "crass commercialism" that has always characterized Times Square while eliminating the squalor and danger that tarnished the area's glitz in recent decades.[37] Those who lament the lost edge of Times Square are simply "romanticizing the gutter," as Dykstra sees it. The new Forty-second Street will not be like a suburban mall, they contend, where one developer imposes a coherent vision; rather, there will be, according to Robertson, "60 different tenants on 42d Street, arguing, fighting for product and advertising space." She envisions Forty-second Street as "a place for the masses," while Cahan would also make room for those at the top of the social ladder in a place for "everybody."

As well meaning and competent as these officials are, the language of the theme park oozes from their vision for Forty-second Street. They operate according to a shared "gestalt of Times Square" as "eclectic, vital, colorful and sort of in your face, a certain esthetic chaos." They formed their vision in part by looking at "what made people love this street, the legendary place with fables and stories." And in true, unabashed Disneyspeak, they declare it their intent to "make sure the magic continues."

Even troubling images of Times Square past can be employed in sanitized form to serve the theme-park vision. For example, the three officials were thrilled about a proposal for a twenty-foot-long, ten-foot-high fiberglass hot dog from which frankfurters would be vended under the name "Between the Buns." "You know," Dykstra opined, "that's a name that might work in Times Square." Dykstra and the others seemed unaware that they were employing a basic theme-park strategy: repackaging disturbing images in nonthreatening forms that would be safe for mainstream consumption. Disney is a master of this tactic. For example, in its animated film adaptation of Victor Hugo's *Hunchback of Notre Dame,* Disney managed to transform a tragic tale involving deeply disturbed and troubled characters into light entertainment fit for the whole family. In its own theme parks, a ride like "Pirates of the Caribbean" can recast a history of pillage, rape, and murder into a safe, thrilling adventure. In parallel fashion, the "Between the Buns" name (affixed to a fiberglass phallic symbol of immense proportions) adds an element of amusement to the act of eating a hot dog through its euphemistic allusion to the troubling history of explicit sexual representations in Times Square. Similarly, respectable tourists in Times Square can titter mischievously at enormous Calvin Klein bill-boards featuring scantily clad, bulging young men and child-like young women without worrying about unpleasant issues of sexual exploitation.

This is not to disparage the theme-park experience or those who enjoy it. Indeed, there may be something very beneficial to the human psyche that comes from the ability to tame those images, experiences, and events that we find most disturbing. The issue, though, is whether the theme-park experience should be the guiding principle behind the construction of public spaces in cities. When the form and content of public spaces are orchestrated in this way to create a marketable environment, they become antithetical to a diversity of uses and users. A $3 hot dog from "Between the Buns" is still, for many people, an overpriced wienie. The theme-park atmosphere itself then becomes a symbol of exclusion to those with limited resources. In this way, the absence of authenticity that comes from market-driven, authoritarian control undermines genuinely democratic social life.

In the final analysis, it is possible to criticize the redevelopment of Forty-second Street with regard to its implications for a democratic public space. In an effort to create a place marketable to mainstream tourists and corporate tenants, a coalition of public and private elites imposed a Disney model of controlled, themed public space on an area of remarkable, if unsettling, diversity. In so doing, they sacrificed the provocative, raw energy produced by the friction of different social groups in close interaction for the stultifying hum of a smoothly functioning machine for commercial consumption. In this way, public and private elites arguably destroyed the essence of Times Square as a contested public space. And this, more than any physical characteristic, may have been the truly meaningful theme of the place.

CULTURAL CONFLICT AND SEGREGATED SPACES

The Times Square case points to a central problem of contemporary urban rede-velopment: the interaction of political discourse and cultural politics that supports urban development often plays on and exacerbates underlying class- and race-based conflicts over urban space. Pro-growth forces utilize the negative imagery of urban decline and the positive imagery of historic preservation and Disneyspace in their attempt to revalue urban spaces by reclaiming them for the use of higher-income residents and tourists. Increasingly, however, historic preservation provides an empty facade that forms a cultural code demarcating a theme-park area for upscale consumption. Preservation thus contributes to the process by which the city is carved into distinct spaces for the affluent and the poor, with their boundaries rein-forced by polarizing cultural codes.

In this way, contemporary political discourse reinforces the belief that segre-gation by class and race is essential to real-estate values, an assumption that has long dictated patterns of urbanization and suburbanization in the United States.[38]

Public- and private-investment policies have made this a self-fulfilling prophesy that undermines the viability of integrated spaces. While many of the legal supports for segregation have been dismantled, pro-growth elites encourage the containment of different social groups within their own segregated spaces by playing on the signs of class- and race-based cultural difference in development efforts. Cultural stereotypes—especially those attributed to lower-income people of color—become the symbols of a threatening turf invasion that is deemed unacceptable in the economically valuable spaces of the city.

The result of this dynamic is a self-perpetuating struggle to reclaim or defend urban spaces, in which people of color and low-income groups are continually displaced and contained. As planning documents revealed, the Forty-second Street project was fundamentally an attempt to dislodge the African-American and Latino populations that visited the street as an entertainment district. This subculture was successfully ousted after some 280 businesses on West Forty-second Street were condemned and closed down. But the result of this short-sighted victory was to move the cultural conflicts from Forty-second Street into other city neighborhoods.

It was hardly a coincidence when, in the summer of 1993, *New York* featured a cover story declaring that Greenwich Village was "under siege" from the "urban pathologies of the late Twentieth Century."[39] According to the article, this liberal bastion was being strained to the limits of tolerance by "the black and Latino denizens of rap culture" who were flocking to the Village for entertainment, bringing with them boom-boxes, graffiti, and forty-ounce bottles of malt liquor—all potent cultural symbols of an invasion by the "other." In effect, the article characterized the battle lines over the Village in terms remarkably similar to those that defined the conflict over West Forty-second Street. It seemed that the same minority subculture driven from Times Square was now targeted for eviction from Greenwich Village.[40]

To the extent that urban redevelopment works to displace lower-income people of color from central places and confine them to segregated areas, it ultimately undermines the viability of cities. Redevelopment may contribute to the social isolation of the "truly disadvantaged" African-American population described by William Julius Wilson,[41] promoting the containment of lower-income African-Americans in "outcast ghettos."[42] This spatial segregation only makes it more difficult for members of this group to enter mainstream society.[43] The pent-up frustrations in inner-city communities of concentrated poverty pose a real threat to the social order, a fact revealed by the recurring waves of riots, or rebellions, that continue to erupt in American cities. Despite the ongoing efforts to defend safe spaces for upscale consumption, urban residents remain rightfully afraid of the threat posed by some desperate members of chronically disadvantaged populations in cities. Obviously, a new approach to urban development alone will not solve entrenched problems of crime and poverty in cities. But if revitalized urban places can integrate out-groups into mainstream society, and so moderate excessive fears of social difference, they will help dismantle some of the barriers to social mobility.

ENVISIONING NEW URBAN PLACES

Instead of a development agenda that plays on the threat posed by cultural differences in creating segregated spaces, what is needed are new places that bridge, rather than reinforce, the spatial boundaries between social groups. Neighborhoods, entertainment districts, and other public spaces must support the coexistence of different social groups. In order to construct these new areas of cultural diversity, it is necessary to recognize the influence of the micro-level practices that shape the realm of human action. They take the form of the discourses, like that of urban decline and preservation-based redevelopment, that structure how problems are perceived and solved. They also exist in the form of modern disciplines—such as urban planning, economics, and marketing—that reinforce the assumed inevitability of social arrangements.

The existing discourse of urban decline and redevelopment evident in the Times Square case uses cultural symbols in a way that reinforces the segregating impulses at work in cities. Rather than continuing to frame the social dynamics of cities in these terms, we must construct new discourses that articulate a more enlightened vision for the future of cities. For example, faced with an influx of African-American and Latino youth seeking entertainment in Greenwich Village, precisely the wrong response is to declare that battle lines have been drawn as Village residents must fight the plagues of urban decline. This message, conveyed in *New York,* incites class- and race-based conflicts in the city; thus it represents a tragic failure of social commentary. It does no more than locate a complex phenomenon in a simplistic discourse of urban decline. Rather than falling back on the idea that young people of color constitute an unacceptable threat to the social order, why not frame the situation as a problem of balancing competing interests in a big-city neighborhood that serves as both a residential and an entertainment area? In this way, it would be possible to pursue solutions that do not reinforce strategies of class- and race-based segregation.

An important lesson from the Forty-second Street case is that in reconstructing the urban environment, we are trapped by politically constructed definitions of the problems to be overcome. As long as we continue to subscribe to the class- and race-based images of urban decline that are used in the pursuit of economic interests, we will continue to seek solutions in the form of a segregated city. Despite its plethora of social ills, there was much to be learned from the area of Forty-second Street and Times Square in the 1970s and 1980s that combined people of all different classes, races, ethnicities, and nationalities in one central public space. Forty-second Street was an opportunity to be worked with rather than a failure to be destroyed and replaced. An entirely different development agenda could have been pursued if the theme of the place had been defined in terms of its social diversity rather than its social decline. In this respect, the new Forty-second Street is less an abomination than the reflection of a tragically squandered opportunity.

Despite its favorable reviews, the renaissance of West Forty-second Street reveals a failure to learn from the diversity of the area. We already know how to construct commercially successful urban theme parks that promise the reassurance of a controlled environment. We must now learn how to take advantage of the opportunities in a complex area like West Forty-second Street in order to construct new kinds of social spaces that welcome diverse groups and cultures. By vacating all the businesses on Forty-second Street, the existing social fabric was destroyed, and with it the promises as well as the failures of the street. It would now be difficult to create a truly democratic public space without restoring some of the affordable low-brow establishments that were forced out. Contrary to the dictates of planning, marketing, and real estate economics, it would be important to the goal of diversity to include some discount movie theaters, greasy spoons, and shops selling cheap electronics, jewelry, and martial-arts supplies along with the new theaters, trendy theme restaurants, and retail chains. A progressive approach to redevelopment would have to be guided by social goals rather than economic interests.

The idea of real integration among classes and races will strike many as truly utopian. But if we look around carefully, we will find that diverse groups coexist in some neighborhoods, parks, workplaces, schools, mass-transit systems, gymnasiums, fast-food outlets, and other public environments. The challenge is to nurture these places of diversity and foster the development of new ones. There are already elements of our culture that point the way to overcoming the fear of difference. Professional sports, for example, provides a kind of spaceless cultural realm that transcends the barriers of race and income, although not yet gender. Unfortunately, the high price of tickets to sports events restores patterns of segregation in the stadium, thereby preventing this cultural system from supporting integrated public spaces. Still, unifying cultural realms like sports can provide the basis for strategies to improve the flawed spaces of social diversity, such as Times Square.[44] Certainly there are other possibilities as well.

Perhaps the greatest lesson that Jane Jacobs had to offer was not so much a substantive one as the simple fact of her heretical challenge to the orthodoxies of urban planning and commercial real-estate investment. Human action is structured by vast systems of discursive and disciplinary practices. If we are to find ways to unite diverse populations in the urban realm, we must break out of the constraints on social vision that are formed by these practices. We must violate established planning principles and investment doctrines by combining incompatible economic uses, replacing homogeneity with heterogeneity as a goal of real estate development, and finding other ways to create new spaces that offer people many choices. A healthy public place whose theme is genuine diversity—now there's a truly meaningful undertaking for an inspired new breed of urban theme-park developers!

Appendices

1976   42nd Street Development Corporation formed as nonprofit local development corporation (LDC) to spur economic growth on West Forty-second Street.

1976   Mayor Abraham Beame creates Office of Midtown Enforcement to crack down on adult-entertainment businesses in Times Square.

1978   Private corporations fund preliminary study of renewal possibilities for Times Square. Ford Foundation pursues plan for redevelopment of Forty-second Street between Seventh and Eighth Avenues.

1978   42nd Street LDC completes Phase I of Theater Row project on West Forty-second Street.

1978   Manhattan Plaza opens on West Forty-second Street with 70 percent of units set aside for people in theater industry.

1979   Ford Foundation unveils preliminary plan for "world's fair"–type development on Forty-second Street between Seventh and Eighth Avenues called Cityscape.

1979   The City at 42nd Street, Inc., formed as offshoot of 42nd Street LDC to pursue revised Cityscape plan, now called The City at 42nd Street. Formal proposal submitted to City Planning Commission (CPC) for approval.

1980   Work begins on Phase II of Theater Row project.

1980   Mayor Edward I. Koch refuses to support The City at 42nd Street.

1980   City and state officials announce intent to pursue joint publicly sponsored redevelopment effort for West Forty-second Street. (Coordinated effort of state Urban Development Corporation [UDC] and city's Department of City Planning [DCP], City Planning Commission [CPC], and Public Development Corporation [PDC].)

1981   City and state officials release design guidelines for 42nd Street Development Project (prepared by Cooper Eckstut Associates), issue request-for-proposals, and receive responses from developers. Plan calls for construction of four office towers, a hotel, and a merchandise mart, as well as restoration of nine historic theaters and improvements to Times Square subway station.

1982   City and state officials designate developers of project sites. George Klein named developer of office towers.

1982   City approves Special Midtown Zoning District to spur West Side office development in and around Times Square.

1983	Designs by architects Philip Johnson and John Burgee for office towers in Forty-second Street project are released and soon criticized for somber design and violation of design guidelines.
1984	New York City Board of Estimate (BoE) unanimously approves 42nd Street Development Project after public hearings.
1989	City and state officials release new "honky-tonk" designs for office towers, by John Burgee with Phillip Johnson.
1990	State UDC receives final court approval to condemn project area through eminent domain, ending lengthy court challenge. Condemnations begin.
1990–92	UDC clears eastern two-thirds of project area, condemning 34 buildings and evicting 240 commercial tenants.
1992	Times Square Business Improvement District (BID) begins providing sanitation, security, and promotional services for Times Square.
1992	Project officials and developers agree to put construction of office towers on indefinite hold because of collapse of real-estate market. Officials announce intent to pursue an interim plan of temporary redevelopment for entertainment uses.
1992	The New 42nd Street, Inc., formed as nonprofit organization to oversee the restoration and operation of historic theaters in project area.
1993	Officials release design guidelines for interim plan, called 42nd Street Now!, produced under direction of architect Robert A. M. Stern.
1993	42nd Street Art Project uses vacated storefronts as backdrop for outdoor art installations. (Exhibition repeated in 1994.)
1993	Walt Disney Company begins negotiations for use of historic New Amsterdam Theater on West Forty-second Street.
1994	Officials and developers reach formal agreement on terms of interim plan: Prudential (partner of Klein in office development) to put up $22.6 million for temporary redevelopment in exchange for right to develop office towers later.
1995	Project officials and Disney announce formal agreement on deal for New Amsterdam (city and state to subsidize restoration). Announcement includes deals with American Multi-Cinemas (twenty-five-screen movie theater) and Madame Tussaud's of London (wax museum) for other historic Forty-second Street theaters (Liberty, Empire, Harris).
1995	Development team with Disney as partner wins right to construct forty-seven-story hotel (with time-share, retail, and entertainment uses) at northeast corner of Forty-second Street and Eighth Avenue.
1995	New Victory Theater opens (first of restored historic Forty-second Street theaters [Victory]), providing live stage productions for children.
1996	Deal sealed with Livent Company to restore two historic theaters (Lyric, Apollo [Academy]) as one stage for major Broadway musicals. Ford Motor Company joins as corporate sponsor in 1997, and restored theater named Ford Center for the Performing Arts.
1996	Disney superstore opens at corner of Forty-second Street and Seventh Avenue (next door to New Amsterdam).
1996	Douglas Durst purchases right (from Prudential/Klein) to construct first of

project office towers at northeast corner of Broadway and Forty-second Street. Condé Nast commits as anchor tenant (receiving $10.75 million in tax breaks). Construction on Condé Nast Building begins in 1997.

1997   Officials reach agreement with Milsteins to build thirty-five-story hotel at southeast corner of Forty-second Street and Eighth Avenue.

1997   Restored New Amsterdam opens with premiere showing of Disney movie *Hercules,* followed by Disney parade along Forty-second Street.

1997   New 42nd Street announces plan to restore Selwyn Theater for Roundabout Theater Company, with ten-story addition providing rehearsal space for nonprofit theater groups.

1998   Ford Center for the Performing Arts opens with production of *Ragtime.*

1998   Deal set for second office tower, thirty-two-story Reuters Building, at northwest corner of Forty-second Street and Seventh Avenue.

1998   Livent wins right to operate the Times Square Theater as 500-seat Broadway stage with restaurant and office space.

B. ORGANIZATIONS INVOLVED IN REDEVELOPMENT

The City at 42nd Street, Inc. Offshoot of the 42nd Street Development Corporation created to pursue a private plan for revelopment of West Forty-second Street called The City at 42nd Street.

42nd Street Development Corporation (Forty-second Street LDC). Nonprofit local development corporation established to promote economic development on West Forty-second Street.

42nd Street Development Project, Inc. Subsidiary of the New York State Urban Development Corporation created to oversee the publicly sponsored plan for West Forty-second Street, known as the 42nd Street Development Project. (In the early 1980s, this entity went by the names Times Square Redevelopment Corporation and 42nd Street Redevelopment Corporation.)

Municipal Art Society (MAS). Civic group concerned with historic preservation, the arts, and urban design.

The New 42nd Street, Inc. (New 42). Nonprofit organization created to oversee the restoration and operation of the historic Forty-second Street theaters.

New York City Board of Estimate (BoE). Legislative body with final authority over land-use decisions in New York. (Authority transferred to City Council with charter revisions adopted in 1989.)

New York City Department of City Planning (DCP). Professional planning staff serving the City Planning Commission.

New York City Landmarks Preservation Commission (LPC). Appointed commission with power to designate and regulate historic landmarks (subject to legislative review).

New York City Planning Commission (CPC). Appointed commission responsible for formal decisions on land uses in New York (subject to legislative review).

New York City Public Development Corporation (PDC). Quasi-public entity promoting economic development projects in New York. (Renamed Economic Development Corporation [EDC] under Mayor Rudolf Giuliani.)

New York State Urban Development Corporation (UDC). State agency sponsoring economic development projects throughout the state. (Renamed Empire State Development Corporation [ESDC] under Governor George Pataki.)

Times Square Business Improvement District (Times Square BID). Privately funded organization (through special tax assessment on area business and property owners) providing security, sanitation, and promotional services.

Times Square Center Associates (TSCA). Development team of George Klein and Prudential Insurance Company formed to develop office towers in Forty-second Street project.

Notes

1. TIMES SQUARE AS TEXT

1. In his review of a show on urban architecture at the Los Angeles Museum of Contemporary Art, Herbert Muschamp stated: "With the exception of architectural preservation, which has become a kind of urban strategy by default, nothing resembling a set of accepted strategies has held the field of urbanism for nearly three decades" ("The Polyglot Metropolis and Its Discontents," *New York Times*, 3 July 1994) (hereafter cited as *NYT*).

2. See, for example, Kevin W. Green, ed., *The City as a Stage* (Washington, D.C.: Partners for Livable Places, 1983); J. Allen Whitt, "The Role of the Performing Arts in Urban Competition and Growth," in *Business Elites and Urban Development*, ed. Scott Cummings (Albany: State University of New York Press, 1988), 49–69; and Franco Bianchini and Michael Parkinson, eds., *Cultural Policy and Urban Regeneration: The West European Experience* (Manchester: Manchester University Press, 1993).

3. Lewis Mumford, *The Culture of Cities* (New York: Harcourt, Brace, 1938).

4. Carl Schorske, *Fin-de-Siècle Vienna: Politics and Culture* (New York: Vintage Books, 1981), chap. 2.

5. Mike Davis, *City of Quartz* (New York: Vintage Books, 1992).

6. Michel Foucault, *Discipline and Punish* (New York: Vintage Books, 1979), esp. part 3.

7. Timothy P. Mitchell, *Colonising Egypt* (Cambridge: Cambridge University Press, 1988).

8. Two other important studies are Ira Katznelson, *City Trenches* (Chicago: University of Chicago Press, 1981), and Richard Sennett, *The Conscience of the Eye* (New York: Norton, 1990).

9. M. Christine Boyer, "Cities for Sale: Merchandising History at South Street Seaport," in *Variations on a Theme Park*, ed. Michael Sorkin (New York: Noonday Press, 1992), 181–204; Boyer, "The Return of Aesthetics to City Planning," *Society*, May–June 1988, 49–56; David Harvey, *The Condition of Postmodernity* (Oxford: Blackwell, 1989).

10. On the consequences of economic restructuring in New York City, see John H. Mollenkopf and Manuel Castells, eds., *Dual City* (New York: Russell Sage Foundation, 1991).

11. Boyer, "Cities for Sale."

12. M. Christine Boyer, "The Great Frame-Up: Fantastic Appearances in Contemporary Spatial Practices," in *Spatial Practices*, ed. Helen Liggett and David C. Perry (Thousand Oaks, Calif.: Sage, 1995), 81–109.

13. Harvey, *Condition of Postmodernity*, chap. 4; see also David Harvey, *The Urban Experience* (Baltimore: Johns Hopkins University Press, 1989), chap. 9.

14. David Harvey, *Consciousness and the Urban Experience* (Baltimore: Johns Hopkins University Press, 1985).

15. Harvey, *Condition of Postmodernity,* 92.

16. Sharon Zukin, *The Cultures of Cities* (Cambridge, Mass.: Blackwell, 1995), ix; see also Zukin, *Landscapes of Power: From Detroit to Disney World* (Berkeley: University of California Press, 1991), and *Loft Living: Culture and Capital in Urban Change* (New Brunswick, N.J.: Rutgers University Press, 1982).

17. Harvey, *Consciousness and the Urban Experience.*

18. Marshall Berman, *All that Is Solid Melts into Air* (New York: Viking Penguin, 1982); Mumford, *Culture of Cities.*

19. John H. Mollenkopf, *The Contested City* (Princeton, N.J.: Princeton University Press, 1983).

20. Jewel Bellush and Murray Hausknecht, eds., *Urban Renewal: People, Politics, and Planning* (Garden City, N.Y.: Anchor Books, 1967).

21. Manual Castells, *The Urban Question* (Cambridge, Mass.: MIT Press, 1977); Norman I. Fainstein and Susan S. Fainstein, "Restructuring the American City: A Comparative Perspective," in *Urban Policy Under Capitalism,* ed. Norman I. Fainstein and Susan S. Fainstein, (Beverly Hills, Calif.: Sage, 1982), 161–189.

22. Edward Relph, *The Modern Urban Landscape* (Baltimore: Johns Hopkins University Press, 1987).

23. Jane Jacobs, *The Death and Life of Great American Cities* (New York: Vintage Books, 1961).

24. Neil Smith, "Gentrification, the Frontier, and the Restructuring of Urban Space," in *Gentrification of the City,* ed. Neil Smith and Peter Williams (Boston: Allen & Unwin, 1986), 15–34; Smith, "New City, New Frontier: The Lower East Side as Wild, Wild West," in *Variations on a Theme Park,* ed. Sorkin, 60–93.

25. Michael Jager, "Class Definition and the Esthetics of Gentrification: Victoriana in Melbourne," in *Gentrification of the City,* ed. Smith and Williams, 78–91.

26. Tom Wolfe, *From Bauhaus to Our House* (New York: Pocket Books, 1981).

27. Shirley Bradway Laska and Daphne Spain, eds., *Back to the City* (New York: Pergamon Press, 1980).

28. Smith and Williams, eds., *Gentrification of the City.*

29. Zukin, *Loft Living.*

30. On the social significance of cultural tastes, see Pierre Bourdieu, *Distinction: A Social Critique of the Judgement of Taste,* trans. Richard Nice (Cambridge, Mass.: Harvard University Press, 1984).

31. See, for example, Green, *City as a Stage,* and Whitt, "Role of the Performing Arts."

32. Paul E. Peterson, *City Limits* (Chicago: University of Chicago Press, 1981).

33. Peterson dismissed the seemingly "deviant case" of New York City—with its historically large redistributive role and conflictual development politics—by maintaining that the city's fiscal crisis in the mid-1970s effectively proved his argument about the decisive authority of economic imperatives in city politics. But without abandoning the neat logic of economics for the less secure terrain of political analysis, Peterson could not explain why New York embarked on such an irrational path.

34. See, for example, Clarence N. Stone and Heywood T. Sanders, eds., *The Politics of Urban Development* (Lawrence: University Press of Kansas, 1987).

35. Martin Shefter, *Political Crisis/Fiscal Crisis: The Collapse and Revival of New York City* (New York: Basic Books, 1985); Stephen L. Elkin, *City and Regime in the American*

Republic (Chicago: University of Chicago Press, 1987); Clarence N. Stone, *Regime Politics: Governing Atlanta, 1946–1988* (Lawrence: University Press of Kansas, 1989); John H. Mollenkopf, *A Phoenix in the Ashes: The Rise and Fall of the Koch Coalition in New York City Politics* (Princeton, N.J.: Princeton University Press, 1992).

36. These and other studies have been linked under the label of regime theory by William Sites, "The Limits of Urban Regime Theory: New York City Under Koch, Dinkins, and Giuliani," *Urban Affairs Review* 32 (1997): 536–557.

37. See, especially, Stone, *Regime Politics.*

38. David A. Rochefort and Roger W. Cobb, eds., *The Politics of Problem Definition* (Lawrence: University Press of Kansas, 1994).

39. E. E. Schattschneider, *The Semisovereign People: A Realist's View of Democracy in America* (New York: Harcourt, Brace & World, 1960), 66.

40. Ibid., 64.

41. Murray Edelman, *Constructing the Political Spectacle* (Chicago: University of Chicago Press, 1988); see also Edelman, *The Symbolic Uses of Politics* (Urbana: University of Illinois Press, 1964).

42. Stuart A. Scheingold, *The Politics of Law and Order* (New York: Longman, 1984).

43. Robert A. Beauregard, *Voices of Decline: The Postwar Fate of U.S. Cities* (Cambridge, Mass.: Blackwell, 1993); Beauregard, "Representing Urban Decline: Postwar Cities as Narrative Objects," *Urban Affairs Quarterly* 29 (1993): 187–202.

44. Beauregard, "Representing Urban Decline," 188.

45. Ibid., 198.

46. Beauregard, *Voices of Decline,* 9.

47. Ibid., 22.

48. For this reason, I use the term "political discourse" rather than "public discourse." In doing so, I do not mean to delineate a particular type of public discourse, but to emphasize the political significance of all public discourses.

49. H. V. Savitch, *Post Industrial Cities* (Princeton, N.J.: Princeton University Press, 1988), chap. 3.

50. Although exact costs are impossible to determine precisely, and reported figures have varied considerably, the $2.5 billion was cited (among other places) in Paul Goldberger, "Times Square: Lurching Toward a Terrible Mistake?" *NYT,* 19 February 1989.

51. John H. Mollenkopf, "The 42nd Street Development Project and the Public Interest," *City Almanac* 18 (1985): 12–13.

52. See, for example, the reported findings of a study by New York University economist Emanuel Tobier in Robert Neuwirth, "A Hundred Years of Subsidy," *Village Voice,* 12 February 1991.

53. Gregory D. Squires, ed., *Unequal Partnerships* (New Brunswick, N.J.: Rutgers University Press, 1989).

54. The Board of Estimate was the legislative body with primary authority over land-use decisions at the time. The BoE—consisting of the five borough presidents (with one vote each), the mayor, the president of the City Council, and the comptroller (with two votes each)—was later ruled unconstitutional on the grounds that it violated the principle of one person, one vote. Its legislative powers were transferred to an expanded City Council with the charter revisions that took effect in 1990.

55. Although Mayors Dinkins and Giuliani had no direct role in the Forty-second Street

redevelopment effort, their conflicting political interests left each with a different relationship to the project. Dinkins had little incentive to link himself directly with the Forty-second Street project. His term of office, from 1989 to 1993, coincided with a low point in the redevelopment effort when there were few signs of progress and the project's future seemed uncertain. Moreover, his political base was the antithesis of Koch's and was more likely to be critical of the redevelopment plan.

In contrast, Giuliani had much to gain from linking himself to the project. He was in office when the redevelopment project finally came to fruition and produced a dramatic transformation of Forty-second Street and Times Square. And because Giuliani was supported by the same political base that had supported Ed Koch, the project served his political interests in much the same way that it had served Koch's. Indeed, Giuliani was unable to resist claiming some credit for the cleanup of Times Square, although he has been criticized for taking credit that is not his due.

56. I use the term "pro-growth alliance" to refer to the particular collection of groups and interests that were joined specifically in support of the 42nd Street Development Project. I use the terms "pro-growth coalition" and "pro-growth regime" to refer to the enduring coalition of interests that were unified behind a broader pro-growth agenda for New York City. In this sense, the Forty-second Street project could serve as a mechanism for drawing groups into a broader pro-growth coalition, or regime.

57. In support of this interpretation, see Goldberger, "Times Square."

58. See, for example, "Five Reasons to Transform 42d Street," *NYT,* 11 September 1989.

59. Beauregard, *Voices of Decline.*

2. FROM URBAN RENEWAL TO HISTORIC PRESERVATION

1. Christopher Gray, "On Preservation, 'I Told You So,'" *NYT,* 12 July 1992.

2. Quoted in Martin Tolchin, "Demo Starts at Penn Station; Architects Picket," *NYT,* 29 October 1963.

3. Ibid.

4. In pursuing this restoration strategy, Amtrak was influenced by the successful adaptations of old railroad stations in other major cities, such as Chicago, Philadelphia, and Washington. Ticket sales at Washington's Union Station reportedly increased by 25 percent after renovation was completed in 1987. An Amtrak spokesperson noted that restored urban train stations "exhibit a sense of optimism and grandeur, an aesthetic beauty which we feel is [a] very important psychological factor in marketing rail service" (quoted in James Dao, "Amtrak's Envious Look at Post Office," *NYT,* 13 May 1992). Inside the new Penn Station, commercial space would be available for trendy shops, boutiques, and restaurants as the station evolved into a new breed of urban mall. A similar transformation was under way across town at New York's Grand Central Terminal.

5. New York City Landmarks Preservation Commission (LPC), *Guide to New York City Landmarks* (Washington, D.C.: Preservation Press, 1992).

6. David W. Dunlap, "Amtrak Unveils Its Design to Transform Post Office," *NYT,* 2 May 1993.

7. Under the prodding of Senator Daniel Patrick Moynihan, President Clinton included $90 million for the project in his proposed budget for fiscal year 1995. Marvin Howe,

"Grand New Amtrak Terminal: Arriving the First $10 Million," *NYT,* 20 February 1994; Dunlap, "Amtrak Unveils Its Design."

8. Herbert Muschamp, "In This Dream Station Future and Past Collide," *NYT,* 20 June 1993.

9. Herbert Muschamp, "The Polyglot Metropolis and Its Discontents," *NYT,* 3 July 1994.

10. John H. Mollenkopf, *The Contested City* (Princeton, N.J.: Princeton University Press, 1983).

11. Department of Housing and Urban Development (HUD), *HUD Statistical Yearbook 1975* (Washington, D.C.: Government Printing Office, 1976).

12. As an example of the how the write-down worked, consider the urban renewal project along the southeastern border of Washington Square Park in New York City. After the city's urban renewal plan received federal approval, the city acquired this attractive real estate for $41 million; it then sold the property to private developers for $20 million. The $21 million difference constituted the write-down. The city recovered two-thirds of this amount in the form of a federal urban renewal grant, and bore the remaining cost itself. The developers received the property at half its value. The land was then used to develop additional facilities for New York University. Jewel Bellush and Murray Hausknecht, "Urban Renewal: An Historical Overview," in *Urban Renewal: People, Politics, and Planning,* ed. Jewel Bellush and Murray Hausknecht (Garden City, N.Y.: Anchor Books, 1967), 3–16.

13. Dennis Gale, "Conceptual Issues in Neighborhood Decline and Revitalization," in *Neighborhood Policy and Programmes,* ed. Naomi Carmon (New York: St. Martin's Press, 1990), 11–35.

14. Bellush and Hausknecht, eds., "Urban Renewal."

15. Roman A. Cybriwsky, David Ley, and John Western, "The Political and Social Construction of Revitalized Neighborhoods: Society Hill, Philadelphia, and False Creek, Vancouver," in *Gentrification of the City,* ed. Neil Smith and Peter Williams (Boston: Allen & Unwin, 1986), 92–120.

16. Norma Nager, "Continuities of Urban Policy on the Poor: From Urban Renewal to Reinvestment," in *Back to the City,* ed. Shirley Bradway Laska and Daphne Spain (New York: Pergamon Press, 1980), 239–251; on Atlanta, see Clarence N. Stone, *Regime Politics: Governing Atlanta, 1946–1988* (Lawrence: University Press of Kansas, 1989).

17. Manuel Castells, *The Urban Question* (Cambridge, Mass.: MIT Press, 1977); Norman I. Fainstein and Susan S. Fainstein, "Restructuring the American City: A Comparative Perspective," in *Urban Policy Under Capitalism,* ed. Norman I. Fainstein and Susan S. Fainstein (Beverly Hills, Calif.: Sage, 1982), 161–189.

18. Martin Anderson, *The Federal Bulldozer* (Cambridge, Mass.: MIT Press, 1964); Jewel Bellush and Murray Hausknecht, "Relocation and Managed Mobility," in *Urban Renewal,* ed. Bellush and Hausknecht, 366–377; Chester W. Hartman, "The Housing of Relocated Families," in *Urban Renewal,* ed. Bellush and Hausknecht, 315–353.

19. Mollenkopf, *Contested City,* 84.

20. Susan S. Fainstein, "Neighborhood Planning: Limits and Potentials," in *Neighborhood Policy,* ed. Carmon, 223–237.

21. Laska and Spain, eds., *Back to the City.*

22. Neil Smith, "Gentrification, the Frontier, and the Restructuring of Urban Space," in *Gentrification of the City,* ed. Smith and Williams, 15–34; Smith, "New City, New Fron-

tier: The Lower East Side as Wild, Wild West," in *Variations on a Theme Park,* ed. Michael Sorkin (New York: Noonday Press, 1992), 60–93.

23. Mollenkopf, *Contested City,* 181.

24. Michael Jager, "Class Definition and the Esthetics of Gentrification: Victoriana in Melbourne," in *Gentrification of the City,* ed. Smith and Williams, 78–91; Castells, *Urban Question.*

25. Tom Wolfe, *From Bauhaus to Our House* (New York: Pocket Books, 1981).

26. Smith and Williams, eds., *Gentrification of the City;* Laska and Spain, eds., *Back to the City.*

27. Paul R. Levy and Roman A. Cybriwsky, "The Hidden Dimensions of Culture and Class: Philadelphia," in *Back to the City,* ed. Laska and Spain, 138–155.

28. Smith and Williams, eds., *Gentrification of the City.*

29. Quoted in James Q. Wilson, "Planning and Politics: Citizen Participation in Urban Renewal," in *Urban Renewal,* ed. Bellush and Hausknecht, 289–290.

30. William L. Slayton, "Report on Urban Renewal," in *Urban Renewal,* ed. Bellush and Hausknecht, 382.

31. Jane Jacobs, *The Death and Life of Great American Cities* (New York: Vintage Books, 1961).

32. Ibid., 14.

33. Herbert Gans, *The Urban Villagers* (New York: Free Press, 1962).

34. Marc Fried and Peggy Gleicher, "Some Sources of Residential Satisfaction in an Urban Slum," *Journal of the American Institute of Planners* 27 (1961): 305–315.

35. Anderson, *Federal Bulldozer.*

36. James Marston Fitch, *Historic Preservation: Curatorial Management of the Built World* (New York: McGraw-Hill, 1982); Kevin Lynch, *What Time Is This Place?* (Cambridge, Mass.: MIT Press, 1972); David Lowenthal, *The Past Is a Foreign Country* (Cambridge: Cambridge University Press, 1985).

37. Christopher Jencks, *Post-modernism: The New Classicism in Art and Architecture* (New York: Rizzoli, 1987), 29.

38. Mollenkopf, *Contested City.*

39. Marshall Berman, *All That Is Solid Melts into Air* (New York: Viking Penguin, 1982).

40. See, for example, M. Christine Boyer, "The Return of Aesthetics to City Planning," *Society,* May–June 1988, 49–56.

41. Advisory Council on Historic Preservation (ACHP), *Report to the President and the Congress of the United States: Twenty Years of the National Historic Preservation Act* (Washington, D.C.: ACHP, 1986).

42. ACHP, *National Historic Preservation Act of 1966, as Amended,* 3rd ed. (Washington, D.C.: ACHP, 1993).

43. Ibid.

44. ACHP, *Report to the President and the Congress of the United States* (Washington, D.C.: ACHP, 1971).

45. ACHP, *Report to the President and the Congress of the United States* (Washington, D.C.: ACHP, 1975).

46. Richard O. Baumbach, Jr., and William E. Borah, *The Second Battle of New Orleans* (University: University of Alabama Press, 1981).

47. ACHP, *Report to the President and the Congress of the United States* (Washington, D.C.: ACHP, 1973).

48. Gale, "Conceptual Issues," 21.

49. Housing and Home Finance Agency, *Historic Preservation Through Urban Renewal* (Washington, D.C.: HHFA, 1963); HUD, *Preserving Historic America* (Washington, D.C.: HUD, 1966).

50. ACHP, *Report* (1986).

51. HUD, *HUD Statistical Yearbook 1970* (Washington, D.C.: Government Printing Office, 1971).

52. HUD, *Programs of HUD* (Washington, D.C.: Government Printing Office, 1977).

53. Mollenkopf, *Contested City.*

54. ACHP, *Report to the President and the Congress of the United States* (Washington, D.C., ACHP 1978), 5.

55. Ibid., 29.

56. ACHP, *Report* (1986).

57. ACHP, *Federal Tax Law and Historic Preservation* (Washington, D.C.: ACHP, 1983); ACHP, *Report* (1973).

58. Stephen F. Weber, *Historic Preservation Incentives of the 1976 Tax Reform Act: An Economic Analysis,* National Bureau of Standards Technical Note 980 (Washington D.C.: Department of Commerce, 1979).

59. Ibid., 1.

60. ACHP, *Federal Tax Law.*

61. General Accounting Office (GAO), *Tax Policy and Administration: Historic Preservation Tax Incentives: Fact Sheet for the Chairman, Subcommittee on Public Lands, Committee on Interior and Insular Affairs, House of Representatives* (Washington, D.C.: GAO, 1986).

62. ACHP, *Report to the President and the Congress of the United States* (Washington D.C.: ACHP, 1989).

63. GAO, *Tax Policy.*

64. ACHP, *Report* (1989).

65. Demetrios Caraley, "Washington Abandons the Cities," in *Critical Issues for Clinton's Domestic Agenda,* ed. Demetrios Caraley (New York: Academy of Political Science, 1994), 1–30.

66. ACHP, *The Contribution of Historic Preservation to Urban Revitalization* (Washington, D.C.: Government Printing Office, 1979).

67. Real Estate Research Corporation, *Economics of Revitalization: A Decisionmaking Guide for Local Officials* (Washington, D.C.: Department of the Interior, Heritage Conservation and Recreation Service, 1981); Selma Thomas, ed., *Rehabilitation: An Alternative for Historic Industrial Buildings* (Washington, D.C.: Government Printing Office, 1978); Randolph Langenbach, *A Future from the Past: The Case for Conservation and Reuse of Old Buildings in Industrial Communities* (Washington D.C.: HUD, 1977).

68. Sharon Zukin, *Loft Living: Culture and Capital in Urban Change* (New Brunswick, N.J.: Rutgers University Press, 1982).

69. The redevelopment of the South Street Seaport in New York City occurred under similar circumstances. Like the SoHo area, the seaport was originally a part of David Rockefeller's Lower Manhattan Plan for urban renewal, but the plan gave way to preservation-

oriented commercial redevelopment. M. Christine Boyer, "Cities for Sale: Merchandising History at South Street Seaport," in *Variations on a Theme Park,* ed. Sorkin, 181–204.

70. Zukin, *Loft Living,* chap. 2.

71. Ibid., 46.

72. The Battery Park City project was one notable exception. But even that massive development attempted to incorporate new planning techniques, like a diversity of building types, that emerged from the urban renewal critique. Indeed, the design guidelines for the project provided for "the constant evocation of historic imagery recalling the civic values of New York's heroic past" (Boyer, "Cities for Sale," 195).

73. Quoted in Zukin, *Loft Living,* 20.

74. In the case *Penn Central Transportation Company* v. *City of New York* (98 S. Ct. 2646 [1978]), concerning local preservation powers, the Supreme Court upheld the position that landmarks laws fall within the realm of local zoning powers.

75. ACHP, *Report* (1986); on Charleston, see Robert E. Tournier, "Historic Preservation as a Force in Urban Change: Charleston," in *Back to the City,* ed. Laska and Spain, 173–186; on New Orleans, see Baumbach and Borah, *Second Battle.*

76. Historic preservation has a particular significance in the South, where slavery was a dominant feature of the region's history. The early interest in historic preservation in southern cities may have been motivated by a nostalgia for traditional patterns of domination. As African-Americans have achieved political power in southern cities, they often have favored unrestricted economic development over preservation goals. Stone, *Regime Politics,* 126–131; Alexander J. Reichl, "Historic Preservation and Progrowth Politics in U.S. Cities," *Urban Affairs Review* 32 (1997): 513–535.

77. U.S. Conference of Mayors, Special Committee on Historic Preservation, *With Heritage So Rich* (New York: Random House, 1966).

78. ACHP, *Report* (1986).

79. On the preservation movement in New York City, see Gregory F. Gilmartin, *Shaping the City: New York and the Municipal Art Society* (New York: Clarkson Potter, 1995).

80. Tolchin, "Demo Starts."

81. "Farewell to Penn Station," *NYT,* 30 October 1963.

82. Thomas W. Ennis, "Landmarks Get City Protection," *NYT,* 11 April 1965.

83. LPC, *Guide to New York City Landmarks.*

84. David Dinkins, Foreword to LPC, *Guide to New York City Landmarks.*

85. Brendan Gill, Introduction to LPC, *Guide to New York City Landmarks.*

86. For an excellent history of the zoning movement and its relationship to capitalism in the United States, see Richard E. Foglesong, *Planning the Capitalist City: The Colonial Era to the 1920s* (Princeton, N.J.: Princeton University Press, 1986).

87. *Penn Central Transportation Company* v. *City of New York,* 98 S. Ct. 2646 (1978).

88. John Brigham, *Property and the Politics of Entitlement* (Philadelphia: Temple University Press, 1990).

89. Penn's case illustrates the powerful effect on social conceptions of space that comes from enframing space through zoning practices. Specifically, it reveals the way in which the abstract zoning framework comes to be perceived as preexisting and absolute. On the concept of "enframing," see Timothy P. Mitchell, *Colonising Egypt* (Cambridge: Cambridge University Press, 1988).

90. Technically, the term "air rights" refers to only the developable air space above a

given lot, while "development rights" refers to the unused development potential that can be transferred from one lot to another.

91. David K. Shipler, "Landmarks Zoning Change Proposed," *NYT,* 7 October 1969.

92. David A. Richards, "Development Rights Transfer in New York City," in *Transfer of Development Rights,* ed. Jerome G. Rose (New Brunswick, N.J.: Center for Urban Policy Research, Rutgers University, 1975), 123–156.

93. *Penn Central Transportation Company* v. *City of New York,* 98 S. Ct. 2646 (1978), 2666.

94. Quoted in Richards, "Development Rights," 136.

95. Ibid.

96. Steven R. Weisman, "Zoning Proposal Would Allow Higher Apartment Structures," *NYT,* 19 November 1970.

97. New York City Department of City Planning (DCP), *Midtown Development* (New York: DCP, 1981).

98. David W. Dunlap, "Transit Agency Seeking to Buy Grand Central," *NYT,* 30 August 1990.

99. David W. Dunlap, "Plan to Ease the Transfer of Air Rights," *NYT,* 15 November 1989.

100. David W. Dunlap, "A Battle Looms over Grand Central's Air Space," *NYT,* 6 July 1989.

101. Richards, "Development Rights."

102. Quoted in Dunlap, "Battle Looms."

103. Dunlap, "Plan to Ease Transfer."

104. Richard F. Babcock and Wendy U. Larsen, *Special Districts* (Cambridge, Mass.: Lincoln Institute of Land Policy, 1990).

105. Dunlap, "Plan to Ease Transfer."

106. David W. Dunlap, "Trump Offers Unusual Plan to Use 'Underwater Zoning,' " *NYT,* 28 June 1989.

107. John J. Costonis, "The Chicago Plan: Incentive Zoning and the Preservation of Urban Landmarks," *Harvard Law Review* 85 (1972): 574–631; Costonis, *Space Adrift;* Costonis, *Icons and Aliens: Law, Aesthetics, and Environmental Change* (Urbana: University of Illinois Press, 1989).

108. Costonis, "Chicago Plan."

109. ACHP, *Report* (1973).

110. Donald H. Elliott and Norman Marcus, "From Euclid to Ramapo: New Directions on Land Development Controls," *Hofstra Law Review* 56 (1972): 72–78.

111. Richards, "Development Rights."

112. See, for example, Paul Goldberger, "Shaping the Face of New York," in *New York Unbound: The City and the Politics of the Future,* ed. Peter D. Salins (New York: Blackwell, 1988) 127–140.

113. Foglesong, *Planning the Capitalist City,* 232.

3. TIMES SQUARE DISCOURSE

1. Tony Hiss, *The Experience of Place* (New York: Knopf, 1990).

2. Quoted in New York State Urban Development Corporation (UDC), *42nd Street*

Development Project: Draft Environmental Impact Statement (New York: UDC, 1984), 2-165.

3. Stanley Buder, "42nd Street at the Crossroads: A History of Broadway to Eighth Avenue," in "West 42nd Street: The Bright Light Zone," ed. William Kornblum (Unpublished study, City University of New York, 1978), 52–80; William Kornblum and Vernon Boggs, "The Social Ecology of the Bright Light District," in "West 42nd Street," ed. Kornblum, 17–51; William Kornblum and Terry Williams, "Book Prospectus: West 42nd Street, the Bright Lights Zone" (Paper presented at the Urban Forum conference "Contested Spaces," New York, 14–15 June 1991).

4. See, for example, "Five Reasons to Transform 42d Street," *NYT,* 11 September 1989.

5. For an excellent history of Times Square, see William R. Taylor, ed., *Inventing Times Square: Commerce and Culture at the Crossroads of the World* (New York: Russell Sage Foundation, 1991).

6. With regard to Times Square, see David C. Hammack, "Developing for Commercial Culture," in *Inventing Times Square,* ed. Taylor, 36–50; more generally, see Paul Kantor, with Stephen David, *The Dependent City* (Glenview, Ill.: Scott, Foresman, 1988).

7. Federal Writers' Project, *The WPA Guide to New York City* (1939; reprint, New York: Pantheon Books, 1982), 146.

8. Ibid.

9. Ibid.

10. Ibid., 147.

11. Hammack, "Developing"; Buder, "42nd Street."

12. Hammack, "Developing," 39–41.

13. Buder, "42nd Street," 59.

14. On the importance of newspapers in urban growth, see John R. Logan and Harvey L. Molotch, *Urban Fortunes* (Berkeley: University of California Press, 1987).

15. Buder, "42nd Street"; UDC, *42nd Street Development Project.*

16. Timothy J. Gilfoyle, "Policing of Sexuality," in *Inventing Times Square,* ed. Taylor, 297–314.

17. Betsy Blackmar, "Uptown Real Estate and the Creation of Times Square," in *Inventing Times Square,* ed. Taylor, 51–65.

18. Gilfoyle, "Policing," 298.

19. UDC, *42nd Street Development Project.*

20. *New York Times* (1881), quoted in Josh Alan Friedman, *Tales of Times Square* (Portland, Ore.: Feral House, 1993), 140.

21. Federal Writers' Project, *WPA Guide,* 155.

22. Quoted in Friedman, *Tales of Times Square,* 140.

23. Federal Writers' Project, *WPA Guide,* 147.

24. Ibid., 155.

25. Ibid., 156.

26. Ibid., 159.

27. Friedman, *Tales of Times Square*; UDC, *42nd Street Development Project.*

28. Peter G. Buckley, "Boundaries of Respectability: Introductory Essay," in *Inventing Times Square,* ed. Taylor, 286–296.

29. Gilfoyle, "Policing."

30. Ibid.; UDC, *42nd Street Development Project.*

31. UDC, *42nd Street Development Project,* 2-161.

32. Brooks McNamara, "The Entertainment District at the End of the 1930s," in *Inventing Times Square,* ed. Taylor, 178–190.

33. Gilfoyle, "Policing," 299.

34. Federal Writers' Project, *WPA Guide,* 147.

35. Gilfoyle, "Policing," 301.

36. Ibid., 299.

37. Ibid., 300.

38. Quoted in Federal Writers' Project, *WPA Guide,* 147.

39. Gilfoyle, "Policing," 297.

40. Buckley, "Boundaries," 288.

41. Margaret Knapp, "Entertainment and Commerce: Introductory Essay," in *Inventing Times Square,* ed. Taylor, 120–132.

42. William Leach, "Commercial Aesthetics: Introductory Essay," in *Inventing Times Square,* ed. Taylor, 234–242.

43. Ibid., 237–238.

44. Ibid., 234.

45. Eric Lampard, "Structural Changes: Introductory Essay," in *Inventing Times Square,* ed. Taylor, 16–35.

46. Neil Harris, "Urban Tourism and the Commercial City," in *Inventing Times Square,* ed. Taylor, 66–82.

47. Leach, "Commercial Aesthetics," 236.

48. Ibid., 240.

49. Blackmar, "Uptown Real Estate."

50. William Wood Register, Jr., "New York's Gigantic Toy," in *Inventing Times Square,* ed. Taylor, 243–270.

51. Dennis Judd and Todd R. Swanstrom, *City Politics* (New York: HarperCollins, 1994), 111–113; Lewis Erenberg, "Impressarios of Broadway Nightlife," in *Inventing Times Square,* ed. Taylor, 158–177.

52. Buder, "42nd Street"; UDC, *42nd Street Development Project.*

53. McNamara, "Entertainment District"; UDC, *42nd Street Development Project.*

54. Buder, "42nd Street;" UDC, *42nd Street Development Project.*

55. Federal Writers' Project, *WPA Guide,* 167.

56. Ibid., 169–170.

57. UDC, *42nd Street Development Project,* 2-164.

58. Buder, "42nd Street"; Lawrence Senelick, "Private Parts in Public Places," in *Inventing Times Square,* ed. Taylor, 329–353.

59. UDC, *42nd Street Development Project,* 2-163.

60. McNamara, "Entertainment District," 181–182.

61. Buckley, "Boundaries," 291.

62. Federal Writers' Project, *WPA Guide,* 167.

63. McNamara, "Entertainment District"; Senelick, "Private Parts."

64. Senelick, "Private Parts."

65. Buckley, "Boundaries," 296.

66. Ibid.; Richard Wightman Fox, "The Discipline of Amusement," in *Inventing Times Square,* ed. Taylor, 83–98.

67. Senelick, "Private Parts"; McNamara, "Entertainment District."

68. McNamara, "Entertainment District."

69. Senelick, "Private Parts."

70. George Chauncey, Jr., "The Policed: Gay Men's Strategies of Everyday Resistance," in *Inventing Times Square*, ed. Taylor, 315–328.

71. See, for example, John Rechy's novel *City of Night* (1963; reprint, New York: Quality Paperback Book Club, 1994).

72. Buder, "42nd Street"; UDC, *42nd Street Development Project;* Senelick, "Private Parts."

73. UDC, *42nd Street Development Project,* 2-164.

74. Senelick, "Private Parts."

75. Friedman, *Tales of Times Square.*

76. Senelick, "Private Parts," 340.

77. UDC, *42nd Street Development Project,* 1-16.

78. Richard F. Babcock and Wendy U. Larsen, *Special Districts* (Cambridge, Mass.: Lincoln Institute of Land Policy, 1990).

79. Senelick, "Private Parts."

80. Jennifer Hunt, "Crime and Law Enforcement in the Bright Light District," in "West 42nd Street," ed. Kornblum, 164–216; UDC, *42nd Street Development Project;* Friedman, *Tales of Times Square,* 145–146.

81. Friedman, *Tales of Times Square,* 146.

82. Hunt, "Crime and Law Enforcement."

83. The City at 42nd Street, *The City at 42nd Street: A Proposal for the Restoration and Redevelopment of 42nd Street* (New York: City at 42nd Street, 1980).

84. UDC, *42nd Street Development Project,* S-3–S-4.

85. Ibid.

86. Planners did virtually nothing in the final environmental-impact statement to address the many objections raised during public hearings on the draft version. Although there were many concerns about the scale and design of the project and its impact on neighboring residents and industries, planners made only two notable changes: they shifted the focus of the merchandise mart from fashion clothing to computers, and they allowed the possibility of preserving the Times Tower from demolition. Susan S. Fainstein, "The Redevelopment of 42nd Street: Clashing Viewpoints," *City Almanac* 18 (1985): 2–8.

87. UDC, *42nd Street Development Project,* 1-8.

88. Ibid., 2-71.

89. Ibid., 2-117.

90. Ibid., 2-101.

91. Ibid., 2-122.

92. Ibid.; Kornblum and Boggs, "Social Ecology."

93. UDC, *42nd Street Development Project,* 2-82.

94. Kornblum and Boggs, "Social Ecology," 21–22; UDC, *42nd Street Development Project,* 2-83.

95. Kornblum, ed., "West 42nd Street."

96. Kornblum and Boggs, "Social Ecology," 22–23.

97. Ibid., 23.

98. Andrew Hacker, *Two Nations* (New York: Ballantine Books, 1992).

99. Such a gender-based pattern of dominance was not unique to Forty-second Street;

along the main shopping areas of Fifth Avenue, the ratio was reversed, with an over-whelming dominance of female pedestrians. Kornblum and Boggs, "Social Ecology," 24.

100. UDC, *42nd Street Development Project,* 2-83–2-94.

101. Ibid., 2-94.

102. Ibid., 2-92.

103. Herbert Gans, "The 42nd Street Development Project Draft EIS: An Assessment" (Report prepared for New York City Board of Estimate on behalf of the Brandt Organization, 1994, photocopy).

104. UDC, *42nd Street Development Project,* 2-94.

105. Ibid., 2-101.

106. Ibid., 2-100–2-101.

107. Gans, "42nd Street Development Project," 7–9.

108. UDC, *42nd Street Development Project,* 2-113–2-114.

109. Ibid., 2-103.

110. Hunt, "Crime and Law Enforcement," 169–171.

111. Samuel Weiss, "Police Cannot Cure 42nd Street, Study Finds," *NYT,* 19 November 1978.

112. William Kornblum et al., "Urban Design and Social Control," in "West 42nd Street," ed. Kornblum, 217.

113. UDC, *42nd Street Development Project,* 2-69–2-70.

114. Kornblum and Boggs, "Social Ecology."

115. Ibid., 39.

116. Ibid., 36.

117. Ibid.

118. Ibid., 38.

119. UDC, *42nd Street Development Project,* 2-90; Charles Winick, "The Sex Entertainment Industries on 42nd Street," in "West 42nd Street," ed. Kornblum, 99–125.

120. UDC, *42nd Street Development Project,* 2-132.

121. Winick, "Sex Entertainment," 117.

122. Senelick, "Private Parts."

123. This point was brought out in discussions that I had with two members of the team of CUNY sociologists studying West Forty-second Street, William Kornblum and Terry Williams.

124. UDC, *42nd Street Development Project,* 2-90, 2-133.

125. Kornblum and Boggs, "Social Ecology," 39.

126. UDC, *42nd Street Development Project,* 2-131–2-145.

127. Winick, "Sex Entertainment," 101–102.

128. UDC, *42nd Street Development Project,* 2-9–2-10.

129. Susan S. Fainstein, *The City Builders* (Oxford: Blackwell, 1994), 130, 136.

130. James R. Brigham, Jr., "The 42nd Street Development Project: The City's Perspective," *City Almanac* 18 (1985): 11.

131. UDC, *42nd Street Development Project,* 2-10–2-16.

132. William Kornblum et al., "Markets in the Bright Light District," in "West 42nd Street," ed. Kornblum, 90.

133. H. V. Savitch, *Post Industrial Cities* (Princeton, N.J.: Princeton University Press, 1988), chap. 3.

134. Kornblum and Boggs, "Social Ecology," 33.

135. Murray Edelman, *Constructing the Political Spectacle* (Chicago: University of Chicago Press, 1988), chap. 4.

136. Gregory F. Gilmartin, *Shaping the City: New York and the Municipal Art Society* (New York: Clarkson Potter, 1995), 455–456.

137. Hiss, *Experience of Place,* 65–66.

138. Gilmartin, *Shaping the City,* 456.

139. Ada Louise Huxtable, "Re-inventing Times Square: 1990," in *Inventing Times Square,* ed. Taylor, 356–370.

140. New York City Department of City Planning (DCP), *Midtown Development* (New York: DCP, 1981). That the DCP report was funded in part by five private foundations, including the Rockefeller Brothers Fund, is an indication of the difficulty of distinguishing distinct realms of public and private action.

141. New York City Planning Commission (CPC), *Midtown Zoning* (New York: Department of City Planning, 1982).

142. DCP, *Midtown Development,* 56.

143. Ibid., 12.

144. DCP, *Midtown Development Review* (New York: DCP, 1987).

145. Fainstein, *City Builders,* 134.

146. Paul Goldberger, "A Huge Architecture Show in Times Square," *NYT,* 9 September 1990.

147. Savitch, *Post Industrial Cities,* 80–89.

148. Ada Louise Huxtable, "Redeveloping New York," *NYT,* 23 December 1979.

149. Office of the Mayor, Edward I. Koch, "Press Release," 17 May 1979.

150. Mel Gussow, "Stage Lights Are Getting Brighter on the Far West Side," *NYT,* 8 February 1980.

151. Ibid.

152. DCP, *42nd Street Study* (New York: DCP, 1978).

153. Ibid., 40.

154. Office of the Mayor, "Press Release."

155. The conversion of SROs as a result of the city's tax incentive programs in the 1980s has since contributed to New York's homeless population by removing these essential housing resources for the poor.

4. PLANNING THE REVALUATION OF TIMES SQUARE

1. Susan S. Fainstein and Norman I. Fainstein, "New York City: The Manhattan Business District, 1945–1988," in *Unequal Partnerships,* ed. Gregory D. Squires (New Brunswick, N.J.: Rutgers University Press, 1989), 59–79; Norman I. Fainstein and Susan S. Fainstein, "The Politics of Planning New York as a World City," in *Regenerating the Cities,* ed. Michael Parkinson, Bernard Foley, and Dennis R. Judd (Glenview, Ill.: Scott, Foresman, 1989), 143–162; H. V. Savitch, *Post Industrial Cities* (Princeton, N.J.: Princeton University Press, 1988).

2. Martin Shefter, *Political Crisis/Fiscal Crisis: The Collapse and Revival of New York City* (New York: Basic Books, 1985); Ester R. Fuchs, *Mayors and Money* (Chicago: University of Chicago Press, 1992).

3. John H. Mollenkopf, *A Phoenix in the Ashes: The Rise and Fall of the Koch Coalition in New York Politics* (Princeton, N.J.: Princeton University Press, 1992); Susan S. Fainstein, *The City Builders* (Oxford: Blackwell, 1994); Fainstein and Fainstein, "New York City."

4. Cited in "Towering Troubles," *Economist,* September 30, 1989, 26.

5. Paul Goldberger, "Shaping the Face of New York," in *New York Unbound: The City and the Politics of the Future,* ed. Peter D. Salins (New York: Blackwell, 1988), 127–140; Savitch, *Post Industrial Cities,* chap. 3.

6. Squires, ed., *Unequal Partnerships.*

7. Lopez, Edwards, Frank & Co., financial statements for 42nd Street Local Development Corporation and Wholly Owned Subsidiary West Side Properties, Inc., 1979–1986; "East Side, West Side, 42nd Street Is Story," *Daily News,* 11 February 1979 (hereafter cited as *DN*).

8. Steven R. Weisman, "U.S. to Provide $1.9 Million for Times Square Renovation," *NYT,* 3 April 1979.

9. Gregory F. Gilmartin, *Shaping the City: New York and the Municipal Art Society* (New York: Clarkson Potter, 1995).

10. Ibid., 406.

11. The following discussion draws on Frederic Papert, interview with author, 2 February 1993.

12. Josh Alan Friedman, *Tales of Times Square* (Portland, Ore.: Feral House, 1993), 148.

13. 42nd Street Development Corporation, *The Renewal of West 42nd Street* (Promotional brochure, 1981).

14. Gilmartin, *Shaping the City,* 449.

15. Friedman, *Tales of Times Square,* 148.

16. Ibid., 143.

17. Mel Gussow, "Stage Lights Are getting Brighter on the Far West Side," *NYT,* 8 February 1980.

18. 42nd Street Development Corporation, *What's a Nice Girl Like Estelle Parsons Doing in a Massage Parlor on 42nd Street?* (Promotional brochure, 1982), 6.

19. Gussow, "Stage Lights."

20. For a critical discussion of how the Mitchell-Lama housing program served to enrich private interests at public expense in the construction of the Manhattan Plaza complex, see Robert Schur, "Manhattan Plaza: Old Style Ripoffs Are Still Alive and Well," in *Critical Perspectives on Housing,* ed. Rachel G. Bratt, Chester Hartman, and Ann Meyerson (Philadelphia: Temple University Press, 1986), 277–291, and Tom Robbins, "Manhattan Plaza Sequel," in *Critical Perspectives,* ed. Bratt, Hartman, and Meyerson, 292–295.

21. Quoted in Robbins, "Manhattan Plaza Sequel," 293.

22. Ibid., 294–295.

23. Quoted in Gussow, "Stage Lights."

24. 42nd Street Development Corp., *What's a Nice Girl Like Estelle Parsons Doing?*

25. Ibid.

26. William Kornblum, a sociologist at CUNY and a consultant for the Ford Foundation at the time, suggests that it was actually the involvement of Ford, with its "deep pockets," that stimulated the owner's speculative appetite.

27. "Companies Aid Times Square Study," *NYT,* 16 June 1978.

28. Ibid.

29. "Koch Swings Porno Ax at Times Square," *City News*, 30 August 1978.

30. This paragraph draws on separate discussions I had with William Kornblum and Terry Williams, CUNY sociologists who were consultants to Ford in the late 1970s, during 1993.

31. The involvement of the Ford Foundation in Forty-second Street redevelopment began to wane in the early 1980s with a changing of the guard that included the replacement of Kennedy and led to a shift in emphasis toward antipoverty efforts under the direction of Frank Thomas.

32. 42nd Street Development Corporation, *42nd Street* (Promotional brochure, 1978).

33. Fred Ferretti, " 'New' Times Square Waiting in the Wings," *NYT*, 14 November 1978; Paul Goldberger, "A New Plan for West 42d St.," *NYT*, 31 January 1979.

34. Goldberger, "New Plan."

35. Ibid.

36. 42nd Street Development Corp., *42nd Street*.

37. The City at 42nd Street, *The City at 42nd Street: A Proposal for the Restoration and Redevelopment of 42nd Street* (New York: City at 42nd Street, 1980).

38. Ibid., 2.

39. Dames & Moore, *The City at 42nd Street Urban Renewal Project: Draft Environmental Impact Statement* (New York: Dames & Moore, 1979); City at 42nd Street, *City at 42nd Street*.

40. City at 42nd Street, *City at 42nd Street*, 2.

41. Ibid., 7; Carter B. Horsley, "Times Square's Potential Inspires the Developers," *NYT*, 23 December 1979.

42. James Carberry and Daniel Hertzberg, "New York Plans Renewal of Sleazy Times Square, but the Planning Stage Is About as Far as It Gets," *Wall Street Journal*, 20 August 1980.

43. Dames & Moore, *City at 42nd Street*.

44. City at 42nd Street, *City at 42nd Street*, 21–22.

45. Ibid., 2.

46. Horsley, "Times Square's Potential."

47. On the ULURP process, see Savitch, *Post Industrial Cities*, 57–59.

48. Robert F. Pecorella, *Community Power in a Postreform City* (Armonk, N.Y.: Sharpe, 1994).

49. Mollenkopf, *Phoenix in the Ashes*.

50. Michael Goodwin, "Roadblocks for a New Time Sq.," *NYT*, 8 June 1980.

51. Ada Louise Huxtable, "Redeveloping New York," *NYT*, 23 December 1979.

52. Ibid.

53. "Koch Favors Competitive Bidding on Development of Times Square Area," *NYT*, 5 June 1980.

54. Goodwin, "Roadblocks."

55. Quoted in "Times Sq. Project," *NYT*, 4 June 1980.

56. Goldberger, "New Plan."

57. Carberry and Hertzberg, "New York Plans Renewal."

58. Quoted in Goldberger, "New Plan."

59. Carberry and Hertzberg, "New York Plans Renewal."

60. Quoted in "Times Sq. Project."

61. Horsley, "Times Square's Potential"; Huxtable, "Redeveloping New York."

62. Open Space Institute, "Times Square South: Pre-Development Analysis" (Prepared by KBS Associates, January 1981). This plan was formulated through the efforts of the Save Our Broadway Committee, a group opposed to John Portman's plan for a hotel on Broadway that would require the demolition of three Broadway theaters. (Portman's Marriott Marquis was ultimately built, with one new Broadway theater to replace the three that were destroyed.) Carter B. Horsley, "New Proposal for Times Square Block," *NYT,* 20 February 1981.

63. Fainstein and Fainstein, "New York City."

64. Savitch, *Post Industrial Cities,* 58.

65. Fainstein and Fainstein, "New York City," 67.

66. Savitch, *Post Industrial Cities,* 58.

67. Ibid., 58; Fainstein and Fainstein, "New York City," 67–68; Mollenkopf, *Phoenix in the Ashes,* 142.

68. Fainstein and Fainstein, "New York City," 68.

69. Goldberger, "Shaping the Face."

70. Marc V. Levine, "The Politics of Partnership: Urban Redevelopment Since 1945," in *Unequal Partnerships,* ed. Squires, 12–34.

71. Gregory D. Squires, "Public–Private Partnerships: Who Gets What and Why," in *Unequal Partnerships,* ed. Squires, 2.

72. New York City Department of City Planning (DCP), *42nd Street Development Project: A Discussion Document* (New York: DCP, 1981).

73. While some developers regarded the signage requirement as an obstacle to leases with corporate tenants, it was estimated that annual revenues from the signs could be as high as $20 million. So the cultural project would serve private profits after all. Mark McCain, "A Mandated Comeback for the Great White Way," *NYT,* 9 April 1989.

74. The following discussion of Klein and his involvement in the 42nd Street Development Project draws on Jonathan Greenberg, "How to Make It Big in New York Real Estate," *Forbes,* 8 October 1984, 43; see also Wayne Barrett and William Bastone, "Klein's Square," *Village Voice,* 15 December 1987.

75. Greenberg, "How to Make It Big."

76. Edward I. Koch, with William Rauch, *Mayor* (New York: Simon and Schuster, 1984), 289. Koch made these statements in the context of citing several examples of policy positions that he had taken that demonstrated his independence from top contributors.

77. Quoted in Greenberg, "How to Make It Big."

78. Wayne Barrett and William Bastone, "Times Square Developer Linked to Payoff Scandal," *Village Voice,* 15 December 1987.

79. Greenberg, "How to Make It Big."

80. In the earliest media accounts, the UDC subsidiary was sometimes referred to as the Times Square Redevelopment Corporation.

81. Greenberg, "How to Make It Big."

82. "Divorce on 42d Street?" *NYT,* 13 August 1983.

83. Rubin Baum Levin Constant & Friedman, letter to members of the New York City Board of Estimate on behalf of the Brandt Organization, 23 October 1984.

84. Barrett and Bastone, "Times Square Developer."

85. New York City Board of Estimate (BoE), "Resolution on Calendar Number 31, Adopted November 8, 1984" (BoE, New York, 1984, photocopy), 1.

86. Huxtable, "Redeveloping New York."

87. Frank J. Prial, "Five Theaters Added to 42d Street Revival Plan," *NYT,* 13 June 1982.

88. "42nd Street Stalemate Killed Tower for Chemical Bank," *New York Observer,* 28 May 1990 (hereafter cited as *NYO*); Guy Trebay, "Times Square: The Sequel," *Village Voice,* 12 September 1989.

89. Brett Pulley, "Key Developer Seeks a Role in Times Sq.," *NYT,* 21 November 1995; Peter Slatin and Paul Tharp, "Condé Nast Seals $11M Tax Deal for Times Square Move," *New York Post,* 8 May 1996 (hereafter cited as *NYP*); "A Star Is Reborn," *Business Week,* 8 July 1996, 102.

90. Pulley, "Key Developer."

91. Susan S. Fainstein, "The Redevelopment of 42nd Street: Clashing Viewpoints," *City Almanac* 18 (1985): 2–8.

92. John H. Mollenkopf, "The 42nd Street Development Project and the Public Interest," *City Almanac* 18 (1985): 12–13.

93. Barrett and Bastone, "Klein's Square."

94. David W. Dunlap, "Times Square Plan Is on Hold, but Meter Is Still Running," *NYT,* 9 August 1992.

95. Carl Weisbrod, "42nd Street Landlords: Greed, Inc.," *NYT,* 17 June 1989.

96. "Squaring Off over Redevelopment," *New York Newsday,* 1 May 1990 (hereafter cited as *NYN*).

97. Richard Levine, "State Acquires Most of Times Square Project Site," *NYT,* 19 April 1990.

98. Alan S. Oser, "Picking Up the Pace of Preparing the Site," *NYT,* 22 July 1990; "Times Square Skyscrapers Face an Uncertain Future," *NYO,* 11 November 1991; "Square Deal for Times Square?" *NYN,* 22 April 1991.

99. David W. Dunlap, "Owners of Times Sq. Tower Seek Bankruptcy Protection," *NYT,* 31 December 1991.

100. Paul Goldberger, "4 New Towers for Times Sq.," *NYT,* 21 December 1983.

101. Quoted in Savitch, *Post Industrial Cities,* 74.

102. James R. Brigham, Jr., "The 42nd Street Development Project: The City's Perspective," *City Almanac* 18 (1985): 9–12.

103. BoE, "Stenographic Record of the Discussion on Calendar Number 86 Held at the Meeting of the Board of Estimate on October 25, 1984" (BoE, New York, 1984, photocopy).

104. Jeffrey Hoff, "Who Should Pay to Transform Times Square?" *Barron's,* 25 September 1989, 64.

105. For an excellent discussion of the city as public and private entity, see Gerald E. Frug, "The City as a Legal Concept," *Harvard Law Review* 93 (1980): 1059–1154.

106. John R. Logan and Harvey L. Molotch, *Urban Fortunes* (Berkeley: University of California Press, 1987).

107. The city's major newspapers in the period since the late 1970s have been the *New York Times, Daily News, New York Post, New York Newsday,* and *Wall Street Journal.* My informal judgment is that this list reflects, in descending order, the degree to which each paper actively contributed to the pro-development discourse on Times Square.

108. "Companies Aid Times Square Study."

109. Ferretti, "'New' Times Square."

110. Alan S. Oser, "Finding Productive Uses for Midtown Properties," *NYT,* 3 January 1979.

111. "East Side, West Side."

112. Ada Louise Huxtable, "The Many Faces of 42nd Street," *NYT,* 18 March 1979.

113. Goldberger, "New Plan."

114. Glenn Fowler, "Restoration of Times Sq. Moving Closer to Reality," *NYT,* 18 June 1979.

115. Gussow, "Stage Lights."

116. Ralph Blumenthal, "A Times Square Revival?" *NYT Magazine,* 27 December 1981.

117. Frank J. Prial, "Can 42d Street Regain Its Showbiz Glamour?" *NYT,* 18 April 1982.

118. "A Look at the Sunny Side of Times Square," *DN,* 11 February 1982.

119. Goodwin, "Roadblocks."

120. "Times Square Stirs While Planning Sleeps," *NYT,* 15 January 1980.

121. "The City Planning Lesson, Contd.," *NYT,* 27 June 1980.

122. "Starting Over in Times Square," *NYT,* 7 July 1980.

123. "Another Opening on 42d Street," *NYT,* 15 July 1980.

124. "Seize the Time for Times Square," *NYT,* 23 June 1981.

125. "Divorce on 42d Street."

126. Susan Chira, "Bank's Withdrawal Deals Major Blow to Times Sq. Plan," *NYT,* 21 April 1989.

127. "Five Reasons to Transform 42d Street," *NYT,* 11 September 1989.

128. Cited in Marshall Berman, "Signs Square," *Village Voice,* 18 July 1995.

129. Wayne Barrett, "A Final Test for Times Square," *Village Voice,* 8 March 1988.

130. Ibid.

131. William R. Taylor, *In Pursuit of Gotham* (New York: Oxford University Press, 1992), 51.

132. Ibid., 52.

133. Goldberger, "4 New Towers."

134. Quoted in "Plans Unveiled for New 42d Street," *DN,* 22 December 1983.

135. Goldberger, "4 New Towers."

136. Paul Goldberger, "Times Square: Lurching Toward a Terrible Mistake?" *NYT,* 19 February 1989.

137. Ada Louise Huxtable, "Times Square Renewal (Act II): A Farce," *NYT,* 14 October 1989; Huxtable, "Re-Inventing Times Square: 1990," in *Inventing Times Square: Commerce and Culture at the Crossroads of the World,* ed. William R. Taylor (New York: Russell Sage Foundation, 1991), 356–370.

138. David W. Dunlap, "New Dispute Tangles Plan on Times Sq.," *NYT,* 18 May 1989.

139. Trebay, "Times Square."

140. Paul Goldberger, "New Times Square Design: Merely Token Changes," *NYT,* 1 September 1989.

141. Susan Chira, "New Designs for Times Square Try to Reflect Neon Atmosphere," *NYT,* 31 August 1989; Trebay, "Times Square."

142. Goldberger, "New Times Square."

143. Ibid.

144. Huxtable, "Times Square Renewal."

5. PUBLIC VOICES AND PRO-GROWTH POLITICS

1. For the definitive account of "the rise and fall of the Koch coalition in New York City politics," see John H. Mollenkopf, *A Phoenix in the Ashes: The Rise and Fall of the Koch Coalition in New York Politics* (Princeton, N.J.: Princeton University Press, 1992). On the Koch regime see also Martin Shefter, *Political Crisis/Fiscal Crisis: The Collapse and Revival of New York City* (New York: Basic Books, 1985).

2. Rufus P. Browning, Dale Rogers Marshall, and David H. Tabb, eds., *Racial Politics in American Cities,* 2nd ed. (New York: Longman, 1997).

3. John H. Mollenkopf, "New York: The Great Anomaly," in *Racial Politics in American Cities,* ed. Browning, Marshall, and Tabb, 95–115.

4. Saskia Sassen, *The Global City* (Princeton, N.J.: Princeton University Press, 1991); H. V. Savitch, *Post Industrial Cities* (Princeton, N.J.: Princeton University Press, 1988); Norman I. Fainstein and Susan S. Fainstein, "The Politics of Planning New York as a World City," in *Regenerating the Cities,* ed. Michael Parkinson, Bernard Foley, and Dennis R. Judd (Glenview, Ill.: Scott, Foresman, 1989), 143–162; Mollenkopf, *Phoenix in the Ashes.*

5. Mollenkopf, *Phoenix in the Ashes,* 47; see also John H. Mollenkopf and Manuel Castells, eds., *Dual City* (New York: Russell Sage Foundation, 1991).

6. Mollenkopf, *Phoenix in the Ashes,* 81–87.

7. Mollenkopf, "New York."

8. Mollenkopf, *Phoenix in the Ashes,* chap. 5.

9. For example, Latinos and African-Americans shared problems of poverty and limited economic opportunities, and both Jews and African-Americans had histories of discriminatory treatment. For insightful analyses of the interests that unite and divide these groups, see James Jennings, "The Puerto Rican Community: Its Political Background," in *Latinos and the Political System,* ed. F. Chris Garcia (Notre Dame, Ind.: University of Notre Dame Press), 65–80; Angelo Falcon, "Black and Latino Politics in New York City: Race and Ethnicity in a Changing Urban Context," in *Latinos and the Political System,* ed. Garcia 171–194; and Nathan Glazer and Daniel P. Moynihan, *Beyond the Melting Pot* (Cambridge, Mass.: MIT Press, 1963).

10. Times Square redevelopment was an important political objective for Mayor Koch since taking office. In 1978, Koch began aggressively courting developer John Portman to complete a Marriott Hotel project for Times Square that had stalled in 1974. Ultimately, Koch orchestrated $100 million in public subsidies to entice Portman back and bring the project to fruition. The city even allowed the demolition of two beloved, historic Broadway theaters to make way for the new hotel. Despite some public protests, Koch was able to secure the support of the preservationist Municipal Art Society, whose president, Fred Papert, was carefully cultivating a working alliance with city public officials. Gregory F. Gilmartin, *Shaping the City: New York and the Municipal Art Society* (New York: Clarkson Potter, 1995), 446–449.

11. Robert A. Beauregard, *Voices of Decline: The Postwar Fate of U.S. Cities* (Oxford: Blackwell, 1993).

12. The Board of Estimate was since declared unconstitutional on the grounds that it violated the principle of one person, one vote. Land-use decisions were transferred to an expanded City Council with the charter revisions that took effect in 1990.

13. The information in this chapter on witnesses and testimony at the Board of Estimate hearings is taken from BoE, "Stenographic Record of the Discussion on Calendar Number

86 Held at the Meeting of the Board of Estimate on October 25, 1984" (BoE, New York, 1984, photocopy); BoE, "Disposition of the Matters on the Calendar of the Board of Estimate Meeting of October 25, 1984" (BoE, New York, 1984, photocopy); BoE, "Transcript of the Stenographic Record (Excerpt) of the Discussion on Calendar Number 31 Held at the Meeting of the Board of Estimate on November 8, 1984" (BoE, New York, 1984, photocopy); BoE, "Disposition of the Matters on the Calendar of the Board of Estimate Meeting of November 8, 1984" (BoE, New York, 1984, photocopy).

14. John R. Logan and Harvey L. Molotch, *Urban Fortunes* (Berkeley: University of California Press, 1987).

15. J. Allen Whitt, "Mozart in the Metropolis: The Arts Coalition and the Urban Growth Machine," *Urban Affairs Quarterly* 23 (1987): 15–36.

16. Except where otherwise noted, the quotes in this chapter are taken from BoE, "Stenographic Record," and "Transcript."

17. UDC, *42nd Street Development Project: Draft Environmental Impact Statement* (New York: UDC, 1984).

18. The Brandt Organization, which owned and operated seven theaters and a small office building in the project area, was one of the most determined opponents. Although no one testified on behalf of Brandt, the company's attorneys submitted a detailed letter of opposition to the BoE. In it, they argued that Brandt had been excluded from participation in the project even though it had proposed a private redevelopment plan for its properties that would have saved the public millions of dollars. In this way, the Brandts challenged the assumption that only large-scale, state-sponsored intervention could stimulate revitalization. Rubin Baum Levin Constant & Friedman, letter to members of the New York City Board of Estimate on behalf of the Brandt Organization, October 23, 1984.

19. Susan S. Fainstein reported that Community Board 5 "issued a catalogue of objections but did not come to a firm stand" ("The Redevelopment of 42nd Street: Clashing Viewpoints," *City Almanac* 18 [1985]: 5).

20. The Presidents' Council also had been an active voice regarding the special midtown zoning revisions a few years earlier. Ironically, though, the group had contributed to the zoning amendment that facilitated the overbuilding of the West Side. Gilmartin, *Shaping the City*, 441–442.

21. Fainstein, "Redevelopment," 2. One of the recommendations presented at the hearings by the Presidents' Council was to make comprehensive Times Square planning a major focus of CPC efforts.

22. Gilmartin, *Shaping the City*, 441.

23. The Lincoln Center project involved the demolition of 7,000 units of low-income housing and the construction of 4,400 new dwelling units, 4,000 of which were luxury housing. Robert Caro, *The Power Broker: Robert Moses and the Fall of New York* (New York: Vintage Books, 1975), 1014.

24. Quoted in Fainstein, "Redevelopment," 6.

25. Even Frederick Papert was distressed at how the MAS's efforts to address the blight in Times Square had mushroomed into "a puffy real estate deal." But he still believed that the group should remain an ally in support of the project it initiated. Gilmartin, *Shaping the City*, 453–454.

26. Jack L. Goldstein, "Development and the Threat to the Theater District," *City Almanac* 18 (1985): 23.

27. Although the new high-rise hotel also included the construction of a new Broadway

theater—for the purpose of a zoning bonus—the design of the building was antithetical to the pedestrian orientation of Times Square. This was hardly surprising from developer John Portman, who lamented, "People are still hung up on the goddamn corny image of what's there in Times Square. There's not one great thing about it" (Gilmartin, *Shaping the City,* 446–449).

28. Goldstein, "Development," 24.

29. Ibid.

30. Mary Brendle, "Negotiating for Clinton," *City Almanac* 18 (1985): 25–26; Robert Neuwirth, "Developers to Clinton Residents: 'Don't Get Too Comfortable,'" *City Almanac* 18 (1985): 27–28; Fainstein, "Redevelopment."

31. Fainstein, "Redevelopment," 5.

32. Brendle, "Negotiating," 26.

33. Ironically, the fact that the housing money came from the city and state, rather than the developers, worked to the advantage of the Clinton neighborhood, because the community was able to receive the money even while the development project became bogged down in lengthy delays.

34. See, for example, David B. Truman, *The Governmental Process* (New York: Knopf, 1951); Robert A. Dahl, *Who Governs?* (New Haven, Conn.: Yale University Press, 1961); and Edward C. Banfield, *Political Influence* (Glencoe, Ill.: Free Press, 1961).

35. UDC, *42nd Street Development Project;* William Kornblum, ed., "West 42nd Street: The Bright Light Zone" (Unpublished study, City University of New York, 1978); Tony Hiss, *The Experience of Place* (New York: Knopf, 1990).

36. Mancur Olson, *The Logic of Collective Action* (Cambridge, Mass.: Harvard University Press, 1965).

37. Peter Bachrach and Morton S. Baratz, "The Two Faces of Power," *American Political Science Review* 56 (1962): 947–952.

38. Mollenkopf, *Phoenix in the Ashes.*

39. Whitt, "Mozart in the Metropolis."

40. J. Allen Whitt, "The Role of the Performing Arts in Urban Competition and Growth," in *Business Elites and Urban Development,* ed. Scott Cummings (Albany: State University of New York Press), 49–69; J. Allen Whitt and John C. Lammers, "The Art of Growth: Ties Between Development Organizations and the Performing Arts," *Urban Affairs Quarterly* 26 (1991): 376–393.

41. Kevin W. Green, ed., *The City as a Stage* (Washington, D.C.: Partners for Livable Places, 1983).

42. Paul E. Peterson, *City Limits* (Chicago: University of Chicago Press, 1981).

43. Ibid.

6. FIN-DE-SIÈCLE FORTY-SECOND STREET

1. James Bennett, "Vibrancy to Vacancy: Remaking the Deuce," *NYT,* 9 August 1992.

2. Paul Goldberger, "Times Square: Lurching Toward a Terrible Mistake?" *NYT,* 19 February 1989.

3. Paul Goldberger, "New Times Square Design: Merely Token Changes," *NYT,* 1 September 1989; Ada Louise Huxtable, "Times Square Renewal (Act II): A Farce," *NYT,* 14 October 1989.

4. Gregory F. Gilmartin, *Shaping the City: New York and the Municipal Art Society* (New York: Clarkson Potter, 1995), 453–461.

5. The "Spectacolor" sign on the Times Tower remained alive, flashing the message: "Hey, Mr. Mayor! It's dark out here. Help keep the bright lights in Times Square" (quoted in Gilmartin, *Shaping the City,* 456–457).

6. The coalition was largely reconstituted by Republican Rudolph Giuliani with his successful challenge to Mayor David Dinkins in 1993.

7. John H. Mollenkopf, "New York: The Great Anomaly," in *Racial Politics in American Cities,* 2nd ed., ed. Rufus P. Browning, Dale Rogers Marshall, and David H. Tabb (New York: Longman, 1997), 95–115.

8. Martin Gottlieb, "State Backing Won for Plan for Times Sq.," *NYT,* 5 October 1984.

9. William Sites, "The Limits of Urban Regime Theory: New York City Under Koch, Dinkins, and Giuliani," *Urban Affairs Review* 32 (1997): 536–557.

10. "Times Sq. Builders Getting Cold Feet," *NYP,* 8 November 1991.

11. David W. Dunlap, "Times Square Redevelopers Seek Delay in Project," *NYT,* 9 November 1991; "Times Square Skyscrapers Face an Uncertain Future," *NYO,* 11 November 1991.

12. "He's Still Standing," *NYN,* 20 April 1992.

13. Ibid.

14. Quoted in David W. Dunlap, "New Times Square Plan: Lights! Signs! Adventure! Dancing! Hold the Offices," *NYT,* 20 August 1992.

15. Robert A. M. Stern Architects, "42nd Street Now!: A Plan for the Interim Development of 42nd Street" (Report prepared for 42nd Street Development Project, Inc., 1993, typescript).

16. David W. Dunlap, "Choreographing Times Sq. into 21st Century," *NYT,* 16 September 1993.

17. Ibid.

18. Herbert Muschamp, "42d Street Plan: Be Bold or Be Gone!" *NYT,* 19 September 1993.

19. Robert Venturi, Denise Scott Brown, and Steven Izenour, *Learning from Las Vegas* (Cambridge, Mass.: MIT Press, 1972).

20. Shawn G. Kennedy, "State and Developer Agree to Refurbish Times Square Storefronts," *NYT,* 3 August 1994.

21. David W. Dunlap, "Rethinking 42d Street for Next Decade," *NYT,* 27 June 1993.

22. Claudia H. Deutsch, "Waiting for Act 2 Around Times Square: A Tale of 3 Buildings Built in Time for the Bust," *NYT,* 2 May 1993.

23. David W. Dunlap, "Owners of Times Sq. Tower Seek Bankruptcy Protection," *NYT,* 31 December 1991.

24. Jerry Adler, *High Rise: How 1,000 Men and Women Worked Around the Clock for Five Years and Lost $200 Million Building a Skyscraper* (New York: HarperCollins, 1993).

25. Under the new agreement, the interest paid to the developers on the amount that they spent for property acquisition in excess of their $88 million cap would be calculated as the yield on ten-year Treasury bills plus 1 percent. In June 1993, this translated into a rate of 7.06 percent, compared with a rate of 7 percent under the old calculation of 1 percent above prime. Dunlap, "Rethinking 42d Street."

26. Thomas J. Lueck, "Financing for Times Square Leads to Harsher Criticism," *NYT,* 28 July 1994; Lueck, "Must Show Go On?" *NYT,* 8 August 1994.

27. UDC, *42nd Street Development Project: Draft Environmental Impact Statement* (New York: UDC, 1984).

28. Muschamp, "42d Street Plan."

29. Quoted in Dunlap, "New Times Square Plan."

30. "A New Opening for Times Square," *NYT,* 10 August 1992.

31. David W. Dunlap, "Times Square's Future May Be Found Back at Its Roots," *NYT,* 4 August 1992.

32. Herbert Muschamp, "For Times Square, a Reprieve and Hope of a Livelier Day," *NYT,* 6 August 1992.

33. Dunlap, "New Times Square Plan."

34. Herbert Muschamp, "Time to Reset the Clock in Times Square," *NYT,* 1 November 1992.

35. "Decorous 'Deuce,'" *NYN,* 28 May 1992.

36. "Glad Reprieve for Times Square," *NYN,* 9 August 1992.

37. Stern, "42nd Street Now!" 1.

38. Ibid., 2.

39. Lueck, "Financing"; Lueck, "Must Show Go On?"

40. The MAS's opposition to the interim plan and the strategies the MAS was considering as a way of challenging it were the subject of a meeting between Emanuel Tobier of New York University and David Nissenbaum, the attorney for the MAS, that was attended by the author in July 1994.

41. Gilmartin, *Shaping the City.*

42. 42nd Street Development Project, *Crossroads* [newsletter], July 1992.

43. James Dao, "A Desire Named Broadway Lingers," *NYT,* 5 May 1992.

44. The boundaries of the business improvement district extend from Fortieth to Fifty-third Street, just west of Sixth Avenue to the west side of Eighth Avenue. Along Forty-sixth Street, the district stretches to Ninth Avenue to cover the Restaurant Row block.

45. Times Square Business Improvement District (BID), promotional brochure (1993?).

46. Times Square BID, *Times Square Sound Bites* 1 (1992); BID, *Times Square Sound Bites* 2 (1994); BID, promotional brochure.

47. Sharon Zukin, *The Cultures of Cities* (Cambridge, Mass.: Blackwell, 1995).

48. Karen DeWitt, "Panel Plans Special Services District for Times Sq.," *NYT,* 27 July 1990; James C. McKinley, Jr., "Business-Tax Zone for Times Sq. Area Is Signed into Law," *NYT,* 24 July 1991.

49. "New Round in Times Sq.," *DN,* 25 March 1992; "Getting a Drop on Times Sq.," *DN,* 30 March 1992.

50. UDC, "Crime in the 42nd Street Development Project Area Decreases by 54 Percent," press release, 20 May 1992.

51. 42nd Street Development Project, *Crossroads.*

52. Ibid., 5.

53. The "42nd Street Art Project" was organized by the 42nd Street Development Project in conjunction with the nonprofit arts organization Creative Time, Inc. Creative Time, "42nd Street Art Project," promotional brochures (1993, 1994); Carol Vogel, "In Times Square, Art Conquers Kung Fu," *NYT,* 7 July 1993; Herbert Muschamp, "A Highbrow Peep Show on 42d Street," *NYT,* 1 August 1993; Vogel, "42d Street Says Move over SoHo," *NYT,* 7 July 1994.

54. Vogel, "42nd Street."

55. Glenn Collins, "42d Street to Get a Theater for Youth," *NYT,* 20 October 1993.

56. Paul Goldberger, "The New Times Square: Magic that Surprised the Magicians," *NYT,* 15 October 1996; Jeanne B. Pinder, "Disney Considers Move into Times Sq.," *NYT,* 15 September 1993.

57. Douglas Martin, "Disney Seals Times Square Theater Deal," *NYT,* 3 February 1994.

58. Goldberger, "New Times Square."

59. Brett Pulley, "A Mix of Glamour and Hardball Won Disney a Piece of 42d Street," *NYT,* 29 July 1995.

60. Marshall Berman, "Signs Square," *Village Voice,* 18 July 1995.

61. Pulley, "Mix of Glamour."

62. Brett Pulley, "Companies Reach Deal for Renewal in Heart of 42d St.," *NYT,* 21 July 1995; Pulley, "Mix of Glamour."

63. Project officials agreed to provide a $21 million loan at 3 percent interest and another $5 million at 3.5 percent, both payable over thirty years; they would also provide a $1.9 million contingency fund for unforeseen costs. The city and state would also split, with Disney, development costs in excess of $32.5 million. In exchange, the city and state would receive from 2 to 3 percent of the New Amsterdam's revenues, plus an additional small percentage for rent and a payment-in-lieu-of-taxes. In real dollar terms, the city and state would receive a modest total of about $600,000 a year in payments in return for a net subsidy valued at one-third of the project cost. Pulley, "Mix of Glamour."

64. David W. Dunlap, "Cuomo Backs Loan Program for Broadway," *NYT,* 7 January 1994.

65. Pulley, "Mix of Glamour."

66. Ibid.

67. Pulley, "Companies Reach Deal."

68. Frank Rich, "The Key to the City: Getting a Lock on Times Square," *NYT,* 15 December 1994.

69. Peter Grant, "Sky's the Limit on 42d," *DN,* 22 February 1996.

70. Thomas J. Lueck, "Hotel Plans Are Submitted for Times Sq.," *NYT,* 30 July 1994.

71. Tom Lowry, "Hotel Square-off on 42d," *DN,* 17 February 1995.

72. Pulley, "Mix of Glamour."

73. Herbert Muschamp, "A Flare for Fantasy: Miami Meets 42d Street," *NYT,* 21 May 1995.

74. Charles V. Bagli, "NBC Rivals Look at Sites on Times Sq.," *NYT,* 19 November 1997.

75. Disney paid the city roughly $500,000 to cover the costs of additional services associated with the event. To accommodate the parade, the city provided almost 2,000 police officers and more than 100 sanitation workers; the city also repaired potholes and blocked traffic on more than thirty blocks. Matthew Purdy, "Disney to Turn Manhattan Goofy," *NYT,* 13 June 1997.

76. Paul Tharp, "Times Square Land!" *NYP,* 7 May 1996.

77. Brett Pulley, "2 Win by Not Quitting 42d Street," *NYT,* 12 January 1996; Thomas J. Lueck, "35-Story Hotel to Be Built on Prime Lot on 42d Street, Ending a Long Legal Battle," *NYT,* 14 January 1997.

78. Thomas J. Lueck, "Developer Buys Rights to Build Times Square Tower," *NYT,* 12 April 1996; Thomas J. Lueck, "3 Prime Sites in Times Sq. Go Up for Sale," *NYT,* 18 March 1997; "A Star Is Reborn," *Business Week,* 8 July 1996, 102.

79. Peter Slatin and Paul Tharp, "Condé Nast Seals $11M Tax Deal for Times Square Move," *NYP,* 8 May 1996.

80. Lueck, "3 Prime Sites."

7. LEARNING FROM FORTY-SECOND STREET

1. Clarence N. Stone, *Regime Politics: Governing Atlanta, 1946–1988* (Lawrence: University Press of Kansas, 1989), 27.

2. Michael A. Pagano and Ann O'M. Bowman, *Cityscapes and Capital* (Baltimore: Johns Hopkins University Press, 1995), 2.

3. Ibid., 3–4.

4. Sharon Zukin, *The Cultures of Cities* (Cambridge, Mass.: Blackwell, 1995); Zukin, *Landscapes of Power: From Detroit to Disney World* (Berkeley: University of California Press, 1991); Zukin, *Loft Living: Culture and Capital in Urban Change* (New Brunswick, N.J.: Rutgers University Press, 1982).

5. Robert A. Beauregard, *Voices of Decline: The Postwar Fate of U.S. Cities* (Oxford: Blackwell, 1993).

6. A popular broadway show during the height of the Times Square revival of the mid-1990s was *Bring in da Noise, Bring in da Funk,* which chronicled African-American music and history. This was another example of how prominent pro-growth forces (in this case, theater owners and producers) could capitalize on the troubling images of Times Square, such as the prevalence of an African-American subculture, by repackaging them in sanitized forms for mass consumption.

7. Paul E. Peterson, *City Limits* (Chicago: University of Chicago Press, 1981).

8. M. Christine Boyer, "Cities for Sale: Merchandising History at South Street Seaport," in *Variations on a Theme Park,* ed. Michael Sorkin (New York: Noonday Press, 1992), 181–204.

9. Alexander J. Reichl, "Historic Preservation and Progrowth Politics in U.S. Cities," *Urban Affairs Review* 32 (1997): 513–535.

10. Stone, *Regime Politics,* 126–131.

11. Reichl, "Historic Preservation," 529–531.

12. Robert K. Whelan, "New Orleans: Mayoral Politics and Economic-Development Policies in the Postwar Years, 1945–1986," in *The Politics of Urban Development,* ed. Clarence N. Stone and Heywood T. Sanders (Lawrence: University Press of Kansas, 1987), 216–229.

13. Richard O. Baumbach, Jr., and William E. Borah, *The Second Battle of New Orleans* (University: University of Alabama Press, 1981).

14. Historic preservation has had a different impact on development politics in San Francisco, where preservationists joined with a diverse progressive alliance to topple a pro-growth regime. Richard E. DeLeon, *Left Coast City* (Lawrence: University Press of Kansas, 1992).

15. On regime change in New Orleans, see Whelan, "New Orleans"; Robert K. Whelan, Alma H. Young, and Mickey Lauria, "Urban Regimes and Racial Politics in New Orleans," *Journal of Urban Affairs* 16 (1994): 1–21; and Christine C. Cook and Mickey Lauria, "Urban Regeneration and Public Housing in New Orleans," *Urban Affairs Review* 30 (1995): 538–557.

16. See, for example, Lewis Mumford, *The Culture of Cities* (New York: Harcourt, Brace, 1938); Friedrich Engels, *The Condition of the Working Class in England in 1844*, ed. and trans. W. O. Henderson and W. H. Chaloner (1845; reprint, Oxford: Blackwell, 1958); Ira Katznelson, *City Trenches* (Chicago: University of Chicago Press, 1981); Carl Schorske, *Fin-de-Siècle Vienna: Politics and Culture* (New York: Vintage Books, 1981), chap. 2; John H. Mollenkopf, ed., *Power, Culture, and Place* (New York: Russell Sage Foundation, 1988); and David Harvey, *The Condition of Postmodernity* (Oxford: Blackwell, 1989).

17. Michael Sorkin, ed., *Variations on a Theme Park* (New York: Noonday Press, 1992); Henri Lefebvre, *The Production of Space*, trans. Donald Nicholson-Smith (Cambridge, Mass.: Blackwell, 1991); Richard Sennett, *The Conscience of the Eye* (New York: Norton, 1990); Timothy P. Mitchell, *Colonising Egypt* (Cambridge: Cambridge University Press, 1988); David Harvey, *Consciousness and the Urban Experience* (Baltimore: Johns Hopkins University Press, 1985); Zukin, *Cultures of Cities.* Two early studies are Katznelson, *City Trenches,* and Mumford, *Culture of Cities.*

18. Even without overt mechanisms of social control, it is office workers—not the homeless—who can be found napping in the comfortable and sheltered public spaces of the seaport.

19. Tom Wolfe, *The Bonfire of the Vanities* (New York: Bantam Books, 1987).

20. Christopher Mele, "Globalization, Culture, and Neighborhood Change: Reinventing the Lower East Side of New York," *Urban Affairs Review* 32 (1996): 3–22; Neil Smith, "New City, New Frontier: The Lower East Side as Wild, Wild West," in *Variations on a Theme Park,* ed. Sorkin, 60–93.

21. Lawrence M. Mead, *The New Politics of Poverty* (New York: Basic Books, 1992).

22. John R. Logan and Harvey L. Molotch, *Urban Fortunes* (Berkeley: University of California Press, 1987).

23. There is an interesting parallel between the politics of Times Square redevelopment and the politics of welfare reform at the federal level in the mid-1990s. Republican-led efforts to reform the welfare system drew heavily on negative cultural images of welfare recipients—as minority populations locked into a culture of poverty—in order to justify a conservative economic agenda of federal retrenchment and tax cuts. In this way, the Republicans were able to define their plan to dismantle the federal welfare guarantee in social terms, as an effort to help the poor themselves. Through masterful control of political discourse, conservatives portrayed the elimination of the safety net as a gift to the poor. But the Republican refusal to provide the poor with resources enabling them to move into the workforce (education, job training, job placement, child care,and so on) exposed the preeminence of conservative economic goals over social ones.

24. Beauregard, *Voices of Decline.*

25. Zukin, *Cultures of Cities.*

26. Paul Tharp, "Times Square Land!" *NYP,* 7 May 1996.

27. See, especially, Michael Sorkin, Introduction to *Variations on a Theme Park,* ed. Sorkin, xi–xv; Sorkin, "See You in Disneyland," in ibid., 205–232; and Zukin, *Cultures of Cities.*

28. On the detrimental impacts of the contemporary urban form for social life, see Sorkin, ed., *Variations on a Theme Park;* Sennett, *Conscience of the Eye;* Harvey, *Condition of Postmodernity;* Mike Davis, *City of Quartz* (New York: Vintage Books, 1992); and M. Christine Boyer, "The Great Frame-Up: Fantastic Appearances in Contemporary Spatial Practices," in *Spatial Practices,* ed. Helen Liggett and David C. Perry (Thousand Oaks, Calif.: Sage, 1995), 81–109.

29. Susan S. Fainstein, *The City Builders* (Oxford: Blackwell, 1994), 224–240.

30. Ibid., 229.

31. Ibid., 233.

32. Dennis Judd and Todd R. Swanstrom, *City Politics* (New York: HarperCollins, 1994).

33. Mike Davis, "Fortress Los Angeles: The Militarization of Urban Space," in *Variations on a Theme Park,* ed. Sorkin, 156.

34. Jane Jacobs, *The Death and Life of Great American Cities* (New York: Vintage Books, 1961).

35. Marshall Berman, "Signs Square," *Village Voice,* 18 July 1995.

36. That they have avoided rather than embraced the theme-park comparison is interesting in itself. It suggests that, in principle, there may be widespread support for the existence of truly democratic public spaces in cities.

37. Bruce Weber, "In Times Square, Keepers of the Glitz," *NYT,* 25 June 1996.

38. Judd and Swanstrom, *City Politics.*

39. Michael Gross, "The Village Under Siege," *New York,* 16 August 1993, 30.

40. Conflicts also erupted in residential neighborhoods across the city as adult-entertainment establishments displaced from Forty-Second Street sought new locations.

41. William Julius Wilson, *The Truly Disadvantaged* (Chicago: University of Chicago Press, 1987).

42. Peter Marcuse, "The Enclave, the Citadel, and the Ghetto: What Has Changed in the Post-Fordist U.S. City," *Urban Affairs Review* 33 (1997): 228–264.

43. William Julius Wilson, *When Work Disappears* (New York: Knopf, 1996).

44. The sociologists studying Forty-second Street in the 1970s recommended sports-related entertainment as part of a balanced revitalization effort. William Kornblum, ed., "West 42nd Street: The Bright Light Zone" (Unpublished study, City University of New York, 1978).

Bibliography

Adler, Jerry. *High Rise: How 1,000 Men and Women Worked Around the Clock for Five Years and Lost $200 Million Building a Skyscraper.* New York: HarperCollins, 1993.

Advisory Council on Historic Preservation. *The Contribution of Historic Preservation to Urban Revitalization.* Washington, D.C.: Government Printing Office, 1979.

_____. *Federal Tax Law and Historic Preservation.* Washington, D.C.: ACHP, 1983.

_____. *National Historic Preservation Act of 1966, as Amended.* 3rd ed. Washington, D.C.: ACHP, 1993.

_____. *Report to the President and the Congress of the United States.* Washington, D.C.: ACHP, 1971–1989.

Anderson, Martin. *The Federal Bulldozer.* Cambridge, Mass.: MIT Press, 1964.

Babcock, Richard F., and Wendy U. Larsen. *Special Districts.* Cambridge, Mass.: Lincoln Institute of Land Policy, 1990.

Bachrach, Peter, and Morton S. Baratz. "The Two Faces of Power." *American Political Science Review* 56 (1962): 947–952.

Banfield, Edward C. *Political Influence.* Glencoe, Ill.: Free Press, 1961.

Barrett, Wayne. "A Final Test for Times Square." *Village Voice,* 8 March 1988.

Barrett, Wayne, and William Bastone. "Klein's Square." *Village Voice,* 15 December 1987.

_____. "Times Square Developer Linked to Payoff Scandal." *Village Voice,* 15 December 1987.

Baumbach, Richard O., Jr., and William E. Borah. 1981. *The Second Battle of New Orleans.* University: University of Alabama Press, 1981.

Beauregard, Robert A. "Representing Urban Decline: Postwar Cities as Narrative Objects." *Urban Affairs Quarterly* 29 (1993): 187–202.

_____. *Voices of Decline: The Postwar Fate of U.S. Cities.* Oxford: Blackwell, 1993.

Bellush, Jewel, and Murray Hausknecht, eds. *Urban Renewal: People, Politics, and Planning.* Garden City, N.Y.: Anchor Books, 1967.

Berman, Marshall. *All that Is Solid Melts into Air.* New York: Viking Penguin, 1982.

_____. "Signs Square." *Village Voice,* 18 July 1995.

Bianchini, Franco, and Michael Parkinson, eds. *Cultural Policy and Urban Regeneration: The West European Experience.* Manchester: Manchester University Press, 1993.

Blackmar, Betsy. "Uptown Real Estate and the Creation of Times Square." In *Inventing Times Square: Commerce and Culture at the Crossroads of the World,* ed. William R. Taylor, 51–65. New York: Russell Sage Foundation, 1991.

Bourdieu, Pierre. *Distinction: A Social Critique of the Judgement of Taste,* trans. Richard Nice. Cambridge, Mass.: Harvard University Press, 1984.

Boyer, M. Christine. "Cities for Sale: Merchandising History at South Street Seaport." In *Variations on a Theme Park,* ed. Michael Sorkin, 181–204. New York: Noonday Press, 1992.

_____. "The Great Frame-Up: Fantastic Appearances in Contemporary Spatial Practices."

In *Spatial Practices,* ed. Helen Liggett and David C. Perry, 81–109. Thousand Oaks, Calif.: Sage Publications, 1995.

_____. "The Return of Aesthetics to City Planning." *Society,* May–June 1988, 49–56.

Brendle, Mary. "Negotiating for Clinton." *City Almanac* 18 (1985): 25–26.

Brigham, James R., Jr. "The 42nd Street Development Project: The City's Perspective." *City Almanac* 18 (1985): 9–12.

Brigham, John. *Property and the Politics of Entitlement.* Philadelphia: Temple University Press, 1990.

Browning, Rufus P., Dale Rogers Marshall, and David H. Tabb, eds. *Racial Politics in American Cities.* 2nd ed. New York: Longman, 1997.

Buckley, Peter G. "Boundaries of Respectability: Introductory Essay." In *Inventing Times Square: Commerce and Culture at the Crossroads of the World,* ed. William R. Taylor, 286–296. New York: Russell Sage Foundation, 1991.

Buder, Stanley. "42nd Street at the Crossroads: A History of Broadway to Eighth Avenue." In "West 42nd Street: The Bright Light Zone," ed. William Kornblum, 52–80. Unpublished study, City University of New York, 1978.

Calvino, Italo. *Invisible Cities,* trans. William Weaver. San Diego, Calif.: Harcourt Brace Jovanovich, 1974.

Caraley, Demetrios. "Washington Abandons the Cities." In *Critical Issues for Clinton's Domestic Agenda,* ed. Demetrios Caraley, 1–30. New York: Academy of Political Science, 1994.

Caro, Robert. *The Power Broker: Robert Moses and the Fall of New York.* New York: Vintage Books, 1975.

Castells, Manuel. *The Urban Question.* Cambridge, Mass.: MIT Press, 1977.

Chauncey, George, Jr. "The Policed: Gay Men's Strategies of Everyday Resistance." In *Inventing Times Square: Commerce and Culture at the Crossroads of the World,* ed. William R. Taylor, 315–328. New York: Russell Sage Foundation, 1991.

City at 42nd Street. *The City at 42nd Street: A Proposal for the Restoration and Redevelopment of 42nd Street.* New York: City at 42nd Street, 1980.

Cook, Christine C., and Mickey Lauria. "Urban Regeneration and Public Housing in New Orleans." *Urban Affairs Review* 30 (1995): 538–557.

Costonis, John J. "The Chicago Plan: Incentive Zoning and the Preservation of Urban Landmarks." *Harvard Law Review* 85 (1972): 574–631.

_____. *Icons and Aliens: Law, Aesthetics, and Environmental Change.* Urbana: University of Illinois Press, 1989.

_____. *Space Adrift: Landmark Preservation and the Marketplace.* Urbana: University of Illinois Press, 1974.

Cybriwsky, Roman A., David Ley, and John Western. "The Political and Social Construction of Revitalized Neighborhoods: Society Hill, Philadelphia, and False Creek, Vancouver." In *Gentrification of the City,* ed. Neil Smith and Peter Williams, 92–120. Boston: Allen & Unwin, 1986.

Dahl, Robert A. *Who Governs?* New Haven, Conn.: Yale University Press, 1961.

Dames & Moore. *The City at 42nd Street Urban Renewal Project: Draft Environmental Impact Statement.* New York: Dames & Moore, 1979.

Davis, Mike. *City of Quartz.* New York: Vintage Books, 1992.

_____. "Fortress Los Angeles: The Militarization of Urban Space." In *Variations on a Theme Park,* ed. Michael Sorkin, 154–180. New York: Noonday Press, 1992.

DeLeon, Richard E. *Left Coast City.* Lawrence: University Press of Kansas, 1992.
Department of Housing and Urban Development. *HUD Statistical Yearbook 1970.* Washington, D.C.: Government Printing Office, 1971.
_____. *HUD Statistical Yearbook 1975.* Washington, D.C.: Government Printing Office, 1976.
_____. *Preserving Historic America.* Washington, D.C.: HUD, 1966.
_____. *Programs of HUD.* Washington, D.C.: Government Printing Office, 1977.
Edelman, Murray. *Constructing the Political Spectacle.* Chicago: University of Chicago Press, 1988.
_____. *The Symbolic Uses of Politics.* Urbana: University of Illinois Press, 1964.
Elkin, Stephen. *City and Regime in the American Republic.* Chicago: University of Chicago Press, 1987.
Elliott, Donald H., and Norman Marcus. "From Euclid to Ramapo: New Directions on Land Development Controls." *Hofstra Law Review* 56 (1972): 72–78.
Engels, Friedrich. *The Condition of the Working Class in England in 1844.* Ed. and trans. W. O. Henderson and W. H. Chaloner. 1845. Reprint. Oxford: Blackwell, 1958.
Erenberg, Lewis. "Impresarios of Broadway Nightlife." In *Inventing Times Square: Commerce and Culture at the Crossroads of the World,* ed. William R. Taylor, 158–177. New York: Russell Sage Foundation, 1991.
Fainstein, Norman I., and Susan S. Fainstein. "The Politics of Planning New York as a World City." In *Regenerating the Cities,* ed. Michael Parkinson, Bernard Foley, and Dennis R. Judd, 143–162. Glenview, Ill.: Scott, Foresman, 1989.
_____. "Restructuring the American City: A Comparative Perspective." In *Urban Policy Under Capitalism,* ed. Norman I. Fainstein and Susan S. Fainstein, 161–189. Beverly Hills, Calif.: Sage, 1982.
Fainstein, Susan S. *The City Builders.* Oxford: Blackwell, 1994.
_____. "Neighborhood Planning: Limits and Potentials." In *Neighborhood Policy and Programmes,* ed. Naomi Carmon, 223–237. New York: St. Martin's Press, 1990.
_____. "The Politics of Criteria: Planning for the Redevelopment of Times Square." In *Confronting Values in Policy Analysis,* ed. Frank Fischer and John Forester, 232–247. Newbury Park, Calif.: Sage, 1987.
_____. "The Redevelopment of 42nd Street: Clashing Viewpoints." *City Almanac* 18 (1985): 2–8.
Fainstein, Susan S., and Norman I. Fainstein. "New York City: The Manhattan Business District, 1945–1988." In *Unequal Partnerships,* ed. Gregory D. Squires, 59–79. New Brunswick, N.J.: Rutgers University Press, 1989.
Falcon, Angelo. "Black and Latino Politics in New York City: Race and Ethnicity in a Changing Urban Context." In *Latinos and the Political System,* ed. F. Chris Garcia, 171–194. Notre Dame, Ind.: University of Notre Dame Press, 1988.
Federal Writers' Project. *The WPA Guide to New York City.* 1939. Reprint. New York: Random House, 1982.
Fitch, James Marston. *Historic Preservation: Curatorial Management of the Built World.* New York: McGraw-Hill, 1982.
Foglesong, Richard E. *Planning the Capitalist City: The Colonial Era to the 1920s.* Princeton, N.J.: Princeton University Press, 1986.
42nd Street Development Corporation. *42nd Street.* Promotional brochure, 1978.
_____. *The Renewal of West 42nd Street.* Promotional brochure, 1981.

_____. *What's a Nice Girl Like Estelle Parsons Doing in a Massage Parlor on 42nd Street?* Promotional brochure, 1982.

42nd Street Development Project. *Crossroads* [newsletter], July 1992.

Foucault, Michel. *Discipline and Punish.* New York: Vintage Books, 1979.

Fox, Richard Wightman. "The Discipline of Amusement." In *Inventing Times Square: Commerce and Culture at the Crossroads of the World,* ed. William R. Taylor, 83–98. New York: Russell Sage Foundation, 1991.

Fried, Marc, and Peggy Gleicher. "Some Sources of Residential Satisfaction in an Urban Slum." *Journal of the American Institute of Planners* 27 (1961): 305–315.

Friedman, Josh Alan. *Tales of Times Square.* Portland, Ore.: Feral House, 1993.

Frug, Gerald E. "The City as a Legal Concept." *Harvard Law Review* 93 (1980): 1059–1154.

Fuchs, Ester R. *Mayors and Money.* Chicago: University of Chicago Press, 1992.

Gale, Dennis. "Conceptual Issues in Neighborhood Decline and Revitalization." In *Neighborhood Policy and Programmes,* ed. Naomi Carmon, 11–35. New York: St. Martin's Press, 1990.

Gans, Herbert. "The 42nd Street Development Project Draft EIS: An Assessment." Report prepared for New York City Board of Estimate, 1984. Photocopy.

_____. *The Urban Villagers.* New York: Free Press, 1962.

General Accounting Office. *Tax Policy and Administration: Historic Preservation Tax Incentives: Fact Sheet for the Chairman, Subcommittee on Public Lands, Committee on Interior and Insular Affairs, House of Representatives.* Washington, D.C.: GAO, 1986.

Gilfoyle, Timothy J. "Policing of Sexuality." In *Inventing Times Square: Commerce and Culture at the Crossroads of the World,* ed. William R. Taylor, 297–314. New York: Russell Sage Foundation, 1991.

Gilmartin, Gregory F. *Shaping the City: New York and the Municipal Art Society.* New York: Clarkson Potter, 1995.

Glazer, Nathan, and Daniel P. Moynihan. *Beyond the Melting Pot.* Cambridge, Mass.: MIT Press, 1963.

Goldberger, Paul. "Shaping the Face of New York." In *New York Unbound: The City and the Politics of the Future,* ed. Peter D. Salins, 127–140. New York: Blackwell, 1988.

Goldstein, Jack L. "Development and the Threat to the Theater District." *City Almanac* 18 (1985): 23–24.

Green, Kevin W., ed. *The City as a Stage.* Washington, D.C.: Partners for Livable Places, 1983.

Greenberg, Jonathan. "How to Make It Big in New York Real Estate," *Forbes,* 8 October 1984, 43.

Gross, Michael. "The Village Under Seige." *New York,* 16 August 1993, 30.

Hacker, Andrew. *Two Nations.* New York: Ballantine Books, 1992.

Hammack, David C. "Developing for Commercial Culture." In *Inventing Times Square: Commerce and Culture at the Crossroads of the World,* ed. William R. Taylor, 36–50. New York: Russell Sage Foundation, 1991.

Harris, Neil. "Urban Tourism and the Commercial City." In *Inventing Times Square: Commerce and Culture at the Crossroads of the World,* ed. William R. Taylor, 66–82. New York: Russell Sage Foundation, 1991.

Hartman, Chester W. "The Housing of Relocated Families." In *Urban Renewal: People, Politics, and Planning,* ed. Jewel Bellush and Murray Hausknecht, 315–353. Garden City, N.Y.: Anchor Books, 1967.

Harvey, David. *The Condition of Postmodernity.* Oxford: Blackwell, 1989.
_____. *Consciousness and the Urban Experience.* Baltimore: Johns Hopkins University Press, 1985.
_____. *The Urban Experience.* Baltimore: Johns Hopkins University Press, 1989.
Hiss, Tony. *The Experience of Place.* New York: Knopf, 1990.
Hoff, Jeffrey. "Who Should Pay to Transform Times Square?" *Barron's,* 25 September 1989, 64.
Housing and Home Finance Agency. 1963. *Historic Preservation Through Urban Renewal.* Washington, D.C.: HHFA, 1963.
_____. "The Housing of Relocated Families." In *Urban Renewal: People, Politics, and Planning,* ed. Jewel Bellush and Murray Hausknecht, 354–360. Garden City, N.Y.: Anchor Books, 1967.
Hunt, Jennifer. "Crime and Law Enforcement in the Bright Light District." In "West 42nd Street: The Bright Light Zone," ed. William Kornblum, 164–216. Unpublished study, City University of New York, 1978.
Huxtable, Ada Louise. "Re-Inventing Times Square: 1990." In *Inventing Times Square: Commerce and Culture at the Crossroads of the World,* ed. William R. Taylor, 356–370. New York: Russell Sage Foundation, 1991.
Jacobs, Jane. *The Death and Life of Great American Cities.* New York: Vintage Books, 1961.
Jager, Michael. "Class Definition and the Esthetics of Gentrification: Victoriana in Melbourne." In *Gentrification of the City,* ed. Neil Smith and Peter Williams, 78–91. Boston: Allen & Unwin, 1986.
Jencks, Christopher. *Post-modernism: The New Classicism in Art and Architecture.* New York: Rizzoli, 1987.
Jennings, James. "The Puerto Rican Community: Its Political Background." In *Latinos and the Political System,* ed. F. Chris Garcia, 68–80. Notre Dame, Ind.: University of Notre Dame Press, 1988.
Judd, Dennis, and Todd R. Swanstrom. *City Politics.* New York: HarperCollins, 1994.
Kantor, Paul, with Stephen David. *The Dependent City.* Glenview, Ill.: Scott, Foresman, 1988.
Katznelson, Ira. *City Trenches.* Chicago: University of Chicago Press, 1981.
Knapp, Margaret. "Entertainment and Commerce: Introductory Essay." In *Inventing Times Square: Commerce and Culture at the Crossroads of the World,* ed. William R. Taylor, 120–132. New York: Russell Sage Foundation, 1991.
Koch, Edward I., with William Rauch. *Mayor.* New York: Simon and Schuster, 1984.
Kornblum, William, ed. "West 42nd Street: The Bright Light Zone," New York: Unpublished study, City University of New York, 1978.
Kornblum, William, and Vernon Boggs. "The Social Ecology of the Bright Light District." In "West 42nd Street: The Bright Zone," ed. William Kornblum, 17–51. Unpublished study, City University of New York, 1978.
Kornblum, William, and Terry Williams. "Book Prospectus: West 42nd Street, the Bright Lights Zone." Paper presented at the Urban Forum conference "Contested Spaces," New York, June 14–15, 1991.
Lampard, Eric. "Structural Changes: Introductory Essay." In *Inventing Times Square: Commerce and Culture at the Crossroads of the World,* ed. William R. Taylor, 16–35. New York: Russell Sage Foundation, 1991.

Langenbach, Randolph. *A Future from the Past: The Case for Conservation and Reuse of Old Buildings in Industrial Communities*. Washington, D.C.: HUD, 1977.

Laska, Shirley Bradway, and Daphne Spain, eds. *Back to the City*. New York: Pergamon Press, 1980.

Leach, William. "Commercial Aesthetics: Introductory Essay." In *Inventing Times Square: Commerce and Culture at the Crossroads of the World*, ed. William R. Taylor, 234–242. New York: Russell Sage Foundation, 1991.

Lefebvre, Henri. *The Production of Space*. Trans. Donald Nicholson-Smith. Cambridge, Mass.: Blackwell, 1991.

Levine, Marc V. "The Politics of Partnerships: Urban Redevelopment Since 1945." In *Unequal Partnerships*, ed. Gregory D. Squires, 12–34. New Brunswick, N.J.: Rutgers University Press, 1989.

Levy, Paul R., and Roman A. Cybriwsky. "The Hidden Dimensions of Culture and Class: Philadelphia." In *Back to the City*, ed. Shirley Bradway Laska and Daphne Spain, 138–155. New York: Pergamon Press, 1980.

Logan, John R., and Harvey L. Molotch. *Urban Fortunes*. Berkeley: University of California Press, 1987.

Lowenthal, David. *The Past Is a Foreign Country*. Cambridge: Cambridge University Press, 1985.

Lynch, Kevin. *What Time Is This Place?* Cambridge, Mass.: MIT Press, 1972.

Marcus, Norman. "Zoning from 1961 to 1991: Turning Back the Clock—But with an Up-to-the-Minute Social Agenda." In *Planning and Zoning New York City*, ed. Todd W. Bressi, 61–102. New Brunswick, N.J.: Center for Urban Policy Research, Rutgers University, 1993.

Marcuse, Peter. "The Enclave, the Citadel, and the Ghetto: What Has Changed in the Post-Fordist U.S. City." *Urban Affairs Review* 33 (1997): 228–264.

McNamara, Brooks. "The Entertainment District at the End of the 1930s." In *Inventing Times Square: Commerce and Culture at the Crossroads of the World*, ed. William R. Taylor, 178–190. New York: Russell Sage Foundation, 1991.

Mead, Lawrence M. *The New Politics of Poverty*. New York: Basic Books, 1992.

Mele, Christopher. "Globalization, Culture, and Neighborhood Change: Reinventing the Lower East Side of New York." *Urban Affairs Review* 32 (1996): 3–22.

Mitchell, Timothy P. *Colonising Egypt*. Cambridge: Cambridge University Press, 1988.

Mollenkopf, John H. *The Contested City*. Princeton, N.J.: Princeton University Press, 1983.

_____. "The 42nd Street Development Project and the Public Interest." *City Almanac* 18 (1985): 12–13.

_____. "New York: The Great Anomaly." In *Racial Politics in American Cities*, 2nd ed., ed. Rufus P. Browning, Dale Rogers Marshall, and David H. Tabb, 95–115. New York: Longman, 1997.

_____. *A Phoenix in the Ashes: The Rise and Fall of the Koch Coalition in New York Politics*. Princeton, N.J.: Princeton University Press, 1992.

_____, ed. *Power, Culture, and Place*. New York: Russell Sage Foundation, 1988.

Mollenkopf, John H., and Manuel Castells, eds. *Dual City*. New York: Russell Sage Foundation, 1991.

Mumford, Lewis. *The Culture of Cities*. New York: Harcourt, Brace, 1938.

Nager, Norma. "Continuities of Urban Policy on the Poor: From Urban Renewal to Reinvestment." In *Back to the City,* ed. Shirley Bradway Laska and Daphne Spain, 239–251. New York: Pergamon Press, 1980.

Neuwirth, Robert. "Developers to Clinton Residents: 'Don't Get Too Comfortable.'" *City Almanac* 18 (1985): 27–28.

_____. "A Hundred Years of Subsidy," *Village Voice,* 12 February 1991.

New York City Board of Estimate. "Disposition of the Matters on the Calendar of the Board of Estimate Meeting of November 8, 1984." BoE, New York, 1984. Photocopy.

_____. "Disposition of the Matters on the Calendar of the Board of Estimate Meeting of October 25, 1984." BoE, New York, 1984. Photocopy.

_____. "Resolution on Calendar Number 31, Adopted November 8, 1984." BoE, New York, 1984. Photocopy.

_____. "Stenographic Record of the Discussion on Calendar Number 86 Held at the Meeting of the Board of Estimate on October 25, 1984." BoE, New York, 1984. Photocopy.

_____. "Transcript of the Stenographic Record (Excerpt) of the Discussion on Calendar Number 31 Held at the Meeting of the Board of Estimate on November 8, 1984." BoE, New York, 1984. Photocopy.

New York City Department of City Planning. *42nd Street Development Project: A Discussion Document.* New York: DCP, 1981.

_____. *42nd Street Study.* New York: DCP, 1978.

_____. *Midtown Development.* New York: DCP, 1981.

_____. *Midtown Development Review.* New York: DCP, 1987.

New York City Landmarks Preservation Commission. *Guide to New York City Landmarks.* Washington, D.C.: Preservation Press, 1992.

New York City Planning Commission. *Midtown Zoning.* New York: Department of City Planning, 1982.

New York State Urban Development Corporation. *42nd Street Development Project: Draft Environmental Impact Statement.* New York: UDC, 1984.

Olson, Mancur. *The Logic of Collective Action.* Cambridge, Mass.: Harvard University Press, 1965.

Pagano, Michael A., and Ann O'M. Bowman. *Cityscapes and Capital.* Baltimore: Johns Hopkins University Press, 1995.

Pecorella, Robert F. *Community Power in a Postreform City.* Armonk, N.Y.: Sharpe, 1994.

Peterson, Paul E. *City Limits.* Chicago: University of Chicago Press, 1981.

Real Estate Research Corporation. *Economics of Revitalization: A Decisionmaking Guide for Local Officials.* Washington, D.C.: Department of the Interior, Heritage Conservation and Recreation Service, 1981.

Rechy, John. *City of Night.* 1963. Reprint. New York: Quality Paperback Book Club, 1994.

Register, William Wood, Jr. "New York's Gigantic Toy." In *Inventing Times Square: Commerce and Culture at the Crossroads of the World,* ed. William R. Taylor, 243–270. New York: Russell Sage Foundation, 1991.

Reichl, Alexander J. "Historic Preservation and Progrowth Politics in U.S. Cities." *Urban Affairs Review* 32 (1997): 513–535.

Relph, Edward. *The Modern Urban Landscape.* Baltimore: Johns Hopkins University Press, 1987.

Richards, David A. "Development Rights Transfer in New York City." In *Transfer of Development Rights,* ed. Jerome G. Rose, 123–156. New Brunswick, N.J.: Center for Urban Policy Research, Rutgers University, 1975.

Robbins, Tom. "Manhattan Plaza Sequel." In *Critical Perspectives on Housing,* ed. Rachel G. Bratt, Chester Hartman, and Ann Meyerson, 292–295. Philadelphia: Temple University Press, 1986.

Robert A. M. Stern Architects. "42nd Street Now!: A Plan for the Interim Development of 42nd Street." Report prepared for 42nd Street Development Project, Inc., 1993. Typescript.

Rochefort, David A., and Roger W. Cobb, eds. *The Politics of Problem Definition.* Lawrence: University Press of Kansas, 1994.

Sassen, Saskia. *The Global City.* Princeton, N.J.: Princeton University Press, 1991.

Savitch, H. V. *Post Industrial Cities.* Princeton, N.J.: Princeton University Press, 1988.

Schattschneider, E. E. *The Semisovereign People: A Realist's View of Democracy in America.* New York: Harcourt, Brace & World, 1960.

Scheingold, Stuart A. *The Politics of Law and Order.* New York: Longman, 1984.

Schorske, Carl. *Fin-de-Siècle Vienna: Politics and Culture.* New York: Vintage Books, 1981.

Schur, Robert. "Manhattan Plaza: Old Style Ripoffs Are Still Alive and Well." In *Critical Perspectives on Housing,* ed. Rachel G. Bratt, Chester Hartman, and Ann Meyerson, 277–291. Philadelphia: Temple University Press, 1986.

Senelick, Lawrence. "Private Parts in Public Places." In *Inventing Times Square: Commerce and Culture at the Crossroads of the World,* ed. William R. Taylor, 329–353. New York: Russell Sage Foundation, 1991.

Sennett, Richard. *The Conscience of the Eye.* New York: Norton, 1990.

Shefter, Martin. *Political Crisis/Fiscal Crisis: The Collapse and Revival of New York City.* New York: Basic Books, 1985.

Sites, William. "The Limits of Urban Regime Theory: New York City Under Koch, Dinkins, and Giuliani." *Urban Affairs Review* 32 (1997): 536–557.

Slayton, William L. "Report on Urban Renewal." In *Urban Renewal: People, Politics, and Planning,* ed. Jewel Bellush and Murray Hausknecht, 380–386. Garden City, N.Y.: Anchor Books, 1967.

Smith, Neil. "Gentrification, the Frontier, and the Restructuring of Urban Space." In *Gentrification of the City,* ed. Neil Smith and Peter Williams, 15–34. Boston: Allen & Unwin, 1986.

———. "New City, New Frontier: The Lower East Side as Wild, Wild West." In *Variations on a Theme Park,* ed. Michael Sorkin, 60–93. New York: Noonday Press, 1992.

Smith, Neil, and Peter Williams, eds. *Gentrification of the City.* Boston: Allen & Unwin, 1986.

Sorkin, Michael, ed. *Variations on a Theme Park.* New York: Noonday Press, 1992.

Squires, Gregory D., ed. *Unequal Partnerships.* New Brunswick, N.J.: Rutgers University Press, 1989.

"A Star Is Reborn." *Business Week,* 8 July 1996, 102.

Stone, Clarence N. *Regime Politics: Governing Atlanta, 1946–1988.* Lawrence: University Press of Kansas, 1989.

Stone, Clarence N., and Heywood T. Sanders, eds. *The Politics of Urban Development.* Lawrence: University Press of Kansas, 1987.

Taylor, William R., *In Pursuit of Gotham*. New York: Oxford University Press, 1992.
_____, ed. *Inventing Times Square: Commerce and Culture at the Crossroads of the World*. New York: Russell Sage Foundation, 1991.
Thomas, Selma, ed. *Rehabilitation: An Alternative for Historic Industrial Buildings*. Washington, D.C.: Government Printing Office, 1978.
Tournier, Robert E. "Historic Preservation as a Force in Urban Change: Charleston." In *Back to the City*, ed. Shirley Bradway Laska and Daphne Spain, 173–186. New York: Pergamon Press, 1980.
"Towering Troubles." *Economist*, 30 September, 1989, 26.
Trebay, Guy. "Times Square: The Sequel." *Village Voice*, 12 September 1989.
Truman, David B. *The Governmental Process*. New York: Knopf, 1951.
U.S. Conference of Mayors, Special Committee on Historic Preservation. *With Heritage So Rich*. New York: Random House, 1966.
Venturi, Robert, Denise Scott Brown, and Steven Izenour. *Learning from Las Vegas*. Cambridge, Mass.: MIT Press, 1972.
Weber, Stephen F. *Historic Preservation Incentives of the 1976 Tax Reform Act: An Economic Analysis*. Washington, D.C.: Department of Commerce, 1979.
Whelan, Robert K. "New Orleans: Mayoral Politics and Economic-Development Policies in the Postwar Years, 1945–1986." In *The Politics of Urban Development*, ed. Clarence N. Stone and Heywood T. Sanders, 216–229. Lawrence: University Press of Kansas, 1987.
Whelan, Robert K., Alma H. Young, and Mickey Lauria. "Urban Regimes and Racial Politics in New Orleans." *Journal of Urban Affairs* 16 (1994): 1–21.
Whitt, J. Allen. "Mozart in the Metropolis: The Arts Coalition and the Urban Growth Machine." *Urban Affairs Quarterly* 23 (1987): 15–36.
_____. "The Role of the Performing Arts in Urban Competition and Growth." In *Business Elites and Urban Development*, ed. Scott Cummings, 49–69. Albany: State University of New York Press, 1988.
Whitt, J. Allen, and John C. Lammers. "The Art of Growth: Ties Between Development Organizations and the Performing Arts." *Urban Affairs Quarterly* 26 (1991): 376–393.
Wilson, James Q. "Planning and Politics: Citizen Participation in Urban Renewal." In *Urban Renewal: People, Politics, and Planning*, ed. Jewel Bellush and Murray Hausknecht, 287–301. Garden City, N.Y.: Anchor Books, 1967.
Wilson, William Julius. *The Truly Disadvantaged*. Chicago: University of Chicago Press, 1987.
_____. *When Work Disappears*. New York: Knopf, 1996.
Winick, Charles. "The Sex Entertainment Industries on 42nd Street." In "West 42nd Street: The Bright Light Zone," ed. William Kornblum, 99–125. Unpublished study, City University of New York, 1978.
Wolfe, Tom. *The Bonfire of the Vanities*. New York: Bantam Books, 1987.
_____. *From Bauhaus to Our House*. New York: Pocket Books, 1981.
Zukin, Sharon. *The Cultures of Cities*. Cambridge, Mass.: Blackwell, 1995.
_____. *Landscapes of Power: From Detroit to Disney World*. Berkeley: University of California Press, 1991.
_____. *Loft Living: Culture and Capital in Urban Change*. New Brunswick, N.J.: Rutgers University Press, 1982.

Index